The Variety
Community Experience

The Variety of Community Experience

Qualitative Studies of Family and Community Life

edited by

Steven J. Taylor, Ph.D., Director and Professor,
The Center on Human Policy, School of Education,
Syracuse University, Syracuse, New York

Robert Bogdan, Ph.D., Professor and Associate,
The Center on Human Policy, School of Education,
Syracuse University, Syracuse, New York

and

Zana Marie Lutfiyya, Ph.D., Faculty of Education,
Department of Educational Psychology, University of Manitoba,
Winnipeg, Manitoba, Canada

·P A U L·H·
BROOKES
PUBLISHING CO

Baltimore • London • Toronto • Sydney

Paul H. Brookes Publishing Co.
Post Office Box 10624
Baltimore, Maryland 21285-0624

Typeset by Brushwood Graphics, Inc., Baltimore, Maryland.
Manufactured in the United States by
The Maple Press Co., York, Pennsylvania.

With the exception of Karen Mihalyi and the principal characters in the Ward case and the Mcgough story, all names in this book are pseudonyms. Some organization names are also pseudonyms. Interview with Karen Mihalyi used by permission.

Library of Congress Cataloguing-in-Publication Data
The variety of community experience : qualitative studies of family
  and community life / edited by Steven J. Taylor, Robert Bogdan, and
  Zana Marie Lutfiyya.
       p.   cm.
  Includes bibliographical references and index.
  ISBN 1-55766-191-X
  1. Developmentally disabled—United States—Social conditions—
Case studies.   2. Social integration—United States—Case studies.
3. Developmentally disabled—Services for—United States.
I. Taylor, Steven J., 1949–   . II. Bogdan, Robert. III.   Lutfiyya,
Zana Marie.
HV1570.5.U65V37   1995
362.1'968—dc20   94-45944
                                                               CIP

British Library Cataloguing-in-Publication data are available from the British
Library.

Contents

The Contributors

THE EDITORS

Steven J. Taylor, Ph.D., Director and Professor, The Center on Human Policy, School of Education, Syracuse University, 200 Huntington Hall, Syracuse, NY 13244-2340

Steven J. Taylor is Director of The Center on Human Policy and the Research and Training Center on Community Integration. He is Professor of Cultural Foundations of Education and Sociology at Syracuse University. His interests include social policy, qualitative research methods, sociology of disability, advocacy, and community integration. He is the author or editor of numerous published articles and books, including *Life in the Community, Introduction to Qualitative Research Methods, The Social Meaning of Mental Retardation,* and *Community Integration for People with Severe Disabilities.* He is currently the editor of the journal *Mental Retardation.*

Robert Bogdan, Ph.D., Professor and Associate, The Center on Human Policy, School of Education, Syracuse University, Syracuse, NY 13244-2340

Robert Bogdan has worked in the area of disability since obtaining his doctorate in sociology. He is Director of the Interdisciplinary Doctoral Program in Social Science at Maxwell School, Professor of Sociology and Cultural Foundations of Education at Syracuse University, and an associate at The Center on Human Policy. He has written on qualitative research and its relation to special education and on the social history of the "freak show."

Zana Marie Lutfiyya, Ph.D., Faculty of Education, Department of Educational Psychology, University of Manitoba, Winnipeg, Manitoba, R3T 2N2, CANADA

Zana Marie Lutfiyya is Assistant Professor in the Faculty of Education at the University of Manitoba. Prior to this appointment, she worked at The Center on Human Policy, Syracuse University, where she was a member of a team of researchers who conducted a long-term study of the social networks and relationships of people with disabilities. Her interests include the facilitation of personal relationships between people with and without disabilities, social policy, qualitative research methods, advocacy, and inclusive education.

THE AUTHORS

Scott S. Andrews, Ph.D., 350 Sausalito Boulevard, Sausalito, CA 94965

After receiving his undergraduate degree at Dartmouth, Scott S. Andrews attended Temple University, where he received a degree in Visual Anthropology. He received his Ph.D. in Education at Stanford University. In addition to *And Then Came John*, his film credits include *Last Images of War* and the recent Frontline special *School Colors*.

Ellen S. Fisher, J.D., Counseling and Human Services, Syracuse University, 259 Huntington Hall, Syracuse, NY 13244-2340

Ellen Fisher practiced law in Pennsylvania prior to becoming an administrator of housing options for people with psychiatric labels or developmental disabilities. She is currently a doctoral candidate in Rehabilitation Counseling at Syracuse University. Her major research focus has been how people with disabilities are supported to participate in generic community groups.

Susan O'Connor, M.S., Augsburg College, 2211 Riverside Avenue, Minneapolis, MN 55454

Susan O'Connor is Assistant Professor of Education at Augsburg College and is completing her doctoral studies at Syracuse University, where her main research focus has been related to issues of multiculturalism and family supports. In addition to working with adults with disabilities in this country, she has taught in both Morocco and the West Bank with teachers and human services professionals.

Bonnie Shoultz, M.A., The Center on Human Policy, School of Education, Syracuse University, 200 Huntington Hall, Syracuse, NY 13244-2340

Bonnie Shoultz is Associate Director for Information and Training at the Research and Training Center on Community Integration at The Center on Human Policy. She previously worked in a variety of professional and volunteer capacities in Nebraska's community service system. Her personal and research interests are in the areas of empowerment (for parents and people with disabilities) and community regeneration.

Rannveig Traustadottir, Ph.D., Faculty of Social Science, University of Iceland, Oddi, IS-101 Reykjavik, ICELAND

Rannveig Traustadottir is Research Fellow at the Research Center at the University College of Iceland and a lecturer in sociology at the University of Iceland. During her 6 years of doctoral studies at Syracuse University, she was involved in a range of research projects at The Center on Human Policy. In her research, she combines issues of gender and disability to examine the situation of women with disabilities; the gendered nature of caring for people with disabilities; the social construction of women as caregivers; and women's role in the current reform effort toward full inclusion of people with disabilities.

Pam Walker, The Center on Human Policy, School of Education, Syracuse University, 200 Huntington Hall, Syracuse, NY 13244-2340

Pam Walker is Research Associate at The Center on Human Policy, Research and Training Center on Community Integration. She is a doctoral candidate in the Special Education Program at Syracuse University. Her research interests include family supports, residential supports for adults, and social integration into neighborhoods and communities.

Preface

Since its establishment in 1971, The Center on Human Policy at Syracuse University in Syracuse, New York, has used qualitative research methods to study the lives and experiences of people with disabilities in society. Much of the Center's research has had an evaluative focus. In the 1970s, the Center studied and evaluated institutions for people labeled mentally retarded and mentally ill and documented abusive and dehumanizing practices. Toward the latter part of the 1970s and into the 1980s, the Center evaluated strategies and practices to integrate students with disabilities into regular school programs (Biklen, 1985; Taylor, 1982). More recently, the Center has devoted attention to community integration for people with severe developmental disabilities. Beginning in 1985, the Center started to study practices and policies used by public and private agencies to integrate people with disabilities in the community (Taylor, 1985; Taylor, Biklen, & Knoll, 1987; Taylor, Bogdan, & Racino, 1991).

While much of the Center's research has focused on evaluation, we have also attempted to contribute to a general understanding of the meaning of disability and mental retardation in society. Based on our studies of institutions, we attempted to understand how they operate and what effects they have on the people who live and work at them (Bodgan, Taylor, deGrandpre, & Haynes, 1974; Taylor, 1987; Taylor & Bogdan, 1980). If we understand the nature of institutions, we are in a better position to avoid the creation of institutional conditions in ostensibly noninstitutional settings.

In our recent research on community integration, we have attempted not only to identify and document promising practices and innovative policies, but to advance our understanding of community acceptance of people with developmental disabilities. We have begun to develop a theory of acceptance and to explore the types of accepting relationships between people with and without disabilities and the perspectives of the people without disabilities in these relationships (Bogdan & Taylor, 1987, 1989; Taylor & Bogdan, 1989).

Many of the recent books and monographs based on The Center on Human Policy's research have examined community participation in terms of policies, practices, agency organization, and human services frameworks (Taylor, Biklen, & Knoll, 1987; Taylor et al., 1991; Taylor, Racino, Knoll, & Lutfiyya, 1987). These books addressed the general question of how policies and services should be designed and implemented.

This book looks at life in the community from a different viewpoint. Instead of taking human services agencies and frameworks as a point of departure, the studies contained in this book look at community participation from the vantage point of people with developmental disabilities, their families, and the community. The purpose of this book is not to describe or promote specific support strategies or practices or other good ideas, but to explore how life in the community is experienced directly by those with developmental disabilities and their families, whether or not they are involved in the human services system.

The studies in this book attempt to advance our general understanding of what living in the community means and how it is experienced. Good practice should be informed by new ways of understanding and thinking about the community. We hope that this book will not only contribute to general understandings but also provide useful insights and lessons to policy makers, people with developmental disabilities, family members, professionals, advocates, and others interested in life in the community.

REFERENCES

Biklen, D. (1985). *Achieving the complete school: Strategies for effective mainstreaming.* New York: Teachers College Press.

Bogdan, R., & Taylor, S.J. (1987). Toward a sociology of acceptance: The other side of the study of deviance. *Social Policy, 18*(2), 34–39.

Bogdan, R., & Taylor, S.J. (1989). Relationships with severely disabled people: The social construction of humanness. *Social Problems, 36*(2), 135–148.

Bogdan, R., Taylor, S.J., deGrandpre, B., & Haynes, S. (1974). Let them eat programs: Attendants' perspectives and programming on wards in state schools. *Journal of Health and Social Behavior, 15,* 142–151.

Taylor, S.J. (1982). From segregation to integration: Strategies for integrating severely handicapped students in normal school and community settings. *Journal of The Association for Persons with Severe Handicaps, 7*(3), 42–49.

Taylor, S.J. (1985). *Site visit report: State of Michigan.* Syracuse, NY: Center on Human Policy, Syracuse University.

Taylor, S.J. (1987). "They're not like you and me": Institutional attendants' perspectives on residents. *Child and Youth Services: Qualitative Research and Evaluation in Group Care, 8*(3/4), 109–125.

Taylor, S.J., Biklen, D., & Knoll, J.A. (Eds.). (1987). *Community integration for people with severe disabilities.* New York: Teachers College Press.

Taylor, S.J., & Bogdan, R. (1980). Defending illusions: The institution's struggle for survival. *Human Organization, 39*(3), 209–218.

Taylor, S.J., & Bogdan, R. (1989). On accepting relationships between people with mental retardation and nondisabled people: Towards an understanding of acceptance. *Disability, Handicap & Society, 4*(1), 21–36.

Taylor, S.J., Bogdan, R., & Racino, J.A. (Eds.). (1991). *Life in the community: Case studies of organizations supporting people with disabilities.* Baltimore: Paul H. Brookes Publishing Co.

Taylor, S.J., Racino, J.A., Knoll, J.A., & Lutfiyya, Z. (1987). *The nonrestrictive environment: On community integration for people with the most severe disabilities.* Syracuse, NY: Human Policy Press.

Acknowledgments

Many individuals contributed directly or indirectly to this book. First, we thank Paul H. Brookes Publishing Co., and especially Elaine Niefeld for her excellent editorial assistance and Melissa Behm for her continued support of and interest in the work of The Center on Human Policy. Second, we are grateful to the Office of Special Education and Rehabilitative Services and the National Institute on Disability and Rehabilitation Research for support of the Research and Training Center on Community Integration and the Research and Training Center on Community Living. The research reported in this book was supported, in large measure, through Cooperative Agreement H133B00003-90 awarded to The Center on Human Policy, Syracuse University, and Cooperative Agreements H133B80048 and H133B89948 awarded to the Institute on Community Integration, University of Minnesota, by the U.S. Department of Education. Of course, the opinions expressed in this book are those of the authors and no endorsement by the National Institute on Disability and Rehabilitation Research or the U.S. Department of Education should be inferred. We want to single out the Project Officers at the National Institute on Disability and Rehabilitation Research who have been assigned to these Research and Training Centers, Naomi Karp, David Esquith, and Roseann Rafferty, for our special appreciation. Third, we continue to enjoy outstanding support of our research and other activities from Cyndy Colavita, Debbie Simms, and Rachael Zubal at The Center on Human Policy. Finally, we owe a special debt of gratitude to the people with disabilities, families, community members, and professionals who have openly shared their lives and experiences with us.

The Variety of
Community Experience

Introduction

Steven J. Taylor, Robert Bogdan, and Zana Marie Lutfiyya

What is life in the community like for people with developmental disabilities and their families? This question can be answered in different ways. For one, we can listen to the reflections of people with developmental disabilities, their families, their service providers, and their advocates. In the field of developmental disabilities since the late 1980s, "stories" have become an important vehicle for communicating the nature of the community experience (Amado, 1993; O'Brien & Mount, 1991; Schwartz, 1992). Yet another way to answer the question is through activities commonly referred to as *research*, or disciplined inquiry by an independent observer.

The chapters in this book share common elements with both of these approaches. Like the "storytellers" in this field, we are interested in the personal, subjective experiences of people with developmental disabilities and those around them. The question about what life in the community is like ultimately must be answered in terms that are meaningful to the individuals themselves. Also like the storytellers, we believe that experiences are best captured in narratives that reflect the complexity and richness of human existence. Like all researchers, however, we pursue the question about community life based on a particular methodology and world view, and we then filter others' experiences through our own lens.

This book follows in the tradition of qualitative or ethnographic research, an approach that bridges the gap between stories and research (Ferguson, Ferguson, & Taylor, 1992). While the researchers' stories may be collected and analyzed in a manner that is different from that of other storytellers, they are told in such a way as to remain close to the individual's personal, subjective experiences.

Edgerton (1967) was the first researcher in the field of mental retardation and developmental disabilities to popularize qualitative or ethnographic research in his classic study *The Cloak of Competence*. Edgerton and his colleagues and students at the University of California–Los Angeles (UCLA) continue to publish influential qualitative studies in the field (Bercovici, 1983; Edgerton, 1984, 1988, 1993; Edgerton & Bercovici, 1976; Edgerton, Bollinger, & Herr, 1984; Edgerton & Gaston,

1991; Goode, 1980, 1984, 1992; Langness & Levine, 1986). Beginning in the 1970s, another group with roots at Syracuse University began publishing qualitative studies of the lives of people with developmental disabilities (Biklen & Moseley, 1988; Bogdan, 1988; Bogdan & Taylor, 1976, 1982, 1987, 1989, 1994; Bogdan, Taylor, deGrandpre, & Haynes, 1974; Ferguson, 1987, 1994; Ferguson et al., 1992; Foster, 1987; Harry, 1992; Lutfiyya, 1992; Schnorr, 1990; Taylor & Bogdan, 1980, 1989). Syracuse researchers also applied these methods to evaluations of schools and community services (Biklen, 1985; Taylor, 1982; Taylor, Bogdan, & Racino, 1991). By the mid-1980s, qualitative research in developmental disabilities had spread beyond UCLA and Syracuse to become increasingly popular in the field (Murray-Seegert, 1989; Stainback & Stainback, 1984, 1988, 1989).

It is no longer necessary to defend or justify the use of qualitative methods in developmental disability research circles. Yet this book takes on a different challenge because it is written not only for researchers but for practitioners and others working in the field. What might professionals, parents, people with disabilities, advocates, or policy makers learn from a series of qualitative studies of life in the community?

Public policies, agency practices, service ideologies, and professional interventions are based on stereotypes and assumptions about what people with developmental disabilities, families, and communities are like. Take, for example, our images of people with developmental disabilities. Once viewed as eternally childlike, objects of pity, or menaces to the community, those with mental retardation and related disabilities are portrayed differently today. One school of thought and practice automatically associates mental retardation and developmental disabilities with skills training, programs, and interventions. Another depicts individuals with developmental disabilities as powerless, dependent clients of the human services system—victims, as it were, of the very structures ostensibly created to support them.

Or consider some assumptions about families of people with developmental disabilities. Are we to approach them as though they are undergoing a process of grieving and denial, or should we view them in terms of their strengths and capacities? When we think of families, what image do we have in mind? How do matters of class, race, cultural background, and gender roles fit into the picture?

With the recent emphasis on person- and family-centered approaches as well as new paradigms of support, we need to examine the role of human services agencies and professionals. Do human services help or hurt? What is the reality behind the rhetoric?

Finally, how do we think about the community itself? Is community a supportive web of associations and relations available to take over responsibility for the care of dependent members, if only human services agencies would step out of the way? Or is it a hostile and heartless environment, devoid of caring and neighborly concern?

Qualitative studies can provide a yardstick by which to evaluate conventional wisdom, common-sense assumptions, and popular images. When we look closely at the actual experiences of people with developmental disabilities and their families, we find that life in the community is vastly more complex than prevailing views lead us to believe. By understanding and respecting this complexity, we are in a better position to assist and support individuals and families on their own terms.

This book contributes to an understanding of what life in the community is like for some individuals and their families. Each chapter examines a relatively small slice of life in the community. None claims universal or definitive truth. Taken together, though, the chapters fill in a picture of how people with developmental disabilities and their families experience their lives.

The studies reported in this book address one or more of three major themes. The first theme relates to family life. The chapters by Shoultz, Taylor, Traustadottir, and O'Connor examine adults and children with developmental disabilities in the context of their families.

In "'But They Need Me!': The Story of Anna London," Shoultz examines the situation of a young woman with multiple disabilities who, in contrast to commonly held notions, is not a passive recipient of others' help but actively cares for and supports other family members. Taylor's chapter, "'Children's Division Is Coming to Take Pictures': Family Life and Parenting in a Family with Disabilities," contrasts insider and outsider views of a family with disabilities and argues against a presumption of parental incompetence due to mental retardation. Traustadottir's chapter, "A Mother's Work Is Never Done: Constructing a 'Normal' Family Life," shows how families of children with disabilities attempt to conform to what they see as typical life for any family in the community. O'Connor's "'We're All One Family': The Positive Construction of People with Disabilities by Family Members" explores how an African American family views a child with autism and interprets his behavior without regard to his disability category.

The second theme has to do with the nature of community, whether defined in terms of associations and groups or geographically. Each of these chapters highlights examples of acceptance and membership of people with developmental disabilities.

Bogdan's "A 'Simple' Farmer Accused of Murder: The Case of Delbert Ward" and Andrews's "Life in Mendocino: A Young Man with Down Syndrome in a Small Town in Northern California" present case studies in which people with mental retardation were accepted as full-fledged members in small-town communities. The following chapters by Lutfiyya, Fisher, Bogdan, and Shoultz shift attention from acceptance in communities to membership in groups and associations. Lutfiyya's chapter, "Baking Bread Together: A Study of Membership and Inclusion," shows how a man with mental retardation and a history of criminal behavior was incorporated into and supported by a bakery with roots in the Catholic Worker movement. In "A Temporary Place to Belong: Inclusion in a Public Speaking and Personal Relations Course," Fisher examines how the ethos and structure of a public speaking and human relations course facilitated the full participation of two people with disabilities. Bogdan's "Singing for an Inclusive Society: The Community Choir" addresses how a community choir's ideology of social justice and inclusion was extended to accommodate people with disabilities. In her intensely personal chapter, "'My Heart Chose Freedom': The Story of Lucy Rider's Second Life," Shoultz explores the relationship between personal identity and networks of social support.

The third theme touched on in this book is the nature of human services. Although this theme appears throughout many of the chapters, it is addressed most explicitly in the contributions by Walker and O'Connor.

Walker's "Community Based Is Not Community: The Social Geography of Disability" looks at community participation from the vantage point of social geography and explores how people with developmental disabilities can be physically but not socially integrated into the community. O'Connor's "More Than They Bargained For: The Meaning of Support to Families" shows how contemporary family support programs may depart from a family-centered rhetoric and exact a significant toll on families as a cost of seeking help.

As a final note, we want to comment on the language used in this book to refer to people with mental retardation or developmental disabilities. We share a theoretical perspective that considers mental retardation and developmental disabilities to be social constructs. Although we do not deny that physical and intellectual differences among people exist, who does or does not have mental retardation or a developmental disability is a matter of social definition (Bogdan & Taylor, 1994). A person may be considered to have mental retardation or a developmental disability in one context but not in another. The terminology "person labeled mentally retarded or developmentally disabled" represents our theoretical perspective. However, for the sake of readability, we have used the commonly accepted "people-first" language throughout this book. However, by doing so we do not endorse the assumptions and stereotypes underlying contemporary diagnostic categories.

Now we turn to the variety of community experience.

REFERENCES

Amado, A.N. (Ed.). (1993). *Friendships and community connections between people with and without developmental disabilities.* Baltimore: Paul H. Brookes Publishing Co.

Bercovici, S. (1983). *Barriers to normalization: The restrictive management of retarded persons.* Baltimore: University Park Press.

Biklen, D. (1985). *Achieving the complete school: Strategies for effective mainstreaming.* New York: Teachers College Press.

Biklen, S.K., & Moseley, C.R. (1988). "Are you retarded?" "No, I'm Catholic": Qualitative methods in the study of people with severe handicaps. *Journal of The Association for Persons with Severe Handicaps, 13*(3), 155–163.

Bogdan, R. (1988). *Freak show: Presenting human oddities for amusement and profit.* Chicago: University of Chicago Press.

Bogdan, R., & Taylor, S.J. (1976). The judged, not the judges: An insider's view of mental retardation. *American Psychologist, 31*(1), 47–52.

Bogdan, R., & Taylor, S.J. (1982). *Inside out: The social meaning of mental retardation.* Toronto, Ontario, Canada: University of Toronto Press.

Bogdan, R., & Taylor, S.J. (1987). Toward a sociology of acceptance: The other side of the study of deviance. *Social Policy, 18*(2), 34–39.

Bogdan, R., & Taylor, S.J. (1989). Relationships with severely disabled people: The social construction of humanness. *Social Problems, 36*(2), 135–148.

Bogdan, R., & Taylor, S.J. (1994). *The social meaning of mental retardation: Two life stories.* New York: Teachers College Press.

Bogdan, R., Taylor, S.J., deGrandpre, B., & Haynes, S. (1974). Let them eat programs: Attendants' perspectives and programming on wards in state schools. *Journal of Health and Social Behavior, 15,* 142–151.

Edgerton, R.B. (1967). *The cloak of competence: Stigma in the lives of the mentally retarded.* Berkeley: University of California Press.

Edgerton, R.B. (1984). Anthropology and mental retardation. Research approaches and opportunities. *Culture, Medicine, and Psychiatry, 8,* 25–48.

Edgerton, R.B. (1988). Aging in the community—A matter of choice. *American Journal on Mental Retardation, 92*(4), 331–335.

Edgerton, R.B. (1993). *The cloak of competence: Revised and updated.* Berkeley: University of California Press.

Edgerton, R.B., & Bercovici, S.M. (1976). The cloak of competence: Years later. *American Journal of Mental Deficiency, 80*(5), 485–497.

Edgerton, R.B., Bollinger, M., & Herr, B. (1984). The cloak of competence: After two decades. *American Journal of Mental Deficiency, 88*(4), 345–351.

Edgerton, R.B., & Gaston, M.A. (Eds.). (1991). *"I've seen it all!": Lives of older persons with mental retardation in the community.* Baltimore: Paul H. Brookes Publishing Co.

Ferguson, D.L. (1987). *Curriculum decision making for students with severe handicaps: Policy and practice:* New York: Teachers College Press.

Ferguson, D.L. (1994). Is communication really the point? Some thoughts on interventions and membership. *Mental Retardation, 32*(1), 7–18.

Ferguson, P.M., Ferguson, D.L., & Taylor, S.J. (Eds.). (1992). *Interpreting disability: A qualitative reader.* New York: Teachers College Press.

Foster, S.B. (1987). *Politics of caring.* London: The Falmer Press.

Goode, D. (1980). The world of the congenitally deaf-blind: Towards the grounds for achieving human understanding. In J. Jacobs (Ed.), *Mental retardation: A phenomenological approach* (pp. 187–207). Springfield, IL: Charles C Thomas.

Goode, D. (1984). Socially produced identities, intimacy and the problem of competence among the retarded. In S. Tomlinson & L. Barton (Eds.), *Special education and social interests* (pp. 228–248). London: Croom-Helm.

Goode, D.A. (1992). Who is Bobby? Ideology and method in the discovery of a Down syndrome person's competence. In P.M. Ferguson, D.L. Ferguson, & S.J. Taylor (Eds.), *Interpreting disability: A qualitative reader* (pp. 197–212). New York: Teachers College Press.

Harry, B. (1992). *Cultural diversity, families, and the special education system: Communication and empowerment.* New York: Teachers College Press.

Langness, L.L., & Levine, H.G. (Eds.). (1986). *Culture and retardation.* Boston: D. Reidel Publishing Co.

Lutfiyya, Z.M. (1992). "A feeling of being connected": Friendships between people with and without learning difficulties. *Disability, Handicap & Society, 6*(3), 233–245.

Murray-Seegert, C. (1989). *Nasty girls, thugs, and humans like us: Social relations between severely disabled and nondisabled students in high school.* Baltimore: Paul H. Brookes Publishing Co.

O'Brien, J., & Mount, B. (1991). Telling new stories: The search for capacity among people with severe handicaps. In L. Meyer, C. Peck, & L. Brown (Eds.), *Critical issues in the lives of people with severe disabilities* (pp. 89–92). Baltimore: Paul H. Brookes Publishing Co.

Schnorr, R.F. (1990). "Peter? He comes and goes . . .": First graders' perspectives on a part-time mainstream student. *Journal of The Association for Persons with Severe Handicaps, 15*(4), 231–240.

Schwartz, D.B. (1992). *Crossing the river: Creating a conceptual revolution in community and disability.* Cambridge, MA: Brookline Books.

Stainback, S., & Stainback, W. (1984). Broadening the research perspective in special education. *Exceptional Children, 50*(5), 400–408.

Stainback, S., & Stainback, W. (1988). *Understanding and conducting qualitative research.* Dubuque, IA: Kendall/Hunt Publishing Co.

Stainback, W., & Stainback, S. (1989). Using qualitative data collection procedures to investigate supported education issues. *Journal of The Association for Persons with Severe Handicaps, 14*(4), 271–277.

Taylor, S.J. (1982). From segregation to integration: Strategies for integrating severely handicapped students in normal school and community settings. *Journal of The Association for Persons with Severe Handicaps, 7*(3), 42–49.

Taylor, S.J., & Bogdan, R. (1980). Defending illusions: The institution's struggle for survival. *Human Organization, 39*(3), 209–218.

Taylor, S.J., & Bogdan, R. (1989). On accepting relationships between people with mental retardation and nondisabled people: Towards an understanding of acceptance. *Disability, Handicap & Society, 4*(1), 21–36.

Taylor, S.J., Bogdan, R., & Racino, J.A. (Eds.). (1991). *Life in the community: Case studies of organizations supporting people with disabilities.* Baltimore: Paul H. Brookes Publishing Co.

1

"But They Need Me!"

The Story of Anna London

Bonnie Shoultz

Anna London's story contradicts much of what is written about people with developmental and/or psychiatric disabilities. Such people are usually portrayed solely as recipients of care rather than as caregivers themselves (Barton, 1989; Bulmer, 1987; Hillyer, 1993; Singer & Irvin, 1989). Even the recent literature on families having a member with a developmental or psychiatric disability, which often describes people with disabilities making a contribution to the family, emphasizes how the family constructs that contribution (Summers, Behr, & Turnbull, 1989; Turnbull et al., 1993). In this literature, family members are often depicted as experiencing growth, joy, courage, and other benefits simply as a result of the presence of the person with disabilities in their lives, not necessarily as a result of his or her specific qualities or actions. The older literature recognized only the burdens on the family as caregivers (Farber, 1986; Olshansky, 1962). Anna London, however, has given extensive help and support to others, especially members of her family. The literature on people with disabilities as caregivers is small and very recent, and it is based on studies in England (Morris, 1993; Walmsley, 1993). This literature reveals that women with disabilities sometimes assume a helping or caregiving role.

Anna's story also contradicts the other commonly held notion that people with developmental and/or psychiatric disabilities have little control over their own fates—that they are victims or passive clients of service systems that decide for them or, at best, "give" them choices about certain aspects of their lives. For many years, the literature has delineated the oppression and abuse of people with disabilities (Blatt & Kaplan, 1974; Wehman, 1993; Wolfensberger, 1975). More recently, writers have begun to emphasize empowerment and community participation (Lord, 1991; Taylor, Bogdan, & Racino, 1991), but often within a larger framework that assumes service system and family responsibility for people. This assumption may block our awareness that many people with developmental and/or psychiatric disabilities actively manage their own lives.

Anna London helps the people in her life directly and extensively. She is, within limits, master of her own destiny, a person who actively changes the circumstances of her life according to what works best for her at the time. I met Anna as part of a study of the community connections of people with disabilities (the Community Study). Through the self-advocacy movement, I had had a long involvement with people with developmental disabilities as a friend, self-advocacy group advisor, and admirer of their achievements. I am also the mother of a young man with a psychiatric disability. These involvements had intertwined in my life—I was a parent and friend, as well as a professional—but I had never "studied" a person before I met Anna in 1988. Anna welcomed me into her life and was eager to have someone learn about her and tell her story.

AN INTRODUCTION TO ANNA LONDON

Anna London is a European American in her 40s who was nominated for our study by Sara Baxter, director of a program that pairs people with disabilities with people without disabilities. Sara recommended Anna because Anna is well connected in the community. Anna lives by herself in a subsidized apartment building in Salt City; she has lived alone for nearly 2 years. When I met her in 1988, Anna lived with her mother on the South Side. At the time this chapter was written, Anna divided her time between her boyfriend, her mother, a friend who is blind, and the family of her brother, for whose ex-wife she babysat every day after school.

Anna has a number of health problems, including a heart condition (recently diagnosed) and an esophageal dysfunction that required surgery and ongoing treatment to facilitate swallowing. She also has a hearing impairment. As a child she was labeled mildly mentally retarded, and after moving to Salt City as an adult she was diagnosed as having a psychiatric disorder. She has received services from two mental health agencies and another agency that provides community support to people with developmental and/or psychiatric disabilities. She has been an inpatient in a psychiatric hospital on a few occasions.

Anna has a cheerful personality, which many people take at face value. For example, her "companion" (a volunteer who was matched with her through a mental health agency) described her as a cheerful, happy person. However, Anna has told me that beneath her cheery exterior are her "real feelings," feelings of not trusting people or of sadness or anxiety, and she reveals these to the mental health professionals with whom she meets more than to her other acquaintances.

ANNA'S TWO FAMILIES

The first of five children born to her mother and father in a medium-sized city in New York's southern tier, Anna was removed from her parents' custody at 3 months due to "failure-to-thrive syndrome." After a neighbor called the authorities on her behalf, a state agency responsible for child welfare intervened and she was taken to a hospital. Anna had a number of physical disorders as an infant and child, including a cleft palate and ear problems that later led to a mastoidectomy and a hearing impairment. The cleft palate, which resulted in swallowing difficulties, was probably the reason for her failure to thrive. Even in the hospital, it took a long time to correct her condition. Her mother said, "They tube-fed her, but it didn't seem like she grew right. Her stomach got real big but her arms and legs were still like toothpicks."

Reflecting on Anna's removal from her home, her mother said, "She was my first baby, and I didn't know any better. I just trusted what my husband said, because I figured he was experienced. They made me feel real bad in the hospital, like it was my fault, and my husband could see how it hurt me. He told me not to go up there, so I stopped." Her husband, who was in his late 50s when Anna was born, had nine children from his previous marriage, and he had said the baby was fine.

Later, Anna was placed with a foster family. She grew up in that home and had very little contact with her birth parents during her childhood, although her mother tried to regain custody at least twice after the death of Anna's father. Although Anna knew she was a foster child, she regarded her foster parents, an older couple who had 23 different children while she was with them, as her mother and father. Her most vivid childhood memories are of this family, which was large and also included many extended family members. As a child, Anna went to a local school for children with hearing impairments. At age 14 she was placed in an orphanage in Salt City, where she could have a mastoid operation. At age 16 she was sent to a residential school for youth with mild mental retardation, and she stayed there until she was almost 19.

She went back to live with her foster parents in 1967 or 1968 and stayed with them until 1977, when both of them died. She lived at the YWCA in their city for a time but then decided to try to reunite with her birth family in Salt City, which was 90 miles north of where she had lived most of her life. In 1979, when Anna was 30, she came to Salt City to attend a large revivalist meeting, and while she was there she called her grandmother. Her grandmother invited her over and called other family members to meet Anna. They encouraged her to move to Salt City, and, because she was lonely, she did. She and her birth mother decided to try living together. They lived together for several years, after which Anna moved to an apartment with a roommate, with the support and encouragement of a local agency. Later, she moved back with her mother because her mother could not afford to live by herself, and they lived together until late 1991. They moved a number of times and lived in three different places between 1988, when I met her, and 1991.

While Anna was in the foster home, she didn't know much about her birth family, except for the few times her mother came to see her. As her mother now says, "They made me feel bad, like she was their child and not mine, so I stayed away. . . . I did try to get her back, but it didn't work out." Clearly Anna's mother had many difficulties as Anna was growing up. When Anna's mother married Mr. London, she was 18 and he was in his late 50s. He and his young wife had three children after Anna was removed from their home. They were extremely poor. When he was 67, he contracted pneumonia, and his wife (pregnant with a fifth child) had to tell the hospital they had no money to pay the bills. County welfare workers went to their home, found they had no electricity or running water, and removed their children to foster homes and Mrs. London to a "county home," which was a kind of poorhouse for destitute people. She called her mother in Salt City for help and was able to leave the county home after a few days, but her husband died on the day she left. She only saw him once before he died.

She moved to Salt City, had her baby, and began to try getting the other three children back. It took several years for her to do so. After she did, they lived together in Salt City for a couple of years. Then she placed an ad for a husband in a national tabloid and went to Texas with her children to marry one of the two men who responded. She told me, "I showed the children their pictures, and they picked the man I married." She tried to get Anna back before they left, but the welfare department said she would have to prove that her marriage would work. She couldn't prove that, so she and the other children went to Texas without Anna.

The family later moved to Florida. She left her second husband when she discovered that he had been sexually abusing her middle daughter. She and three of her children came back to Salt City, leaving her oldest son in Florida where he had entered the military. One by one, her children married, and she lived alone until she and Anna were reunited and decided to live together.

Anna's mother has been very religious, belonging to various fundamentalist churches since 1965, when, as she says, "I gave myself to the Lord." She feels the Lord has helped her through many trials. At present, Anna's mother has heart problems, having had four episodes of congestive heart failure. She had triple bypass surgery in September 1988. She has also had pneumonia and various other health problems, but is doing quite well now. For years Anna has belonged to the same church as her mother. They have both participated actively in church events, including retreats and church suppers.

ANNA AND HER FAMILY TODAY

Today Anna is poor, as are her family members. She and her mother live in separate rent-subsidized apartments in different parts of the city. They both receive Supplemental Security Income (SSI), and Medicaid pays their medical bills. A brother, married when I met Anna in 1989, has divorced and now lives with a girlfriend and her son. He is unemployed and apparently has extreme mood swings that interfere with his work and relationships. Anna has been the babysitter for his three children for 11 years, ever since the oldest was born. Back then, she took care of the children during the day while both parents worked. They paid her what they could, but much less than they would otherwise have had to pay a sitter. Until recently, she came after school and stayed with the children until their mother came home from work.

When I first met Anna and her mother, Anna's middle sister had not spoken to her mother for years because of a disagreement over religion that involved several family members. This sister had always felt bad about having been left in foster care longer than the others (except for Anna), and she is the one who was sexually abused by her stepfather. She and her mother made up about a year later. She has four children, all of whom have been removed from her custody in the past three years after she discovered that her husband, their father, was sexually abusing them. The father is in prison, but Anna believes that the children and the child welfare system place some of the blame on her sister.

Until fairly recently, one of her sister's children, a boy who is labeled seriously emotionally disturbed, was still with his mother. Anna babysat for him every night while her sister worked. The two babysitting jobs meant that she was away from home 12 hours a day or more during the week, and she was also babysitting some weekends. Later this boy was removed from the home, and Anna had only one babysitting commitment. She took responsibility for quite a bit of her mother's personal care and some housework until they each got their own apartment. Anna arranged her schedule around the needs of her mother, brother, and sister and their families.

ANNA'S CONNECTIONS

Today Anna's primary involvements are with a boyfriend she has been seeing for about 2 years, various family members, a volunteer recruited for her by a local program, and church members, several of whom I have met when I have been out with Anna or her mother. (Anna no longer attends this church because they disapproved of her relationship with her boyfriend who now lives with her.) She also sees a number of health and mental health professionals. Except for the church members, who have behaved in a warm and caring fashion toward Anna and her mother whenever we have encountered them, her only friends without disabilities during the years I have known her were assigned to her as volunteers or mental health professionals. Her boyfriend and other friends have disabilities.

Anna is involved with a few community mental health agencies, each having a different role in her life. When I met her, she had regular appointments with a therapist and a service coordinator. Then, she said, the agency that had been providing her therapy told her that she "wasn't crazy anymore" and terminated her treatment, so she entered into individual counseling with another agency that accepts Medicaid. At various times her mother has become involved in her counseling because they have had problems getting along with each other. Anna sees a case manager who works for an agency that provides community support services to people with psychiatric disorders. This agency has supported her over the years, helping her find apartments, arranging recreational opportunities, and just listening as she made decisions on major or minor changes in her life. She is also involved in a program that recruits community members to advocate for people with disabilities.

Anna sees a number of doctors for her health problems and seems to have fairly frequent medical appointments. In the spring of 1989, she had surgery on some muscles that were constricting her esophagus. She is still seeing doctors for her esophageal condition, which is getting worse again, and for her heart condition. She is very knowledgeable about medical procedures and about the purposes of medications. While she was in the hospital for her surgery, I watched in awe as she and her mother discussed her medications, the machines and equipment she had to use, and the procedures, such as a variety of breathing exercises using three different pieces of equipment, that were employed to help her heal.

Finally, Anna's church is very important to her. She has a special relationship with a woman who is blind and who goes to this church. She says she helps this woman with various tasks during church programs and retreats. While Anna was hospitalized, church members wrote to her, and I have been with her on several occasions when she encountered a "sister in the Lord."

The various health and mental health professionals she sees, the volunteers recruited for her, other people with disabilities, and her church constitute a separate world that Anna, with help, constructed for herself when she was most deeply involved in trying to meet her family's needs. A mental health worker who has been her friend and worker for 10 years described this world as an alternative community of her own and actively worked to support her in developing it. He felt that Anna needed an alternative to be able to see choices other than her role as helper within the family.

ON THE ROLES THAT ANNA FILLS

Many people with disabilities, especially those whose lives are circumscribed by their role as recipient of human services, appear to have attained just one status, that of client or disabled person. Their lives are often profoundly affected by this status, which determines everything that happens to them (Goffman, 1963). Anna, on the other hand, has a number of valued roles. She is a helper, a daughter, a sister, and an active church member. She also has a number of client roles, such as medical patient, mental health system participant, and recipient of volunteer attentions (through two programs that have recruited people who would be involved with her).

To her family, her major roles seem to be as caregiver and family member. To members of her church, she is a "sister in the Lord." To some workers, she is a client. To herself, I believe she is all of these things. She moves easily from role to role, the way most of us do, and makes her own decisions, often in consultation with others. Anna experiences some tension between some of her roles (such as between her role as caregiver and her role as recipient of mental health and volunteer services), but her life is basically under her own control.

However, the control she exercises is tempered by her complex relationships with her family members. There are times when she feels she has no choice but to help out; for example, several times she wanted to get a place of her own but decided to continue living with her mother, who said that she (Anna's mother) could not afford a place of her own. Anna talked to people about her various options and knew that she had choices, but finally felt that "I had no choice." When her mother was accepted for subsidized housing, they did separate, and the community support agency helped Anna pay the rent on the apartment she had shared with her mother until she too could get into subsidized housing.

Thus, Anna's role within the family is somewhat complex. In many ways, the help she has given has allowed the other family members to function—to hold jobs, to feed themselves and their families, and, in her mother's case, to stay out of an adult home or nursing home when her health was at its worst. One worker described Anna as having "held that whole family together." Sometimes Anna expressed some longing to have a life away from them, but she worked hard to keep them from going under, from divorcing, and from losing their children. Now she has attained a life apart. She visits her family members and helps them out when they say they need her, but she is on her own.

Anna's role as member of a congregation is different. It appears to be a role she shares with her mother, due to the fact that she and her mother attend the same church and used to go there together. It would be difficult for Anna to create her own church community, separate from her mother, unless she were to join a different church. She does have one church friend, the woman who is blind, who lives in the apartment building where Anna lives and is a friend outside of church as well as within it. The other church members appear to be friendly to both Anna and her mother. Even when she and her mother have experienced conflict over a church event (such as the time Anna arranged transportation for herself, and her mother was upset because she could not find anyone to take her to the event), Anna has never expressed to me a wish that either she or her mother should join another church. Her church membership and her fellowship with her sisters and brothers in the Lord are extremely important to her.

ON GIVING AND RECEIVING HELP

Anna views herself as a person whose main purpose in life is to help and give care to others. When asked about growing up in her foster home, she described herself as having "helped to raise 23 foster children." When asked about her time as a student in the residential school, the only experience she recalled was helping another new student who was frightened and could not understand the school situation. Anna provides extensive help to her family and provided even more several years ago, when she was living with her mother.

Now that Anna is doing less for her family, she is doing more for friends. She has a boyfriend and other associates, all of whom have disabilities, and she helps them in many ways. She lends her boyfriend money and lets him stay at her apartment much of the time. She helps her other friends with disabilities in any way she can, such as packing for a move, accompanying them to the doctor, and so forth.

When she is relating to people whose role is to help her (mental health workers and volunteers), she helps them by doing or being what they expect—a person who opens up to them about her problems and her feelings, a person who accepts their help. I interviewed representatives of two agencies with which she has been involved, and both said that she frequently called first thing in the morning to wish them a nice day and to say "I love you." Both representatives said they appreciated these calls and felt that they illustrated what a sweet person she is.

It would appear, from what she has told me, that Anna's world view is that relationships comprise helping and getting help, going places together, and showing affection. For example, the reason she gave for coming home early from a trip to visit her brother in Florida with her mother in January 1991 was that her brother's wife did not want her help. She told me, "I guess sometimes helping can be more of a hindrance," as though that were the only basis for her to be there. Even the "other world" she constructed while she was most involved with her family was built around the dynamic of helping. Helping is a way for Anna to have a place in the world, but it also causes problems for her, because she spends so much of her time in this role and finds it difficult to say "no." A contrasting view on the help Anna gives to others holds that she is exploited by the people she helps. Some workers and volunteers have stated or hinted at this view.

However, from Anna's perspective, helping is her core identity. It is what she does best, it lets her know she is needed, and, even when it feels overwhelming to help so much, it has its rewards. For her, helping began when she was a foster daughter, and it became her life's purpose. To take helping away from her, to recommend that she think only of herself, would be to undermine a major aspect of her life.

Anna gets something that is meaningful to her when she helps others. Those who feel that she has been exploited may fail to take that into account or to see the ways in which her mother and other family members give to Anna. I saw her mother's dedication to her when she was in the hospital. Her mother, poor and recovering from congestive heart failure, boarded their dog so that she could take the bus to the hospital every day to be with Anna. She slept in the waiting room the night before Anna's surgery and was present for Anna throughout the recovery period. More importantly, her family and friends give Anna a sense that she is part of a complex network of relationships rather than an individual on her own. In other words, she belongs.

In the early years of my study, workers and volunteers seemed to admire Anna and accept her decisions about her life, but they also saw her as a victim. Yet surely a view of oneself as being needed by and helpful to others is more satisfying than a view of oneself as a client, patient, or victim. I have witnessed her family's grave troubles and their impact on Anna and her mother, and I am aware of how hard her life has been. However, I do not believe that many of the alternatives available within the human services world (living in a group home or certified apartment program, working in a sheltered workshop, or having a menial job—i.e., being a client rather than creating her own life) would have improved things for her. Anna's decision not to pursue these alternatives but rather to wait until her family's circumstances improved is responsible for the opportunities (her apartment, especially, and having a boyfriend) that she has since pursued.

ON BEING POOR AND DIFFERENT

The subject of money came up again and again during my visits. Anna's mother describes living from check to check, back-dating checks at the end of the month, food shopping for an hour to make $11 stretch until the next check comes, and so forth. Anna must sometimes borrow money to make ends meet, although she always pays it back. Both women receive SSI checks, which make up the largest part of their income. Before Anna's mother moved into the subsidized apartment, she could not have made it financially without Anna's check. Workers and volunteers seemed to worry about this, thinking that Anna's mother was taking advantage of her.

The fact is, however, that Anna's mother accepts her own circumstances with grace and dignity. For example, she puts money aside to buy presents for her grandchildren (always including the children of her daughter in Syracuse, who had not, until a couple of years ago, spoken to her for years). As mentioned earlier, she boarded their dog for 8 days so that she could spend time with Anna in the hospital. This cost $87, which is a large sum for people who don't have much money.

Money, or the lack of it, has a big effect on Anna's capacity to do things for others. The help she gives has to be the kind that doesn't cost money—for example, she can't provide car fare or buy things for others, and she can't spend much when she goes out with someone. For years it meant that she and her mother had to live together even when they were not getting along well and that they had to live in small apartments in poor neighborhoods. Lack of money makes it more difficult for her to get out to see people; it affects her appearance (she wears inexpensive dresses); and it limits what she can do for herself. It has also affected her health, and that of her mother. There is a great deal of stress in not having much money, and most of the health problems they have are statistically associated with high levels of stress. On the other hand, they get health care and counseling, paid for by Medicaid, because they are so poor. They have not complained about the quality of the care they receive.

ON HUMAN SERVICES AND THEIR IMPACT ON PEOPLE'S LIVES

Anna has been involved with human services since infancy, when she was taken from her parents and placed in foster care. While the human services system has profoundly affected Anna, she has evolved into a "user" of services who makes her own decisions about how much involvement she wants to have. An example from an interview:

> I have been in the respite program, which is part of [the psychiatric hospital]. It's an emergency housing, where a person can go for five days and just be away from everybody for a while. To get away from all the stress. But I told my therapist . . . that I'm trying to keep myself out, because whenever I get out, I'm right back in the same situation again, so . . . I don't put myself in the hospital at all.

When she speaks of her relations with human services workers, Anna generally sees herself as an actor, not as acted upon. The two human services professionals I interviewed corroborated my feelings about this. Both of them saw themselves as important in Anna's life in the sense that their role was to make her aware of choices, to support her right to choose for herself, and to offer her a community outside her family. Neither saw themselves as needing to control her or were disapproving of the choices she made. One human services worker wondered whether Anna feels loved by her family but tried hard not to judge her or them. His sense was that Anna makes a community out of mental health workers, volunteers, and consumers (people who receive services through the mental health system).

It is possible that the health care world is another community Anna has made for herself. She has many appointments with doctors, is familiar with medical terminology, and in the hospital was very interested in understanding the procedures to which she was subjected. Her interactions with people in the health care setting are meaningful to her, as indicated by her tone of voice and by the way she and they interacted during her hospital stay.

ON CLASS AND RELIGION

Anna's family has always been poor. She may have been brought up by working or middle-class people, but her family of origin would probably be classified as lower working class. Her brothers and sisters are working class people also, and at least two of them continue to have major crises in their lives. Class issues undoubtedly affect the kinds of people with whom Anna could make reciprocal friendships.

Anna's mother "gave herself to the Lord" in 1965, and this decision seems to have affected her life profoundly and to have mediated some of the class issues as well. With the support of their church, Anna and her mother try to abide by religious and moral principles for living. If nothing else, this has given them another source for guidance, separate and different from the all-pervasive human services world that had so much influence when the children were young and also separate from the stresses and negative forces experienced by so many poor people.

ON BEING CONNECTED

What is "being connected" from the perspective of various people who know Anna? Anna was originally nominated for this study because she was seen as a person who is well connected, as a person with at least one good relationship. The definition of "being connected" is somewhat fluid. To some it means having a rich network of unpaid, freely given relationships with people other than family. To Anna it means something very different.

Anna has had two "friends" who were recruited for her while she was living with her mother but who saw themselves as volunteers. For about a year, she went out once a week with Grace, who acted as a service provider in the sense that she saw her role as getting Anna to "open up" to her or as helping Anna. Anna's other recruited friend, May, became more involved in her own life and limited the time she spent with Anna, taking her out once a month to shop for groceries. Apparently, it was hard for Anna's mother to accept that these friendships were Anna's and not hers. According to Grace, her relationship with Anna ended because Anna's mother kept wanting Grace to take her out too. Grace was not able to manage the situation and retain her good feelings for Anna, so she asked to be assigned to someone else.

Anna's view of connectedness was expressed to me in her first interview. She considers her workers, her therapists, her doctors, her recruited friends, and her boyfriend to be her connections. As she once said, "My mother has to understand that I have my own life." The extrafamily life of which she speaks is with these people.

Yet none of these people were particularly responsive when Anna was in the hospital. Neither Grace nor May paid her much attention during her 3-week hospitalization for major surgery, although Grace did visit twice and May sent a card. Her brother visited her once, but that was days before they knew for sure that she would have to have surgery. Only her mother was faithful in visiting. Thus, when she had a real need, her mother was the only one who was truly there for her, in spite of the great inconvenience involved. She told Anna how much the dog missed her and took Anna's comb home so the dog could be comforted by its smell. She did many other little things to cheer Anna and help her feel better.

I am left still pondering the question, what is connectedness? Anna's mother, her case worker, her companion, and others all care for her, in different ways. But there are problems between Anna and her mother, as devoted as her mother can be when Anna is ill, and the other friends limit their presence in her life.

CONCLUSION

Anna London is a woman who in many ways contradicts the idea that disability implies dependence. Although she and her mother are in many ways isolated and just barely surviving, she creates many opportunities to live up to the self-image that she developed at an early age and maintains to this day. That is, she helps: She holds her family together, she is generally cheerful and loving, and she contributes where she can. However, she also has periods of sadness and stress and does not always get back what she gives.

In her life outside the family, Anna determines how and for what she lives. She seeks advice from some people and is influenced by or pressed on by others who want her help, but she has learned how to limit her giving based on her own best interests. She utilizes the human services that she trusts. She is poor and often has to borrow money to get through the month, but she remains—has had to learn how to be—in charge.

REFERENCES

Barton, L. (Ed.). (1989). *Disability and dependency*. London: Falmer Press.

Blatt, B., & Kaplan, F. (1974). *Christmas in purgatory*. Syracuse, NY: Human Policy Press.

Bulmer, M. (1987). *The social basis of community care*. London: Allen & Unwin.

Farber, B. (1986). Historical contexts of research on families with mentally retarded members. In J. Gallagher & P. Vietze (Eds.), *Families of handicapped persons: Research, programs, and policy issues* (pp. 3-23). Baltimore: Paul H. Brookes Publishing Co.

Goffman, E. (1963). *Stigma: Notes on the management of spoiled identity*. Englewood Cliffs, NJ: Prentice Hall.

Hillyer, B. (1993). *Feminism and disability*. Norman: University of Oklahoma Press.

Lord, J. (1991). *Lives in transition: The process of personal empowerment*. Kitchener, Ontario, Canada: Centre for Research and Education in Human Services.

Morris, J. (1993). *Independent lives? Community care and disabled people*. New York: Macmillan.

Olshansky, S. (1962). Chronic sorrow: A response to having a mentally defective child. *Social Work, 43*, 190–193.

Singer, G.H.S., & Irvin, E.K. (Eds.). (1989). *Support for caregiving families: Enabling positive adaptation to disability*. Baltimore: Paul H. Brookes Publishing Co.

Summers, J.A., Behr, S.K., & Turnbull, A.P. (1989). Positive adaptation and coping strengths of families who have children with disabilities. In G. Singer & L. Irvin (Eds.), *Support for caregiving families: Enabling positive adaptation to disability* (pp. 27–40). Baltimore: Paul H. Brookes Publishing Co.

Taylor, S.J., Bogdan, R., & Racino, J.A. (Eds.). (1991). *Life in the community: Case studies of organizations supporting people in the community*. Baltimore: Paul H. Brookes Publishing Co.

Turnbull, A.P., Patterson, J.M., Behr, S.K., Murphy, D.L., Marquis, J.G., & Blue-Banning, M.J. (Eds.). (1993). *Cognitive coping, families, and disability*. Baltimore: Paul H. Brookes Publishing Co.

Walmsley, J. (1993). Contradictions in caring: Reciprocity and interdependence. *Disability, Handicap & Society, 8*(2), 129–141.

Wehman, P. (Ed.). (1993). *The ADA mandate for social change*. Baltimore: Paul H. Brookes Publishing Co.

Wolfensberger, W. (1975). *The origin and nature of our institutional models*. Syracuse, NY: Human Policy Press.

2

"Children's Division Is Coming to Take Pictures"

Family Life and Parenting in a Family with Disabilities

Steven J. Taylor

Parents who are mentally retarded have long been a source of professional and public concern. Beginning with the eugenics movement around the turn of the century, professionals and policy makers raised public alarm about the spread of defective genes resulting from procreation among people with mental retardation and especially among "high-grade defectives" (Goddard, 1912). During the late 1800s and early 1900s, the federal and state governments enacted laws to prevent the propagation of "defective offspring" through restrictive immigration laws, segregation, involuntary sterilization, and restrictive marriage laws (Smith, 1985; Taylor & Searl, 1987).

By the late 1920s and early 1930s, however, leaders in the field of mental retardation began to express serious reservations about the eugenics movement and its campaign to rid the population of the alleged menace to society posed by people with mental retardation (Wolfensberger, 1975). Public revulsion of the eugenics policies and mass extermination practiced in Nazi Germany served to further discredit the more extremist theories and proposals of the eugenics movement in America. By the 1960s and 1970s, the growing recognition of the importance of normalization (Wolfensberger, 1972), or social role valorization (Wolfensberger, 1983), led to increased acceptance of the human and civil rights of people with mental retardation, including the rights to marry and bear children.

Attention has shifted gradually from the prevention of sexual expression and reproduction among people with mental retardation to questions regarding their parental adequacy. When the words *parent* and *mentally retarded* are paired, concern for the welfare of the children automatically arises in the minds of many child protective agencies, developmental disability agencies, and agents of the law. According to one family court judge, "[This] is a problem for a whole society. . . . The question is: how well are children cared for in the homes of parents with mental disabilities?" (Forder, 1990, p. ix). Reflecting common professional opinion, Whitman and Accardo (1990) write, "Mentally retarded adults in the community are having children and are experiencing significant problems in parenting" (p. 203).

This chapter examines family life in a family in which the parents and children have mental retardation as well as other disabilities. The immediate family, which I refer to as the Dukes, consists of four members—Bill and Winnie and their two children, Sammy and Cindy; however, the Dukes are part of a much larger network of extended family members and friends. Each member of the Duke family has mental retardation or other disabilities, and child protective agencies have frequently intervened in the family's life.

In order to appreciate the Duke family, one has to juxtapose how they look from the outside—that is, from a distance—with how they look from the inside—how they see themselves and how they look once one has gotten to know them well. At first glance, the Dukes and their kin remind one of the Kallikaks (Goddard, 1912), the Jukes (Dugdale, 1910), or one of the other notorious families studied during the eugenics period as representing the hereditary transmission of feeblemindedness, disability, social pathology, and pauperism. Bill, Winnie, and their two children have all been diagnosed as mentally retarded or disabled by schools and human services agencies, and a sizable number of their kin and friends have been similarly diagnosed. Mental retardation, physical disabilities, mental illness or emotional disturbance, speech impediments, seizure disorders, and miscellaneous medical problems are common among Bill and Winnie's brothers and sisters, nieces and nephews, cousins, in-laws, and friends. With few exceptions, kin and friends are poor or living at the edge of poverty. The men look seedy, the women look hard, and the children look dirty. But this is only at first glance.

As I have gotten to know Bill and Winnie and their family, I have come to see them as kind, gentle, resourceful, and respectable. They have created for themselves decent lives given their circumstances and experiences. Not all of Bill and Winnie's family and friends are as kind and decent as Winnie and Bill. Some drink too much, steal or have run-ins with the law, or take advantage of other members of the network. Yet, like Bill and Winnie, they are struggling to survive in a society in which they are at a distinct competitive disadvantage socially and economically.

THE DUKE FAMILY

Bill and Winnie Duke live with their young adult son, Sammy, and sometimes their daughter, Cindy, and her family, right outside of Central City, a medium-sized city in the Northeast.

Bill

Bill, 45, describes himself as a "graduate of Empire State School," a state institution originally founded in 1894 as Empire State Custodial Asylum for Unteachable Idiots. Born in a small rural community outside of Eastern City, Bill was placed at the institution as an adolescent. Bill talks about his years at the institution with mixed emotions. While he says that the institution "helped me get my head together," he recalls the bitterness he felt at the time about being separated from his family.

Bill was placed on "probation" and lived for a period of time in a halfway house in Central City, approximately 150 miles from his family's home. He was officially discharged from the institution in 1971.

Bill is "on disability" and receives government Social Security and Supplemental Security Income (SSI) benefits. Shortly after his release from the institution, he held several short-term jobs, but he has not worked at a regular, tax-paying job since the mid-1970s. As Bill explains,

I haven't worked for years because of my disability. Last time I went to my doctor he said I couldn't work because I have seizures. Now that's something I can't understand. I can't work, but it's OK to drive a car. If you can't work, you shouldn't be able to drive a car.

Like other members of the Dukes' network of family and friends, Bill regularly goes "junking," picking up scrap metal, furniture, old appliances, bikes, and other items from the trash that he brings home, sells, or gives away. He also does odd jobs and has worked at least twice at a local garage. He worked at the garage in exchange for service and parts on his cars and also got paid a little "under the table." Bill buys or trades for old cars that he drives until they no longer run or become too expensive to fix. He spends much of his time tinkering on his cars.

Bill is an avid fan of professional wrestling or, as he puts it, a "wrastlin' freak." In addition to attending live events, he watches wrestling videotapes on his VCR and occasionally orders live pay-per-view wrestling on cable television. Bill also likes to fish and does so as often as possible during warm weather.

Bill takes prescription medications for seizures, diarrhea, headaches, and nervousness. He has also said on various occasions that doctors have told him that he has life-threatening brain tumors and lung cancer. (Since Bill has survived his supposedly terminal medical conditions, it is unclear as to whether he fully understands what doctors tell him.)

Winnie

Winnie, 43, runs the household, manages the family's finances, and negotiates relations with schools, government programs, and human services workers. Winnie was born and raised in Central City. She dropped out of school early to help raise her brother, stepbrothers, and stepsisters, but she reads well and prides herself on both her memory and her math skills.

Winnie has a speech impediment, which renders her speech very difficult to understand until one has known her for a while. She also has a host of medical problems. She had convulsions until she was 9 years old and has arthritis, heart problems, and a "club foot." She recently went on a diet when her weight topped 200 pounds.

When I first met the Dukes, Winnie was on public assistance, or welfare, but was subsequently deemed eligible for SSI. She also previously received spouse's benefits from Bill's Social Security. She is eligible for vocational rehabilitation because she has "a disability which results in a substantial handicap to employment," according to her individualized written rehabilitation plan (IWRP), and has participated in numerous job training programs. In the past several years, she has worked twice at a large sheltered workshop, Federated Industries of Central City. She took the job under the threat of losing her welfare benefits, but she no longer works there because Federated ran out of work and laid off most of its clients.

Winnie frequently babysits for the children of family members, friends, and neighbors. She was penalized by welfare several years ago for failing to report money earned from babysitting a neighbor's child.

Winnie has been involved in many parenting and homemaking programs and has had a parent aide, in addition to protective service workers, assigned to the family. Winnie describes herself as a "knick-knack freak" and has a large collection of statues, busts, and knick-knacks of every conceivable kind.

Winnie and Bill

Winnie and Bill met when Winnie's family was living across the street from Bill's halfway house. Winnie had told her stepmother, "I'm going to meet a blue-eyed, blond-haired man who looks just like me," and she did.

When she and Bill met, Winnie recalls, "it was love at first sight." Bill's social worker posed a problem, however. Since Bill was still on "probation" (actually this was called "parole" at the time and entailed a program of strict supervision), his worker told him that he was not allowed to date and went to speak to Winnie to tell her to break off the relationship. Bill eventually got off probation, and he and Winnie were married within a couple of weeks. Winnie still has her wedding dress and a wedding ring that cost $4.95.

Bill and Winnie's first child, Sammy, was born about a year later. Between Sammy and Cindy, who is 2½ years younger, Winnie lost another child.

As Winnie has said to me, "You think me and Bill have a perfect marriage, but we don't." When Sammy and Cindy were young, the couple was separated and both Bill and Winnie confess to infidelity around this time. Yet they reconciled and are looking forward to celebrating their 23rd anniversary. Winnie points out, "We've had our ups and downs, but we've been married longer than any of our brothers and sisters."

Sammy

Sammy, 22, was born with cerebral palsy (which is not currently noticeable), a cleft palate, and heart problems. According to Winnie, he has had over 90 operations for hearing, heart, and other problems. As an infant, he had a tracheostomy and was fed through a tube in his stomach. Winnie proudly recalls how she learned to handle his trach. Sammy has a severe speech impediment and can be understood only with extreme difficulty.

Sammy dropped out of school at age 16. He was enrolled in a special education program for students with multiple disabilities, and specifically mental retardation and hearing impairments. He receives SSI, and his application for Social Security disability benefits is under reconsideration. Winnie is the representative payee for Sammy's SSI; that is, Sammy's check comes in Winnie's name, and she must periodically report how the funds are spent.

Like his father, Sammy enjoys tinkering with bikes, cars, and just about anything else with an engine. While he does not have a driver's license or even a learner's permit, he has owned many cars and motor-cycles. Sammy collects model cars and goes to wrestling matches with his father.

Sammy has never held a regular job, although he worked for a very brief period at the same garage where his father worked. He is very shy and seems sullen until one has known him for a while. He has a number of friends but spends most of the time with his family.

Cindy

Cindy, 18, has a seizure disorder and receives SSI. Prior to dropping out of school at age 17, she was enrolled in an intensive special educa-tion class and her federally mandated individualized education pro-gram (IEP) indicated that she has mild mental retardation. Both Bill and Winnie were proud of how Cindy was doing in school and were disappointed when she dropped out.

One summer while she was in high school, Cindy was placed at the Federated Industries sheltered workshop as part of a job training program. Through her school program, she had job placements at fast food restaurants and a human services agency. Cindy has a family sup-port worker who is funded through the state office of mental retarda-tion and developmental disabilities. I was introduced to the family by this worker. Cindy speaks clearly but has difficulty reading. Like Sammy, she is very shy among strangers and acts withdrawn in public.

Since I started studying the Duke family, Cindy has changed from a girl to a young adult, wife, and mother. About 3 years ago, Bill and Winnie started to worry that Cindy was becoming sexually active. Their fears were not unfounded. She became pregnant, broke up with her boyfriend, and then married a 26-year-old man, Vinnie, shortly af-terward. Cindy's baby, Mikey, was born in the spring of 1993, and a second baby, Joey, was born in the summer of 1994. Cindy, Vinnie, Mikey, and Joey have lived off and on with the Dukes, but currently they have their own apartment not far from Winnie and Bill's home.

The Duke household is usually larger than just their immediate family. Winnie's brother John lived with the family for more than 2 years and as many as 10 additional adults and 4 children have stayed with them for weeks or even months at a time.

The Duke Household

The Dukes moved into a mobile home in a trailer park in a small vil-lage outside of Central City in the summer of 1993. After less than a year there, they moved to another mobile home in the same complex. This is their eighth home in the past 8½ years.

Before moving to their current trailer park, the Dukes lived in two sections of Central City: the North End, a lower and working class area identified as an ethnic community (but today diverse); and the West End, a lower class and racially diverse area. Both parts are characterized by low-income housing, and all of Winnie and Bill's family and friends in the city live in one of these two sections. When I first met the Dukes in 1989, they were living in a small rented house in a factory and warehouse district on the North End. A railroad track ran along the front yard of the house, and slow-moving trains passed by the house two or three times a day.

Household arrangements are usually the same in most of the Dukes' homes. The master bedroom is reserved for one of their boarders or for Cindy, her husband, and baby; Sammy also has his own bedroom; Winnie and Bill sleep in their own room, if a bedroom is left over, or in the living room.

As the Dukes settle into each new home, it slowly begins to resemble their former homes. Floors are strewn with litter, cigarette butts, cat or dog food bowls, and sometimes machine and car parts. The ever-changing living room is furnished with two or three sofas, an easy chair or two, coffee and side tables, and lamps. Just about all of the furniture comes from someone else's trash.

The old furniture stands in sharp contrast to the new television and VCR leased from rent-to-own companies. Stacks of papers are on top of the tables; a dozen prescription pill bottles are on top of the VCR. The walls are covered with brightly colored paintings and tapestries of Christ, a matador, and Elvis Presley. Knick-knack shelves are crammed full of figurines, salt and pepper shakers, religious statuettes, and other objects.

Bill's Family Background

Bill comes from a large family and is one of nine children. Bill has three older sisters, a younger brother, and four younger sisters; he can name 29 nieces and nephews and 9 great-nieces and nephews on his side of the family. His brother, who is divorced and has three children by his wife, has had five children with another woman, but Bill does not consider these to be his nieces and nephews.

Bill is proud of the fact that two of his grandparents were Indian, one Cherokee and one Mohawk, but he does not identify with Native American culture. Bill's father died a number of years ago, but his mother is still living outside of Eastern City.

According to Bill, "When you talk about my family, you're talking down. I mean, down, man." Part of the folklore of Bill's family, shared by his siblings, is that his mother slept around with different men, including a milkman and the "welfare man," and that only three of his siblings can trace their paternity to their father.

Bill's mother was on welfare when her children were young. Bill's three older sisters were eventually placed in foster care and Bill, his sister Betty, and his brother were placed at Empire State School. Bill was the first member of his family to move to Central City when he was placed on probation by Empire State School. Three of his sisters, two nephews, and a niece subsequently moved to Central City. His brother lived in Central City for a while before returning to the Eastern City area.

Bill speaks of his deceased father with deep fondness and respect. He says that he did not get along with his mother for a long time but is on good terms with her now. His mother's current boyfriend is his sister Iris's ex-husband and the brother of Bill's biological father; he refuses to call his mother's boyfriend "Dad." Bill visits his mother every couple of years.

Winnie's Family Background

Like Bill, Winnie comes from a very large family. She has three brothers, five stepbrothers, and three stepsisters, but it is only when explaining her family background that she distinguishes between full and step-siblings. Winnie can count 24 nieces and nephews and 6 great-nieces and nephews. Her mother died when Winnie was young and her father married her current stepmother. Her father died several years ago. Winnie's father had three brothers and one sister.

According to Winnie, her family lived all over the Central City area when she was growing up. Most of her family continues to live in Central City, but her stepmother, brother, stepbrother, and stepsister moved to Tennessee a number of years ago. Winnie's stepmother, with whom she and everyone else in her family has a stormy relationship, has moved back and forth between Central City and Tennessee several times. She currently lives in Central City. Winnie's stepsister also moved back from Tennessee. Winnie's brother John, who had lived with the Dukes at three of their former homes, moved to Tennessee in 1993.

Disabilities Among Kin and Friends

Many of the Dukes' kin and friends have been identified as having mental retardation, mental illness, or another disability by human services agencies or government programs. Of Bill and Winnie's 19 siblings, at least 7 have received treatment for disabilities or have been considered disabled by agencies or programs. Many of the Dukes' other relatives and friends receive SSI or have been served by sheltered workshops, developmental disability programs, or mental health agencies. To my knowledge, virtually all of the children of the Dukes' extended family members and friends have been placed in special education programs.

Within the Duke network, people do not view themselves or others as disabled or mentally retarded, except for two of Bill's nieces who have physical disabilities and are referred to as "handicapped" or "crippled." For example, Bill describes himself as being "on disability," but not as being "disabled" or "having a disability"; in the same manner, Winnie has referred to herself as being "on welfare." Being "on disability" or "on welfare" simply refers to the source of one's entitlement check.

Since people do not think of themselves in terms of disability categories, it is difficult to say exactly how many individuals have actually been defined as disabled by government programs or formal agencies. It is only when the Dukes happen to make reference to someone's SSI or placement in a disability program that one learns that a member of their social network has been defined as having a disability. Many of the Dukes' other kin and friends leave the impression of being slow or vulnerable to being defined as disabled by human services agencies.

Social Relations Among Kin and Friends

Bill and Winnie not only come from sizable extended families, but also have a large and ever-expanding network of friends and acquaintances. The Dukes make friends easily and bring friends of friends, family of friends, and friends of family into their immediate social network.

Social relations within the Duke network are characterized by mutual support, on the one hand, and arguments and feuds, on the other. In contrast to the conventional view of upwardly mobile American families (Mintz & Kellogg, 1988), members of the Dukes' network maintain close kinship ties. Like female-headed African American families (Stack, 1974), the Dukes and their kin and friends depend on each other for help and assistance; mutual support networks are a means of coping with their marginal economic and social status. The Dukes, as well as their relatives and friends, take in homeless family members and friends, lend food or money, and help each other out in other ways.

People within the Dukes' network also regularly complain about and argue with each other or become embroiled in all-out feuds. At any point, someone in the network is fighting with someone else. Hardly a month goes by that Bill and Winnie are not involved in a dispute with relatives or friends. Once an argument begins, other family members and friends are likely to be drawn into it.

Feuds can be emotionally charged and vehement, but they seldom last long. People can be bitter enemies one day and be friendly to each other the next. For example, when I first met the Dukes, Lisa and Gary and their three children were staying with them because they were homeless. Bill and Winnie grew tired of Lisa and Gary, had an argument with them, and threw them out of their house. Within months, however, Lisa and Gary were again close friends of the Dukes and frequent visitors to their home. Then another argument erupted, followed by a reconciliation a short time later. The Dukes are similarly very close to Bill's sister Betty and her family, but they feud with them at least every few months.

THE STUDY

When I first heard about the Duke family, I was interested in meeting them. Cindy's family support worker, Mary, had casually told me about the family and how each member had a disability. Mary described how Bill referred to himself as a "graduate of Empire State School" and bought old junk cars and how Winnie hustled money and free tickets to the Ice Capades, circuses, and other shows from the family's many family support and social workers.

Mary agreed to introduce me to the Duke family in February 1989. I have been studying them ever since and, to date, have completed well over 100 sets of detailed field notes based on my observations. I also talk frequently with them on the telephone.

Early in my study, I told the Dukes that I was writing a book on families and wanted them to be in it. Bill and Winnie took the idea of a book very seriously and asked Sammy and Cindy if it was okay with them to be part of the book. By the end of this visit, it was clear that Winnie and Bill were thrilled and proud of the idea of being included in a book. News that I was writing a book spread rapidly through the Duke network. Bill and Winnie proudly told family members and friends about the book, and people occasionally gave me advice about what I should put in my book.

My relationship with the Duke family has evolved over time. I started out as "Mary's friend" and a teacher or professor who was writing a book. I next became the family's "lawyer." I started helping family members interpret and fill out the confusing and cumbersome paperwork they received from Social Security, welfare, and other government offices. Then one day Winnie received a copy of Cindy's IEP along with a list of organizations to call if parents wanted to dispute the contents of the IEP. My name and The Center on Human Policy were listed on the form. Winnie was impressed.

From that point on, Winnie and Bill referred to me as their lawyer and came to me for advice on everything from Social Security, SSI, and welfare to educational programs, evictions, insurance, and a will for Bill. On numerous occasions, I accompanied Winnie and Bill to the Social Security office to try to help straighten out problems with their benefits. Before long, they started referring other family members and friends to me for advice. Today the Dukes introduce me to others as a "friend of the family." I am invited to all family gatherings, and the Dukes are disappointed if I cannot come.

My study has followed the traditional participant observation mold: hanging out with people and doing whatever they happen to be doing. I have never formally interviewed the Dukes but rather ask questions that seem appropriate at the time. Especially in the beginning of my study, most of my observations occurred in their home. Over the years, I have spent increasing amounts of time with the Dukes outside of their home, visiting kin or friends, attending professional wrestling matches with Bill, running errands, and accompanying Winnie to Cindy's middle school graduation. I also drove Bill and Sammy for a day-long visit to his relatives outside of Capital City.

I have never been made to feel unwelcome by the Dukes. Winnie and Bill are open and honest people and never balk at answering any question I ask. They readily volunteer information about themselves and their family that most people would hide. I know more about the intimate details of the Dukes' lives than about most of my closest friends' and relatives' lives.

Throughout my study, Mary has maintained contact with Bill and Winnie and some of their relatives who have been her clients. With the Dukes' knowledge and consent, she has helped fill in gaps in my information about the family. She has also been available to confirm many of my impressions and observations.

This is a study that so far has a beginning but no end. I cannot foresee cutting off contact with the family, both because I enjoy them and because I want to see how their lives will continue to unfold.

"CHILDREN'S DIVISION"

To the average family, the prospect of being investigated for child abuse or neglect is frightening and shameful. For the Dukes, their kin, and their friends, it is a routine occurrence. Child abuse agencies, or "Children's Division" and "CD" as it is known within the Duke network, are regularly involved with many of Bill and Winnie's extended family members and friends, as well as their own family. Many have been investigated by Children's Division at one time or another and have been assigned protective workers and parent aides.

The Family History

The intervention of child welfare agencies in the Duke network extends at least as far back as to Bill's family when he was a child. Bill's records at Empire State School document the state's and county's constant interventions in his family's life. Bill's Case Summary and Abstract upon admission to Empire describe his parents as deficient and his home environment as deplorable (excerpts appear in Figure 1).

Bill, his older sister Betty, and his younger brother Joey were placed at Empire at the same time. When their mother requested that the three children return home for a summer visit, a social worker from

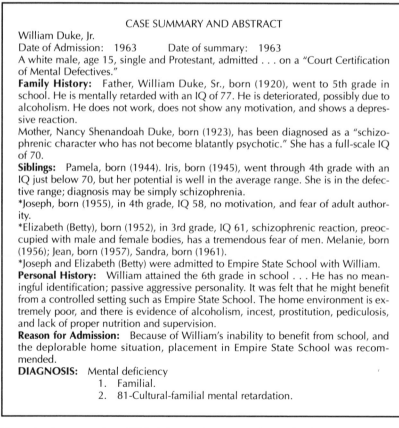

CASE SUMMARY AND ABSTRACT

William Duke, Jr.

Date of Admission: 1963   Date of summary: 1963

A white male, age 15, single and Protestant, admitted . . . on a "Court Certification of Mental Defectives."

Family History: Father, William Duke, Sr., born (1920), went to 5th grade in school. He is mentally retarded with an IQ of 77. He is deteriorated, possibly due to alcoholism. He does not work, does not show any motivation, and shows a depressive reaction.

Mother, Nancy Shenandoah Duke, born (1923), has been diagnosed as a "schizophrenic character who has not become blatantly psychotic." She has a full-scale IQ of 70.

Siblings: Pamela, born (1944). Iris, born (1945), went through 4th grade with an IQ just below 70, but her potential is well in the average range. She is in the defective range; diagnosis may be simply schizophrenia.

*Joseph, born (1955), in 4th grade, IQ 58, no motivation, and fear of adult authority.

*Elizabeth (Betty), born (1952), in 3rd grade, IQ 61, schizophrenic reaction, preoccupied with male and female bodies, has a tremendous fear of men. Melanie, born (1956); Jean, born (1957), Sandra, born (1961).

*Joseph and Elizabeth (Betty) were admitted to Empire State School with William.

Personal History: William attained the 6th grade in school . . . He has no meaningful identification; passive aggressive personality. It was felt that he might benefit from a controlled setting such as Empire State School. The home environment is extremely poor, and there is evidence of alcoholism, incest, prostitution, pediculosis, and lack of proper nutrition and supervision.

Reason for Admission: Because of William's inability to benefit from school, and the deplorable home situation, placement in Empire State School was recommended.

DIAGNOSIS: Mental deficiency
      1. Familial.
      2. 81-Cultural-familial mental retardation.

Figure 1.   An excerpt from Bill Duke's records at Empire State School.

Empire visited the home along with a county social worker. The Empire social worker reported that the family's "mountain top home was broken by the County's efforts" because of "poor supervision and unstableness displayed by the parents . . . physical abuse, incest, improper use of welfare funds and immorality." The social worker proceeded to explain, however, that the family's situation had improved considerably due to the county case worker's efforts: "This family is being helped and studied intensively by the Commissioner of [County] to prove that if all the welfare resources in the county coordinated their services to a family of this type, much could be done to help the family situations socially and financially."

A mixed picture of Bill's parents emerges from the records at Empire State School. On the one hand, summaries characterize the family as disreputable and defective. Vague accusations that appear early in the records are passed down as fact in later entries. On the other hand, home observations, interviews with county workers and family members, and other firsthand information provide few specific instances of abuse or neglect. That the family was poor, the parents had mental retardation or at least appeared slow, and Bill's mother sometimes drank excessively seem beyond dispute. Bill recalls that welfare placed his three older sisters in a "home" (presumably foster care), while he and his two siblings were sent to Empire:

> See, my mother was on P.A. [Public Assistance]. She was drinking real heavy then. The place we were living in didn't have electricity or a toilet. . . . We didn't even have an outhouse. You had to shit in a bucket.

According to Bill's records, charges of incest and physical abuse within the family were never substantiated upon further investigation. Perhaps the most indicting information contained in the records is that after Betty returned to the home from Empire, her mother encouraged older men to take her out in exchange for groceries or a case of beer. Bill says that his mother "sold" Betty to her first husband for a six-pack. After Betty married this 55-year-old man when she was 16, she wrote Empire asking if Bill could be released to live with her, and her home and family situation were investigated by an Empire social worker. The social worker reported that Betty's husband was kind and generous to her and that it was a good situation despite their age difference.

Every once in a while, Bill's records shed a positive light on his family. In the report on a home visit, an Empire social worker wrote, "Patient's father and mother are very fond of one another." The county public welfare department wrote Empire State School to support the return home of Bill, Joey, and Betty less than a year after they had been placed there. Bill's records also contain dozens of the original copies of letters from Bill's mother requesting that her children be permitted home for visits or released from the institution. One letter read: "We have enjoyed every minute of the times we have had them home before." Many of her requests were denied "in view of the problems you had in supervising them before admission."

So the picture that emerges of Bill's family is that it was neither exemplary nor despicable, but somewhere in between. While evidence of child abuse or neglect contained in the records is unclear and contradictory, social welfare agencies intervened in the family's life and separated the children from their parents. This pattern of agency intervention was repeated in successive generations of the Duke family.

The Current Generation

The Dukes have been investigated by Children's Division on at least four occasions. In at least two instances, the investigations resulted in formal intervention in the family and the assignment of parent aides. Bill and Winnie's involvement with child protective agencies began when Sammy and Cindy were young children. Bill recalls that he was investigated for child abuse (hitting Cindy) and that he was not even living with his family at the time (this was during a 2-week separation between Bill and Winnie). Winnie says she was investigated when Cindy got hurt as a baby.

According to Winnie, she called the child protective agency and requested a parent aide when Sammy and Cindy were both young and having medical problems. I asked what the parent aide did for her and she answered, "Same thing you do. Sit here and talk. Then if they see abuse they report you to CD." When I first met the Dukes, they had a protective services worker from a private agency assigned to them (through a contract with the county).

In the late spring and early summer of 1989, Bill and Winnie were investigated by CD for "dog shit on the floor" and "no food in the refrigerator." During one of my visits around this time, I commented on how clean and tidy the home looked. Bill explained, "Children's Division is coming to take pictures." As it turned out, Children's Division did not return for a month. The day after this visit, Winnie showed me a snapshot of herself, Bill, Sammy, and Cindy and said:

> Children's Division is closing the case on us. The worker came here and took pictures. She said as far as she's concerned the case is closed, but it has to be approved by Capital City.

Bill and Winnie have come to expect investigations for child abuse or neglect and try to make sure that they are always covered. Shortly after the last investigation, Bill told Winnie to put some money aside to keep in the house: "That way we'll always have money for food so nobody can come in here saying we don't have food in the house." Winnie and Bill were worried about where Cindy would go on one of the occasions when they were being evicted. They were prepared to live in a car and thought Sammy could move in with one of Winnie's brothers, but they did not know if they could find a place for Cindy to stay. Bill explained what they did:

> I did something smart. I reported us to Children's Division. I called and told them we were being evicted. . . . They said we did the right thing by calling. They said they'd have to do something about Cindy if we don't find a place, but Sammy's OK. See, he turned 18.

On one occasion when Cindy was hit and bruised by a kid, Bill and Winnie reported the incident to the police so that no one would think that they abused her.

Many of the Dukes' kin and friends have regular involvements with Children's Division and child protective agencies. The Dukes' friends, Lisa and Gary, were visited by a protective worker after their children contracted head lice. Children's Division was involved with Bill's brother Joey's three children while they were living with his exwife and continued its involvement after the children were taken in by Bill's sister Betty. Then the agency started to question how Betty cared for her own two children. Betty complained bitterly, "First they're telling me how to raise my nieces and nephews. Now they're telling me how to raise my own kids." Betty subsequently had a protective service worker from a private child abuse agency assigned to her family. Betty's daughter Judy by a previous marriage lost custody of her child because she was living in a dirty, run-down home. Bill's nephew Wes was threatened by CD with having his two children taken away when he faced eviction and had nowhere to live. Children's Division has investigated at least one of Bill's other sisters and two of Winnie's brothers. Winnie reports that her cousin Earl's children were removed from his home on the basis of abuse and neglect.

People within the Duke network become involved with Children's Division and other child abuse agencies in one of three ways. First, people within the Duke network report each other to places like Children's Division when they are feuding. Everyone knows something about everyone else, so there is usually something they can report about their kin and friends. Both the state and the county have child abuse hotlines, and anonymous allegations of abuse and neglect are investigated. Once an investigation is under way, a child abuse agency can usually uncover some shortcoming (poor housekeeping, lack of food reserves, pending eviction) among families in the Duke network.

Second, although not frequently, people have called child abuse agencies either to ask for help or to report themselves. As noted above, Winnie called an agency to get a parent aide, and Bill said "I did something smart" when he contacted Children's Division to say that the Dukes were being evicted. When people report themselves, it is usually in anticipation of being reported by someone else.

Third, families are reported for alleged abuse and neglect by schools and other agencies with which they are involved. Reports of child abuse and neglect are kept confidential, so that it is sometimes difficult to determine who reported a family. While members of the Duke network report each other to child protective agencies, it is possible that schools and other agencies have reported families in some instances in which people accuse kin and friends of having done so. For example, when one of Bill's sisters was investigated for child abuse, she accused Bill and Winnie of reporting her, but the Dukes maintained that they had nothing to do with it.

One of Cindy's special education teachers almost reported the Dukes for child abuse, although Bill and Winnie were not aware of this. The specifics of the incident help to explain how families like the Dukes are viewed. Cindy had spent a weekend at a friend's house. When she showed up at school the following Monday morning, she was bruised. Her teacher asked Cindy how she got the bruises and became suspicious when Cindy seemed to give two different accounts. Cindy told her she had fallen at a bowling alley and had then been hit by her friend's boyfriend. Cindy's teacher was ready to report suspected child abuse but called Mary, Cindy's family support worker, for advice because she knew that Mary had been closely involved with the family. Mary immediately vouched for Bill and Winnie and told the teacher that she had never seen any evidence of abuse. She followed up the conversation with a letter confirming what she had said on the telephone. Because Mary was so certain about Bill and Winnie, the teacher decided not to report the family. As it turned out, Cindy had indeed tripped at a bowling alley and then been hit by her friend's boyfriend while she was away for the weekend. (I had visited the Dukes that weekend and could verify that Cindy was not home.)

The Next Generation

Child protective agencies will undoubtedly be involved in future generations of the Duke family network. Because of Cindy's obvious intellectual limitations, it is likely that her child rearing will come under scrutiny. In fact, her first pregnancy was defined as high risk at the hospital where she eventually delivered. When Cindy became pregnant for the second time, according to Winnie, the hospital threatened to have her sterilized:

> The hospital told her she's going to have her tubes tied after she delivers the baby. They said if she didn't get it done on her own, they'd get a court order to do it.

Cindy and her family have lived off and on with the Dukes. Even when they are not living with Winnie and Bill, they spend a lot of time with them. Winnie instructs Cindy on child care and plays a major role in caring for the children. The children probably are given more juice and were started on solid food earlier than child-rearing books advise (Winnie bragged that Mikey was eating solids at 3 months), but they are thriving and gaining weight steadily.

FAMILY LIFESTYLE AND PARENTING

Certainly, from the vantage point of child rearing experts, Bill and Winnie have had shortcomings as parents. This does not make them abusive or neglectful or necessarily justify intervention in the family's life.

When it comes to child-rearing practices and the home atmosphere, the Dukes and many of their kin and friends depart from middle-class standards. Adults use profanity around children. Child rearing is characterized by permissiveness, on the one hand, and threats or yelling ("I'll smack you if you keep that up") and verbal put-downs ("stupid") on the other. Bill occasionally roughhouses with adults and children alike in ways that would be disapproved of by many people.

The Dukes' housekeeping is poor, and they often face food shortages or even the lack of housing. Each of these factors—poor housekeeping, lack of food reserves, and pending eviction—has been cited by agencies as grounds to intervene in families within the Duke network.

Looking beneath the surface, however, Winnie and Bill have been loving and caring parents. As Bill explained, "Kids need a lot of love." Even if a lack of food or homelessness justifies intervention by child abuse agencies (as opposed to giving families food or helping them find homes), the Dukes always find a way to eat and a place to live.

Contrary to generalizations about parents with mental retardation (Forder, 1990; Whitman & Accardo, 1990), the Dukes are adept at their community survival skills. Despite their frequent evictions, they have never been forced to live on the street or even in a shelter. Just as the Dukes take in homeless kin and friends, so have they been taken in by members of their social network. On one occasion when homelessness loomed as a real possibility for the Dukes, Bill and Winnie made arrangements for their children to live with other family members.

While the Dukes sometimes lack food reserves and have an empty refrigerator, they never go without food. When money is short, they turn first to family members and friends to repay debts or to lend them food or money. If this fails, Winnie makes the rounds at community food banks and charitable organizations. When she is turned down, she contacts the family's current or former teachers, social workers, or even a participant observer until she finds someone willing to help out the family. Child abuse agencies seem to look for food in the refrigerator, but the important question is whether children are malnourished or regularly hungry.

The Dukes' housekeeping is poor and is even remarked on by other members of the network. The family does not get around to dusting, washing dishes, sweeping, or scrubbing bathroom fixtures regularly, although Winnie frequently complains about all the time she spends doing housework. When, in their previous homes, their female dog had puppies, the house occasionally smelled of animal urine. The state of the Dukes' home violates aesthetic standards, but it has never been shown to be unhealthy or dangerous.

For all of their shortcomings in child rearing, Bill and Winnie have always looked out for the welfare of their children and do their best to impart societal values. Winnie makes sure Sammy and Cindy receive adequate medical care and visited Cindy's school program more than many parents. Both Winnie and Bill lecture their children that they should not steal, fight, use drugs, or overindulge in alcohol. Sammy did not drink a full can or bottle of beer until he was 19 years old. Notwithstanding Cindy's pregnancy, Bill and Winnie tried to curtail her sexual activity in their own way.

Profanity is common in the Duke household (although Sammy is scolded if he says "fuck" a lot), but Bill and Winnie do not discuss sex in front of children. Bill uses the term "privates" to refer to genitals when children are around. He was appalled when a male family friend and his woman friend talked about having sex in front of Winnie's brother's two young children and scolded them for talking that way.

Within the Duke network, parents threaten unruly or disobedient children but do not follow through on the threats. Betty has accused Bill of slapping Sammy and Cindy on a handful of occasions. Both Bill and Winnie dispute this, and I have never witnessed anything that could be considered physical abuse. Whether or not Bill and Winnie follow the best child-rearing practices, there is not the slightest evidence that they have ever abused or neglected their children.

As parents, Bill and Winnie have also helped their children construct positive identities as typical or "normal" persons. They do not view Sammy and Cindy as mentally retarded, disabled, or handicapped. For every message their children has gotten from schools or human services agencies that they have disabilities or are different from others, Bill and Winnie convey multiple messages that they are just like everyone else.

One day several years ago when I was visiting the Dukes, Bill was prodding Cindy to sweep the floor. Avoiding the job, Cindy would sweep for a minute or two and then sit down. After being scolded repeatedly by Bill, she laughed and said, "I'm a retard." Bill responded, "You're not a retard, you're just wise." Cindy replied, "I'll be a retard if I don't do my homework."

On another occasion, Cindy showed me a book her teacher had given her from the school library. The title was, "Your Handicap: Don't Let It Handicap You." Commenting on the book, Bill told Cindy,

Cindy, you should read that book. You're going to be a parent some day and you could have a handicapped child. When I was at Empire there was a kid there with his head out to here (motions a very large head). He had tumors and his head just grew. He was a pretty nice kid, too. You should know about handicaps, so you're prepared if you have a handicapped child.

Throughout Sammy's and Cindy's childhood and young adulthood, Winnie and Bill have communicated ordinary expectations for them. When Sammy turned 16, they approved when he bought his first car, even though he did not then and does not now have a driver's license. Bill and Winnie have always communicated to their children that they expected them to get married, raise their own families, and pursue careers. Winnie even talked at one point about Cindy attending college.

Winnie and Bill have given their children something that they would not receive in many families: identities as ordinary people who are like everyone else. In a society in which having a disability, and especially an intellectual disability, is a stigmatizing and potentially discrediting characteristic (Bogdan & Taylor, 1994; Edgerton, 1967), this is no trivial parental contribution.

CONCLUSION

The Duke family presents complex and challenging lessons for human services professionals concerned about families of children with disabilities in general and parents with mental retardation in particular. In this conclusion, I address four questions raised by this study of the Duke family.

First, do families like the Dukes need help in surviving in the community and fulfilling parental roles? The emerging ideology in family support services in the field of developmental disabilities stresses family-centered services in which the family determines the kinds of supports they receive (Center on Human Policy, 1987; Taylor, Bogdan, & Racino, 1991). By contrast, much of the literature and practice regarding parents with mental retardation seems based on the assumption that such parents are inadequate and incapable of making choices about what they need (Whitman & Accardo, 1990). As a consequence, services for parents with mental retardation are oriented toward training and education in parenting skills (Keltner, 1994; Whitman & Accardo, 1990; Whitman, Graves, & Accardo, 1987).

Winnie and Bill often need help and, as a parent, Cindy does also. When viewed from their perspective, however, what they need is advocacy assistance in dealing with government bureaucracies, schools, landlords, and sometimes even child protective agencies; emergency cash assistance; help in locating safe and affordable housing; health care; and, occasionally, transportation. With the exception of the training that Winnie received in changing Sammy's trach when he was an infant, the Dukes have never experienced any kind of general training or education that they found helpful or that supported their self-perceptions as competent parents.

Virtually all parents might benefit from parent education and training. No parent is perfect or knowledgeable about all aspects of child rearing. For people like the Dukes, any education or training that would challenge their definitions of themselves as loving and competent parents or place them in the role of clients with mental retardation would be a disservice to both the parents and the children. Here, the "cure" would be worse than the "disease."

A practical implication of this study is that parents with mental retardation should be approached with the same assumption underlying family-centered support programs; that is, offer assistance, but help the family in ways in which they want to be helped and on their own terms.

Second, when is intervention in the family life of parents with mental retardation justified? Put another way, when should public and private agencies step in to save children from abuse or neglect? The answer seems simple: when there is evidence that children are being abused or neglected. Attention should shift from general impressions of parental competence or fitness to the health, well-being, and safety of the children themselves.

According to Whitman and Accardo (1990), "Mentally retarded parents in the community contribute more than a simple head count to the statistics for illiteracy, homelessness, child abuse, child neglect, failure to thrive, child sexual abuse, medical neglect, malnutrition, unemployment, and poverty" (p. 203). Statements like this can lead to a presumption that children of parents with mental retardation will be at risk of abuse or neglect and can be used to justify intervention and intrusion in family life. Not only is this type of assumption flawed, but it is contrary to democratic ideals. By analogy, crime statistics demonstrating a higher rate of criminal activity among certain socioeconomic or racial groups cannot be used to justify the deprivation of civil liberties among individual members of these groups.

From a professional standpoint, the same standards should be applied to parents with mental retardation that are applied to all parents. Intervention in the life of any family is warranted when there is evidence of physical mistreatment, sexual abuse, hunger, malnutrition, failure to thrive, untreated medical conditions, or unsafe living conditions. Yet unwanted intrusion cannot be justified on the basis of statistical risk factors in the absence of evidence of abuse or neglect.

Third, how representative is the Duke family? A related question concerns whether the experience of the Duke family has general implications for policy and practice regarding parents with mental retardation. Even if one accepts my findings and conclusions about the parental adequacy of Winnie and Bill, one can question the generalizability of my study.

Compared to many parents with mental retardation, Bill and Winnie have some obvious advantages. For one, despite their histories as clients of mental retardation and developmental disability agencies, they have managed to escape the social stigma associated with mental retardation and disability and have learned to define themselves and their children in nonstigmatizing ways. Further, they are part of a large and ever-expanding social network of kin and friends that buffers them from crisis in times of economic hardship and provides support for a positive social status. Finally, they have developed survival skills that enable them to get by on their own in the community.

Certainly, Winnie and Bill are not typical of parents with mental retardation. Like all families, the Duke family is unique. As a qualitative researcher, I cannot claim that my study is generalizable. However, the point is not whether the Duke family is representative of other families but what this particular family's experience tells us about common sense assumptions and generalizations about parents with mental retardation. The Duke family's experience proves many common sense assumptions, generalizations, and stereotypes wrong.

The challenge for professionals is to view and treat people as individuals, not members of categories.

Fourth, how can abusive parents be distinguished from nonabusive ones? Child abuse or neglect is a serious matter; no one can condone the abuse or neglect of children. How are we to differentiate between parents like Winnie and Bill, who are adequate parents despite their shortcomings, and parents who are guilty of abuse and neglect?

Based on my intimate knowledge of the Duke family and detailed experience with them over a number of years, I have concluded that their surface appearance is misleading and that allegations and suspicions of abuse or neglect are unfounded. For example, the Dukes' housekeeping, although substandard, has never placed the children in jeopardy. Similarly, I have evaluated Bill's sister Betty's vague accusations that Bill hit Cindy in the context of a family feud and give them little weight. Cindy's worker Mary, who also knows the family well, has reached similar conclusions. Other agencies and professionals have determined that the Duke children were at risk of abuse and neglect and intervened in the family's life based on second-hand information about the family and brief visits to their home.

Anyone who has taken the time to get to know Bill and Winnie well can easily tell the difference between their family life and abusive and neglectful situations. And those who have not taken the time cannot. Perhaps this is the most important lesson to be learned from this study for those in helping professions.

REFERENCES

Bogdan, R., & Taylor, S.J. (1994). *The social meaning of mental retardation: Two life stories.* New York: Teachers College Press.

The Center on Human Policy, Syracuse University. (September 1987). *Families for all children.* Syracuse, NY: Author.

Dugdale, R.L. (1910). *The Jukes.* New York: Putnam.

Edgerton, R.B. (1967). *The cloak of competence: Stigma in the lives of the mentally retarded.* Berkeley: University of California Press.

Forder, A.C. (1990). Foreword. In B.Y. Whitman & P.J. Accardo (Eds.), *When a parent is mentally retarded* (pp. ix–xii). Baltimore: Paul H. Brookes Publishing Co.

Goddard, H.H. (1912). *The Kallikaks: A study in the heredity of feeblemindedness.* New York: Macmillan.

Keltner, B. (1994). Home environments of mothers with mental retardation. *Mental Retardation, 32*(2), 123–127.

Mintz, S., & Kellogg, S. (1988). *Domestic revolutions: A social history of American family life.* New York: Free Press.

Smith, J.D. (1985). *Minds made feeble: The myth and legacy of the Kallikaks.* Austin, TX: PRO-ED.

Stack, C. (1974). *All our kin: Strategies for survival in a black community*. New York: Harper & Row.

Taylor, S.J., Bogdan, R., & Racino, J.A. (Eds.). (1991). *Life in the community: Case studies of organizations supporting people with disabilities*. Baltimore: Paul H. Brookes Publishing Co.

Taylor, S.J., & Searl, S.J. (1987). The disabled in America: History, policy, and trends. In P. Knoblock (Ed.), *Understanding exceptional children and youth* (pp. 5–64). Boston: Little, Brown.

Whitman, B.Y., & Accardo, P.J. (Eds.). (1990). *When a parent is mentally retarded*. Baltimore: Paul H. Brookes Publishing Co.

Whitman, B.Y., Graves, B., & Accardo, P.J. (1987). The mentally retarded parent in the community: Identification method and needs assessment survey. *American Journal of Mental Deficiency, 91*(6), 636–638.

Wolfensberger, W. (1972). *Normalization: The principle of normalization in human services*. Toronto, Ontario, Canada: National Institute of Mental Retardation.

Wolfensberger, W. (1975). *The origin and nature of our institutional models*. Syracuse, NY: Human Policy Press.

Wolfensberger, W. (1983). Social role valorization: A proposed new term for the principle of normalization. *Mental Retardation, 21*(6), 234–239.

3

A Mother's Work Is Never Done

Constructing a "Normal" Family Life

Rannveig Traustadottir

A number of studies inspired by Goffman (1961, 1963) have high-lighted the significance of stigma in the lives of people with disabilities (Bogdan & Taylor, 1982; Dudley, 1983; Edgerton, 1967). As a result of these studies, we have gained insight into the strategies of coping and adaptation by people who bear the stigma. Most of the studies have focused on the rejection and exclusion of stigmatized people. Although stigmatized individuals generally face an unaccepting world, they also find that there are usually sympathetic others who are ready to accept them (Bogdan & Taylor, 1987, 1989; Taylor & Bogdan, 1989). One such group consists of the family of the stigmatized person. Goffman (1963, p. 30) states that this group is "obliged to share some of the discredit of the stigmatized person to whom they are related." He refers to this as "courtesy stigma."

A handful of studies have examined how families of children with disabilities try to lead ordinary lives. Based on Goffman's theoretical framework, these studies have examined how families cope with the courtesy stigma presented by the child's disability (Birenbaum, 1968, 1970, 1971; Booth, 1978; Schmid, 1977; Voysey, 1972). These studies have mainly focused on the mothers in the families being studied. For example, Birenbaum (1971, p. 56) argues that the mother is "the major agent responsible for the everyday care of the retarded child" and the most important person in responding to the child's discrepancy from typical expectations. This leads Birenbaum to study "the way in which the mother constructs a normal-appearing lifestyle through her direct concern with the everyday management of the child . . . and . . . the everyday management of the impression the family makes in the community" (1971, p. 57). Although these studies both reflect and report that the mothers have the main responsibility for constructing "normalcy" in the families, this is not seen as problematic; it is reported in a matter-of-fact way, thus reinforcing the notion that women's caring work in the family is a "natural" part of family life.

This chapter is about a study of how parents of children with disabilities try to construct an ordinary or "normal" family life. The terms "normal" and "ordinary" refer not to what is most typical or statistically most common but rather the families' ideal of how a family should function.

Rather than emphasizing the family's interactions with the outside world, this chapter examines everyday life within the family. The "naturalness" of the mother's work in constructing an ordinary family life in the face of deviance is not taken for granted, but rather the gendered organization of the work of constructing and maintaining a normal family life is analyzed.

The analysis in this chapter is based on a qualitative study of 26 mothers and 5 fathers of children with disabilities. In-depth interviews were conducted with 14 mothers (5 of their husbands were also interviewed). These mothers varied with regard to social class, race, ethnicity, and other social dimensions. Four of them were upper-class, six were middle-class, and four were lower-class. Four were African American and 10 were white. Three of the mothers were single mothers, and 11 were married or lived with a partner. The children with disabilities ranged in age from 2 to 16 years, and their disability had been identified as ranging from "mild" to "severe." Many of the children had multiple disabilities.

In addition, I spent 2 years of participant observation in a support group for parents of children with disabilities. The group consisted of a core group of 12 mothers who, except for their racial background (all participants were white), represented the same diversity as the 14 families who were interviewed.

"A PART OF THE FAMILY"

The mothers in this study decided that the most acceptable way to deal with having a child with a disability was to keep the child at home and attempt to create a family life that is as ordinary as possible, with the child as a member of the family. The decision to keep the child at home is rooted in their image of what constitutes a family, their basic family values, and a strong belief that families should take care of their own.

It is usually the mother who makes the final decision to keep the child within the family. Included in this decision seems to be the understanding that if the child stays at home, it will be the mother's role to take the responsibility for the extra, and often extraordinarily difficult, work entailed in caring for a child with a disability and in maintaining as ordinary a family life as possible.

Ellen and Richard Spencer have two children, 3-year-old Helen and 7-year-old Paul, who has multiple problems, including severe mental retardation, a severe seizure disorder, and behavior problems. The Spencer family lives in a nice house in a middle-class neighborhood. Richard is a researcher at a large research company, and Ellen has a degree in nursing. Paul has always lived with his family, and his mother has not worked outside the home since he was born. His mother finds it difficult to care for Paul at home. At one point, about a year before I met the family, she felt as though she could not handle Paul's behavior any longer and considered

> placing him somewhere. I called the residential school and I had it all set up to place Paul. It was really a difficult thing for the family. Richard is really in love with his little boy and Helen has a brother and I thought, what would she think? That we would send her away if she wasn't okay? So I decided I could not send him away. I just could not do it. I want to keep Paul at home; he is a part of this family and I'm gonna do the best I can.

Ellen's description reflects the social organization of everyday life within her family where she is responsible for the well-being of the family as a whole and each of its members. The reason Ellen considered "placing him somewhere" was that Paul's behaviors had become increasingly difficult for her to handle. He was in danger of hurting himself, and she did not know how to help him. She was tired and frustrated. Her decision to keep Paul at home, despite the difficulties, reveals how caring for a child with a disability is an inseparable part of constructing and maintaining a family. Ellen's decision is not based on her own need for a break from caring for Paul at home or on Paul's educational needs. Rather, the basis for the decision is the family as a whole and the well-being of each member. Ellen takes into consideration her husband's love of their son as well as the possible effect on their 3-year-old daughter of seeing her brother sent away. Ellen fears that sending Paul away would seriously damage the sense of basic trust and security among members of the family.

Ellen's viewpoint also reflects who is responsible for the family. She describes her decision in terms of "I," not "we." Ellen feels responsible for maintaining the family's well-being, even if it means added difficulties for her. Keeping Paul at home means that her "family work" is more difficult, but she takes on these difficulties in order to maintain the kind of family she wants. Ellen's notion of a family is that families take care of their own. This means that a child with a disability is a part of the family just like any other family member. From Ellen's point of view, it is unacceptable to send her son away because sending him away violates her image of what family is and what family life is based on.

Most of the mothers who participated in this study share Ellen's view. Ann Lepan is another example. Ann and Peter Lepan have three young children: 4-year-old Bob, 2-year-old Tim, and 6-month-old Viola. Ann has a degree in psychology, but she is a full-time wife and mother. Her husband Peter is an architect who runs his own business. Their 2-year-old, Timmy, has multiple disabilities—cerebral palsy, mental retardation, and visual impairment. Ann's older son, Bob, sometimes complains that he doesn't want Timmy in the house because Timmy makes too much noise. Ann responds to such complaints as follows:

> Timmy is a part of our family and he belongs here. And what is best for everybody is that no one is kept out because they have a problem. . . . I think he would survive someplace else but not as well as with us, and we just have to cope with it.

When Ann responds to her older son's complaint about the noisiness of his younger brother, she is in fact constructing a definition of their family: In their family, parents take care of children; they do not send them away. To be a family, you do what families should do. The family is a place where you are loved and cared for. When people are family, you have to accept them, even if their behavior causes problems.

FAMILY LIFE

Creating the sense of being an ordinary family requires that the family be able to do the things that other families do. At the outset of the study, I assumed that the nature and severity of the children's disabilities would be one of the most important factors with regard to the everyday experiences of their respective families. What I learned, however, is that the limitations the child brings to the family depend only partially on the actual severity of the disability. Parents tend to evaluate the disability in terms of the limitations it imposes on the family as a unit, and they describe the restrictions of the child's disability in terms of how much they see the child as restricting or limiting their family life.

From the parents' point of view, the most important issue is for the family to be able to function as a unit. When the parents describe this, it becomes clear that there are certain critical components of a family life that they judge to be most important. These are activities that families do together "as a family" both within the home and outside the home.

The families in this study describe meals as an essential part of family life. The family dinner is perhaps the most critical family event and the one most often mentioned by parents. The family dinner seems to be a symbol of family unity. It is one of the few events for which all family members gather on a regular basis. Many parents described difficulties in eating together as a family. If the child's disability disrupts the family dinner, the parents see the event as seriously disrupting their family life and sense of being an ordinary family.

The Hardings have two sons, 12-year-old Donald and 15-year-old Eric, who has autism. When I first met the Harding family, they had been going through a period of great difficulty with Eric's behavior. Eric's parents see this behavior as having a negative influence on the family as a whole. The father, Derrik, describes the family's problems with Eric's behavior in terms of how it disrupts family dinners:

> It was difficult to deal with. Maybe we would all sit down at the dinner table to eat and suddenly Eric is throwing things across the table and trying to pinch someone. It was no fun.

Family meals are not only essential for families who have children with disabilities. DeVault (1991, p. 39) found that the parents she interviewed (none of whom had a child with a disability) often described meals, and especially dinner, as organizing elements of family life:

> The parents who spoke about the importance of family meals recognize that meals do more than [provide] sustenance; they are also social events that bring family members together. Such rituals provide a basis for establishing and maintaining family culture, and they create a mutual recognition of the family as a group. . . . Indeed, a "family" is not a naturally occurring collection of individuals; its reality is constructed from day to day through activities like eating together.

Some of the parents interviewed for this study receive in-home family support services. These parents tend to evaluate the family support program in terms of whether or not the program has helped them lead an ordinary family life. One issue mentioned by many parents is how effectively the program has helped them deal with problems around the dinner table. If the family support program has managed to help them to eat together "as a family," they describe the family support program as very helpful.

Besides family meals, the parents mentioned other important components of family life. These are most often activities families do together outside the home, such as going on a vacation, eating at a restaurant, shopping, and so on. If the child's disability hinders the family in doing these things, it is seen as hindering family life. Ellen Spencer, Paul's mother, told me that her family has not been able to take a vacation since his birth. She said, "There is a lot of resentment around not being able to lead a normal mobile family life."

Derrik Harding also talked about how difficult it is for them to go out as a family because of Eric's behavior:

> We also have a problem with Eric's behaviors when we go out as a family. And up until a month ago we didn't go out anywhere; in shopping malls, grocery stores, hardware stores, and so on.

Derrik said that the family support program is working with them "on outings." He said he was hoping the program would be able to help them find a way to go out as a family.

One of the mothers who is involved with the same family support program said that her son has very difficult behavior problems in public, and therefore the family never goes out together. The family support program is also working with her family to help them to go out together. The mother emphasized how important this is:

> The resentment was not to be able to function as a normal family . . . not being able to go on a vacation together or go out to dinner together. [The family support program] gave us confidence to take him [her son] out to dinner. The trainer went with us and we ate as a family out at a family-type restaurant, and we had never done that before.

If the child's disability does not restrict the family from doing things as a unit outside the home, the parents often mention that factor. Karen Hutton's 12-year-old son Jonny is autistic. Karen is one of the mothers who emphasized how important it is to her that her son's disability does not prevent the family from doing things together:

> Jonny is very much a part of our lives, and we are lucky in the fact that we can go anywhere. Normally his behaviors are under control. . . . He goes everywhere. He is comfortable going on a vacation with us and things like that. So we can live our lives mostly like we would have except we have to make sure that he has what he needs as far as education.

Other parents made a similar point. For example, Bill and Leslie Brown, who have a 10-year-old daughter with a disability, told me that they go on a vacation with Leslie's parents every year and said they could do that because their daughter "travels very well." The parents also celebrate other occasions that they consider ordinary features of their family life, especially when the child with the disability can be part of an ordinary family situation. Karen Hutton has two sons. Her other son, Carl, does not have a disability. She described the interactions between the brothers:

> Carl is good with Jonny too and is patient, [although] not always. They are typical brothers too and sometimes fight like cats and dogs. But that is kind of nice too and normal.

The sight of brothers fighting is not usually seen as a cause for celebration. But Karen sees the fighting between her sons as a sign of ordinary family life, and so she celebrates it. Thus, what most families would consider a negative event can be interpreted as positive by the families of children with disabilities.

DISABILITY AND THE CONSTRUCTION OF GENDER

Studies of families of children with disabilities typically find that the division of labor within these families tends to follow a traditional pattern whereby the mother becomes a full-time caregiver (Gustavsson, 1985; Wickham-Searl, 1992). Studies also find that fathers seem less likely to become involved in caring for their children with disabilities than their children without disabilities (Parke, 1986). These same patterns of family life were found in this study.

Traditional Family Pattern

The majority of parents in this study follow the most traditional pattern of family life and division of labor with a breadwinning husband and a full-time wife and mother. Many of the parents, both mothers and fathers, describe this traditional division of labor in a matter-of-fact way, like the mother who said, "My husband, of course, has to work and leaves these things to me." By "these things" she was referring to the caring work in the family and the work of searching for appropriate services for their son. The fathers typically have a similar attitude about this traditional division of labor. One of the fathers, Peter Lepan, an architect who has his own business, expressed a similar attitude when I asked him about his involvement in caring for his son with a disability:

> I don't have time . . . I need all the time to make a living. Instead of working with Timmy, I work in the evening. I've got three kids and I have my own business firm.

Feminist studies (Berk, 1985; Coltrane, 1989; DeVault, 1991; West & Zimmerman, 1987) have noted that caring is commonly associated with "womanly" activity. In a study of how parents share household work and child care, Coltrane (1989) suggests that in Western societies "the routine care of home and children are seen to provide opportunities for women to express and reaffirm their gendered relation to men and the world" (p. 473). Coltrane also points out that not only do fathers typically derive their sense of self from activities outside the family but that "their masculinity is even more dependent on not doing the things that women do" (1989, p. 473).

Using the concept of "doing gender" (West & Zimmerman, 1987) to analyze the division of household work, Berk (1985) points out that housework and child care can become "a reaffirmation of one's *gendered* relation to the work and the world" (p. 204; emphasis in original). Because caregiving is commonly understood as women's work, it therefore becomes a way for some women to define themselves.

By the same token, by providing for a family, a man constructs himself as a male. Studies of division of labor in families that do not have children with disabilities have found that when fathers share child care and housework with mothers they may be called to account for such "unnatural" activities (Coltrane, 1989; DeVault, 1991). The fathers in these studies sometimes refrain from telling others about their caregiving activities because they fear being seen as lacking in commitment to their careers and other traditional male activities outside the home.

The presence of a child with a disability seems to increase the pressure on fathers to strengthen their roles as providers for their families and refrain from taking part in the womanly activity of caregiving for a child with a disability. Through their everyday activities and interactions, people construct themselves as male or female. To contend with negative stereotypes of children with disabilities, mothers and fathers are more apt to construct themselves as "normal" men and women. This seems to be one of the reasons why families of children with disabilities tend to follow the most traditional pattern of family life with a breadwinning husband and a full-time wife and mother.

The Devoted Mother

Motherhood is often viewed as the essence of womanhood and mothering as a natural expression of femininity. Although all women who become mothers are under strong cultural expectations to devote themselves to the care of their children, this pressure seems to be unusually strong on mothers of children with disabilities.

Having a child with a disability influences the lives of mothers and fathers differently. At least for two-parent middle-class families, the traditional family pattern with the breadwinning father and the full-time wife and mother offers the father the opportunity to spend much of his time outside the home in a world separate from the child. One of the mothers in this study describes these differences in the following way: "I was jealous that he could walk through that door and be away from what I was going through." She also said that the difficulties presented by their son's disability sometimes made their family life stressful and unpleasant. It was not always pleasant when her husband came home to his family: "I didn't even imagine that he would want to come home." She feels responsible not only for the difficult task of taking care of their son but for constructing a family life and household that her husband enjoys coming home to. This places a great deal of pressure on her to become a devoted mother and wife and to perform her work in such a way that the difficulties concerning her son's disability do not become an overwhelming negative feature of family life.

Mothers are closely associated with their children's successes and failures (Caplan & Hall-McCorquodale, 1984). If the child has an obvious disability, the mother feels the brunt of the blame and is the one who is expected to set things right. In writing about the experiences of families who have children with disabilities, Featherstone (1980) states: "The whole culture supports a mother in the opinion that her children are what she made them" (p. 71). When mothers of children with disabilities devote their lives to caring for their child, it partly serves to construct themselves as good mothers (seen as central to being a woman). The need to establish themselves as good mothers seems to be further reinforced by the fact that many of the mothers are blamed for their children's problems. This is particularly true for the mothers whose children have emotional problems and/or problematic behaviors. The majority of the mothers in the support group have children with emotional problems, and they frequently talk about how they are blamed for their children's problems. When the mothers reflect on their dealings with teachers and other professionals, they commonly say: "They always blame us, the mothers." The professionals would often say things like: "If you only gave him a little more structure, things would be better." To mothers who do provide a structured environment, the professionals would sometimes suggest being "more flexible" in their approach.

Karen Hutton and Linda Fucarro both have children who have problematic behaviors. They both talk about having been blamed for their children's problems and accused of being "bad mothers." Karen described one professional "who said to me I had a terribly behaved child and probably most of it was my fault." When Linda first realized that there was something wrong with her daughter, she went from one doctor to another. The doctors told Linda there was nothing wrong with her daughter; "No one believed me, they just thought I was a bad mother." The doctors implied that her daughter's behavior problems were caused by her lack of parenting skills. Linda's husband took a similar stand: "He always said there was nothing wrong with her and said I was making her nervous by taking her to all these doctors." Linda Fucarro's daughter was later diagnosed as emotionally disturbed and having mental retardation and challenging behaviors.

One way to fight the label of "bad mother" and earn that of "good mother" is to conform as closely as possible to the role of the selfless mother who devotes herself to the welfare of the child and the family. By conforming to a traditional woman's role, these mothers are creating a family pattern that is favored by the larger culture.

Linda Fucarro was a full-time housewife for many years. Her description of what she did highlights how women construct themselves as devoted mothers through their activities. Linda said:

When my daughter was gone during the day I did all the woman things. I learned how to sew more; I knew a little sewing, but I learned more. Also canning, I learned that from books.

Linda also became an active advocate for her daughter and fights hard for appropriate services; she became a member of the parents movement and started doing volunteer work for parent groups. In addition, she has taken on a number of traditional female activities.

Gender Roles and Normal Family Life

All of the mothers in the study have the main responsibility for caregiving within the family. Caring for a child with a disability can be very demanding and hard work, seriously limiting the mother's opportunities to do other things both within and outside of the home. Many of the mothers arrange their whole lives around caring for their child with a disability. Some of the children need constant attention and cannot be left alone for a moment because they can hurt themselves. Others have problems sleeping and keep the mother awake for large parts of the night, and some need to be attended and fed during the night. Elaine Gensberg, one of the mothers, described this in the following way:

As it turned out, because [my husband] basically rejected the child, he didn't do anything. Occasionally, in the middle of the night he would get up and gavage [tube-feed] her and he would sometimes take the midnight ones because I was so tired, and I would have to get up very early in the morning. [My daughter] got up at 4 or 5 usually. But one time out of six or eight is not much when you are doing this on a daily basis.

Besides doing the caregiving, the mothers are also expected to be responsible for other work that needs to be done in order to create an ordinary life with the child as a member. The mothers usually quit their jobs to devote most of their lives to fulfilling these expectations.

Part of this effort is to constantly search for appropriate programs and services. Karen Hutton said:

> Basically I do it because I have the time to investigate things and look into programs and what is available and how we could make things available.

In addition to searching and fighting for services for their children, the mothers also coordinate services, benefits, programs, and people—professionals and others—who are involved with their child. Elaine Gensberg, whose daughter has severe physical disabilities, explained:

> My daughter is seen by 17 professionals, or at least it was the last time I counted. I'm sure it is way up by now because there are all these computer specialists now. Seventeen professionals! Now who is going to take the responsibility for being sure that all these 17 professionals are seen? That whatever they say is followed up on? That they coordinate and talk to each other, that they are paid? If you are going to survive as a mother . . . you become an expert manager.

Although the lives of the mothers in this study are organized around the child, and the work they do for the child restricts and limits their access to other pursuits, neither parent takes this limitation of the mother's life into account when talking about the child's disability as limiting the family. When the parents, both fathers and mothers, describe how the child restricts their family life, they do not bring up how the caring work limits the mother. Thus, it does not seem to be defined as limiting to have a child with a disability if that disability limits only the mother's life; the situation is defined as limiting only if other family members and the family as a whole are prevented from doing things.

DISABILITY SERVICES AND FAMILY LIFE

Many of the mothers expressed a great need for the family support program to help them create strategies to develop interactions and situations that would lead to a more ordinary family life. At the same time, some of the mothers see the program as disrupting family life. To have a stranger come into your house to help you work with your child is not what families normally do. The mothers are caught in a dilemma; the help they need to create an ordinary family life also disrupts their sense of being in an ordinary family. Most of the mothers deal with this by treating the trainer as a family friend or part of the family. One mother described this in the following way:

> When [the trainer] first started coming he was just sitting there at the table, he was not eating. It is much more relaxed now that he eats with us. We felt we were on display or something. Now we are more like a family when we all sit down and eat.

Another mother said:

> Initially it was very difficult to have a stranger come into the house. It disrupts the family, until [the trainer] became a familiar face.

The family support program does not seem to be aware of how important it is for some of the families to be able to incorporate the trainers into the life of the family. Some of the program's rules and policies work against the mothers' attempts to treat trainers as a part of the family. For example, the family support program has a rule that the trainers not eat with the families. Not all of the trainers observe this rule; some have given in to a family's pressure to sit down and eat with them.

Another way of dealing with the presence of a stranger in the house is to treat the trainer as a guest. Two of the mothers described how they used to clean the house before the trainer came. "I felt I had to clean the house before they came," one of them said. She added, "I can understand parents if they don't feel comfortable with having people coming, because if you have a special kid it changes your whole life." Cleaning the house before the trainer came is something both mothers stopped doing after they got to know the trainer better. After a while, these mothers changed their strategy to incorporating the trainer into the family as a friend or family member. Both mothers said that the professionals from the family support program had found out about the extra cleaning, made fun of them for it, and told them it was not necessary. The professionals do not understand why a mother feels the need to clean the house before strangers arrive, not realizing that this helps her to create an ordinary atmosphere of receiving guests.

This family support program relies heavily on behavior management as a way of teaching the parents to deal with their children. For example, the program teaches the mothers diverse behavioral techniques and wants them to "take data" on their child's performance. Some of the mothers resist this approach to dealing with their children. The main reason for the mothers' resistance is that they see some of these techniques as incompatible with family life. Ellen Spencer is one of the mothers who complains about this aspect of the family support program. She said:

> I hate taking data; data taking is terrible. When I sit down with Paul I hate to count how many times he plays with this or that. I'm running a home and I feel it is too professional.

Like many of the other mothers, Ellen Spencer is trying to protect her home and family from being "professionalized" to the extent that it disrupts her sense of leading an ordinary life.

CREATING AN ORDINARY FAMILY IMAGE

According to one mother, having a child with disabilities makes the family "look handicapped." The mothers use different strategies to try to become more like, or at least look more like, ordinary families. One of the strategies is to have another child right away. One mother talked about it in terms of "setting things right":

> We had our daughter very quickly after. I decided I would go right ahead and have another child, and my husband was quite supportive of that. He said that it was fine if that was what I really wanted to do. But it was very much my own decision. . . . I felt that this strange trick had been played on me and that I wanted to set it right.

Many of the other mothers decided to do the same thing, especially if the child with the disability was their first. In fact, the majority went ahead and had another child.

Although this decision to have another child is primarily the mother's decision, this seems to help both parents restore the sense of being an ordinary family. Many of the mothers expressed their relief in having had a child without a disability the second time. Karen Hutton described it in the following way:

> It is easier now that my other son is leading a completely normal life and sometimes it is also fun to go out and do things with him. He is 9 now, very active, very outgoing, the opposite of his brother, and interested in everything.

The decision to have another child seems also to have been made partly to restore the parents' self-image and self-esteem and to reaffirm their biological normality. Some of the mothers said that having the new child helped them feel better about themselves. Miriam Walker's oldest daughter has mental retardation, cerebral palsy, and epilepsy. Miriam and her husband went right ahead and had two other children. Miriam said, "It was a very healing experience to have my other two normal children." Ellen Spencer said that she had felt that her son's disabilities were her fault and she didn't get over that feeling until another child came along. "It was not until I had Helen that I could feel that it was not my fault or people would think, 'You dropped the kid.' "

The idea of what an ordinary family looks like and the importance of conforming closely to that image affects much of what mothers of children with disabilities do. One of the single mothers, Linda Fucarro, has a 16-year-old daughter with mental retardation and emotional problems. Linda divorced her husband when the girl was young and rents an apartment in a low-income neighborhood. She kept her husband's name after the divorce because she considered that to be better for her daughter:

It is hard enough for her to live with a single mother. It is strange, in a way I don't feel like Linda Fucarro because it isn't my own name. It was my husband's name.

CLASS, RACE, AND FAMILY LIFE

Although families of children with disabilities may have many experiences in common, social relations such as race, class, and culture greatly influence the social organization of family life. This section explores how social class and race influence and organize the work of constructing an ordinary family and address the specific issues facing African American families.

African American Families and Disability Services

The differences in the family patterns of African Americans and European Americans have been summarized as follows: "Compared to whites, blacks are less likely to marry, less likely to remain married, more likely to bear children while unmarried, and more likely to reside in households headed by women" (Walker, 1988, p. 87). Because a large number of African American families do not conform to the traditional patterns of marriage and family formation that exist in the white culture, these differences have received a great deal of public attention. This has been defined as a problem because it is widely assumed that life in the traditional nuclear family is an important prerequisite for social and economic success in American society. Scholars as well as policy makers have tended to define these differences as deviant and have joined forces to create social programs to reduce or eliminate them.

As one of the social programs established to "help" dependent populations, the human services system has adopted the dominant view of the African American family as "deviant." This view has influenced how disability services relate to African American families (Kalyanpur & Rao, 1991) and is reinforced by the fact that most professionals are white and from middle-class backgrounds. People's perceptions of "the family" usually reflect their own ethnic, racial, class, and cultural heritage. Therefore, when white, middle-class professionals encounter African American families, they tend to impose their own frame of reference on the situation, which serves to reinforce the dominant view of the African American family as deviant.

The story of Janet Lee, an African American single mother who participated in this study, shows how this can play out in reality. Janet has a 4-year-old son, Frank, who has mental retardation, challenging behaviors, and a communication disorder. When Janet and Frank became involved with a family support program that provides them with in-home services, they were living in an extended family with Janet's parents, two brothers, a sister, and the sister's baby. The family support program saw the collective efforts of this extended family in dealing with Frank's problematic behavior as interfering with the program's efforts. For example, the family support program objected to the way Frank's grandfather dealt with the boy's temper tantrums. The professionals wanted Frank to "work through" the tantrums. The grandfather did not agree because it might mean that the little boy would be left to cry on his own. Instead, the grandfather insisted on hugging and comforting Frank. From the professionals' point of view, the grandfather was a problem because he did not cooperate with them. The professionals claimed that too many people were stepping in and interfering with the program that they were trying to set up for the boy. They therefore encouraged Janet to move away from her extended family and establish her own home with Frank. Janet followed their advice and is now living alone with her son in what both she and the professionals describe as a very bad inner city neighborhood.

Janet's story highlights how the attitudes of white, middle-class professionals can influence the way they relate to poor African American families. Families that include children with disabilities are not the only ones with an image in mind when trying to create an ordinary life. Service providers harbor such images as well. The family support program operated under a definition of "family" that led staff members to identify only Janet and her son as the family with whom they should work. In fact, the program used its influence to break up Janet's existing extended family. Instead of supporting Janet within her existing family, the professionals used their ideal of a "normal" family, along with their influence, to make Janet conform to a stereotype as close to theirs as possible.

In her study of African American family life, Stack (1974) demonstrates how poor African American families form strong networks of cooperation, reciprocity, and support. Stack holds that these support networks were essential to the survival of the families she studied, and her study highlights the importance of such kinship-based exchange networks to cope with poverty. If a service system dominated by the white culture fails to recognize and respect these existing support networks and their importance in the lives of poor African American families, the interventions may in fact damage these networks. A different attitude toward African American families and more knowledge of their life patterns would allow the service system to strengthen and build on existing support networks rather than attempt to replace them with professional help, as seems to have been the case with Janet Lee and her son.

CONCLUSION

Families of children with disabilities devote a great deal of time and energy to trying to lead an ordinary life. The overwhelming majority of the families in this study follow a traditional pattern of family life with a breadwinning husband and a full-time wife and mother. This traditional family pattern contrasts with the family pattern most often found in society today, in which over 60% of all women, and 59% of all mothers, participate in the paid labor force (Russo & Jansen, 1988). Thus, when these families attempt to be ordinary they are responding to an ideal of family and not merely one that is closest to the statistical norm. Most often, the work required to create and maintain this idealized family falls on the mothers.

Although all mothers and fathers may experience cultural expectations to conduct themselves according to traditional gender roles, these expectations become intensified when there is a child with a disability in the family. The presence of the disability seems to suggest something unnatural, and parents of children with disabilities strive to compensate for this by conforming as closely as possible to traditional gender roles, thereby constructing themselves as "normal" men and women, and their family as an ordinary family.

This study indicates that service providers and professionals coming in contact with families that include a member with a disability often lack an understanding and insight into the characteristics and experiences of those families. This chapter illuminates three important insights for such professionals: 1) the importance of making an effort to understand the individual perspectives of families and the dynamics of everyday life within those families, 2) the necessity of being aware of how broader social and cultural issues influence the lives of families of children with disabilities, and 3) the importance of changing the focus of the professional effort on behalf of such families.

Learning to Understand the Perspectives of Families

Most of the professionals who worked with the families in this study seemed to lack in-depth understanding of the impact of a child with a disability on everyday life in the family. For example, they were not aware of how the families strive to achieve an ordinary family life with the child with a disability as a member and thus sometimes (through agency rules and professional actions) disrupted their attempts.

The pressure to construct an ordinary family pulls fathers and mothers toward very traditional patterns. Most service providers and professionals seemed oblivious to this and their actions tended to reinforce the traditional pattern, further locking parents into stereotypical gender roles. It is essential that professionals respect the perspectives of families and appreciate the daily life of families of children with disabilities. Otherwise their actions may disrupt family life and the identities of family members.

Social and Cultural Context

Socioeconomic class, race, ethnicity, and gender are among the social forces that intersect with issues of disability and influence how professionals interact with families. Middle-class professionals tend to have different ideas about child rearing than families from lower socioeconomic groups. Instead of recognizing the possibility of class-based or cultural differences, professionals tend to judge the child-rearing approaches of families from other socioeconomic groups as wrong. Moreover, because the training that professionals receive usually reflects the values of middle-class culture, professionals are receiving reinforcement of their belief that their child-rearing views are correct. As a result, the goal of professional work with families from lower socioeconomic groups too often becomes that of correcting what they see as improper child-rearing approaches. Too often professional practice is carried out from an oversimplified perspective. Service providers and professionals need to increase their cultural competence in order to work effectively with all families of children with disabilities.

The Focus of Professional Work

When professionals come in contact with a family of a child with a disability, they tend to focus on that disability. This study indicates that such narrow focus on the child's disability often prevents professionals from correctly perceiving the dynamics within the family and understanding the family's social and cultural context. It is essential that service providers and professionals adopt a broader focus that would enable them to carry out their work in harmony with the strengths and dynamics of the family.

REFERENCES

Berk, S.F. (1985). *The gender factory: The apportionment of work in American households*. New York: Plenum Press.

Birenbaum, A. (1968). *Non-institutionalized role and role formation: A study of mothers of mentally retarded children*. Unpublished doctoral dissertation, Columbia University, New York.

Birenbaum, A. (1970). On managing a courtesy stigma. *Journal of Health and Social Behavior, 11*(3), 196–206.

Birenbaum, A. (1971). The mentally retarded child in the home and the family cycle. *Journal of Health and Social Behavior, 12*(1), 55–65.

Bogdan, R., & Taylor, S.J. (1982). *Inside out: The social meaning of mental retardation.* Toronto, Ontario, Canada: University of Toronto Press.

Bogdan, R., & Taylor, S.J. (1987). Toward a sociology of acceptance: The other side of the study of deviance. *Social Policy, 18*(2), 34–39.

Bogdan, R., & Taylor, S.J. (1989). Relationships with severely disabled people: The social construction of humanness. *Social Problems, 36,* 135–148.

Booth, T.A. (1978). From a normal baby to handicapped child: Unraveling the idea of subnormality in families of mentally handicapped children. *Sociology, 12*(2), 203–221.

Caplan, P.J., & Hall-McCorquodale, I. (1984). Mother-blaming in major clinical journals. *American Journal of Orthopsychiatry, 55,* 345–353.

Coltrane, S. (1989). Household labor and the routine production of gender. *Social Problems, 36*(5), 473–490.

DeVault, M.L. (1991). *Feeding the family: The social organization of caring as gendered work.* Chicago: University of Chicago Press.

Dudley, J.R. (1983). *Living with stigma: The plight of the people who we label mentally retarded.* Springfield, IL: Charles C Thomas.

Edgerton, R.B. (1967). *The cloak of competence: Stigma in the lives of the mentally retarded.* Berkeley: University of California Press.

Featherstone, H. (1980). *A difference in the family: Living with a disabled child.* New York: Basic Books.

Goffman, E. (1961). *Asylums: Essays on the social situation of mental patients and other inmates.* New York: Doubleday.

Goffman, E. (1963). *Stigma: Notes on the management of spoiled identity.* New York: Simon and Schuster.

Gustavsson, A. (1985). *Samhallsideal och foraldraansvar: En explorative studie av vad det innebar att ha ett forstandshandicappat barn.* (Society's ideals and parental responsibility: An exploratory study of what it means to have a mentally retarded child.) Unpublished doctoral dissertation, University of Stockholm.

Kalyanpur, M., & Rao, S.S. (1991). Empowering low-income black families of handicapped children. *American Journal of Orthopsychiatry, 61*(4), 523–532.

Parke, R.D. (1986). Fathers, families and support systems: Their role in the development of at-risk and retarded infants and children. In J.J. Gallagher & P.M. Vietze (Eds.), *Families of handicapped persons: Research, programs, and policy issues* (pp. 101–113). Baltimore: Paul H. Brookes Publishing Co.

Russo, N.F., & Jansen, M.A. (1988). Women, work, and disability: Opportunities and challenges. In M. Fine & A. Asch (Eds.), *Women with disabilities: Essays in psychology, culture, and politics* (pp. 229–244). Philadelphia: Temple University Press.

Schmid, T.J. (1977). *Parental reactions to the affiliational stigma of mental retardation.* Unpublished doctoral dissertation, University of Minnesota.

Stack, C.B. (1974). *All our kin: Strategies for survival in a black community.* New York: Harper and Row.

Taylor, S.J., & Bogdan, R. (1989). On accepting relationships between people with mental retardation and nondisabled people: Towards an understanding of acceptance. *Disability, Handicap & Society, 4*(1), 21–36.

Voysey, M. (1972). Impression management by parents with disabled children. *Journal of Health and Social Behavior, 13*(1), 80–89.

Walker, H.A. (1988). Black-white differences in marriage and family patterns. In S.M. Dornbusch & M.H. Strober (Eds.), *Feminism, children and the new families*. New York: Guilford Press.

West, C., & Zimmerman, D.H. (1987). Doing gender. *Gender and Society, 1,* 121–174.

Wickham-Searl, P. (1992). Mothers with a mission. In P.M. Ferguson, D.L. Ferguson, & S.J. Taylor (Eds.), *Interpreting disability: A qualitative reader* (pp. 251–274). New York: Teachers College Press.

4

"We're All One Family"

The Positive Construction of People with Disabilities by Family Members

Susan O'Connor

This chapter contrasts the traditional view of families of children with disabilities as going through a process of grieving with a newly emerging view, that of accepting relationships. These are relationships in which individuals are not viewed and judged in terms of their differences, but rather are seen as members of their families and accepted as other children in the family are accepted. This chapter offers an example of one family who views their child, who has been labeled autistic, according to the same values, norms, and rules that they use with their other children.

Much of the family literature written by professionals and by parents of children with disabilities has focused on the deviant characteristics of the family member with disabilities and how parents and siblings are affected (Greenfeld, 1986; Powell & Gallagher, 1993; Samuelson, 1986). Although it is often concluded that the family views the child as having something special to offer and has come to accept the disability, this acceptance often comes after a long process of accustomization to the deviance. Some of this adjustment is made possible through what has been called passing or denial (Goffman, 1963).

Numerous studies of stress on families with a member with a disability have also been reported (Breslau & Davis, 1986; Lazarus & Folkman, 1984; Pahl & Quine, 1987; Roos, 1985; Singer & Irvin, 1989). One predominant framework has suggested that families work through having a member with a disability in stages. This process is described as being similar to how family members experience a death in the family. Families are then approached and intervention is offered in terms of where they are in this grieving process (Drotar, Baskiewicz, Irvin, Kennell, & Klaus, 1975; Seligman & Darling, 1989). Families are also described as working through the four stages of adaptation, which include surviving, searching, settling in, and separating (Miller, 1994).

Positive images, however, may also be constructed by family members, and these often present problems between the family and the professional. From a clinical point of view, families who construct a positive image may be seen as suffering from delusions or denying reality (Booth, 1978; Pollner & McDonald-Wilker, 1985).

Certainly there is stress in every family, and under certain circumstances the nature of a disability could be a cause of stress. It is important, however, to see the disability as it relates to other factors that have an impact on family life. In some families, economic issues, health issues, or issues related to other children may take on greater importance than the disability. An emerging body of literature raises new questions about how families view members with a disability. This perspective, which Bogdan and Taylor (1987) term the *sociology of acceptance*, focuses on families and individuals who have developed caring, loving relationships with people who are seen as different by others. The sociology of acceptance is directed to the understanding of how people with deviant attributes become accepted in individual relationships, families, or communities. In families, reasons for acceptance are often as simple as family membership: the family relationship supersedes the difference (Bogdan & Taylor, 1987, p. 36), and the relationship, not the difference, becomes the binding force. The sociology of acceptance also suggests the idea of the family as based on a sentiment allowing for a very persevering and enduring relationship.

Goode uses anthropological terms to describe two different perspectives of how a person might be seen. An *etic* perspective takes on a clinical or analytical view, whereas an *emic* perspective takes the "insider's view" (Goode, 1980), which would help to account for why some families see skills in their child that professionals do not see. Some families do not approach their child in terms of eradicating flaws, as suggested by a clinical approach, but instead see the role the child plays in the family as a whole. Even after diagnosis, the family interprets information in terms of their particular social context (Booth, 1978, p. 217), and disability may have no greater or lesser impact than the other situations with which the family has to deal. Booth contends that the medicalization of our thinking has been so complete that it has skewed our thinking in relation to children with disabilities (1978, p. 218). He alleges that becoming mentally retarded is a social process and that mental retardation is framed and shaped by social activity.

Given the difference between clinical and family perspectives, it is easy to see how different pictures, descriptions, and identities of the same child can be created. Gallimore, Weisner, Kaufman, and Bernheimer (1989) suggest that families are more than passive victims of the social and economic forces and propose that families take both individual and collective action to change those forces.

Reiss (1981) proposed the idea of family paradigms, whereby a family's assumptions about itself and the world are realized and create the family's reality. This enables members to experience their own values and assumptions as if they were unquestioned components of the outer reality (Pollner & McDonald-Wilker, 1985, p. 241). Thus, a family's acceptance of a member with a disability and how life has evolved is to that family part of the way they have constructed their daily world. Families give their own meaning to the actions of the child whether those actions are as simple as babbling, which they determine as communication, or a physical gesture such as hand flapping, which they interpret as excitement. An example of family acceptance is illustrated by the following case study.

THE HENRY FAMILY: A CASE STUDY

Verna and Nate Henry are the heads of a family that might best be described in one word: proud. They moved up North from the South approximately 25 years ago, and it was here that they began to raise their family. The Henrys are African American and live in a house they own in a community of about 150,000 people. Driving through the neighborhood, especially on a nice day, one can observe people talking on their porches or walking along the sidewalks and children playing or riding bicycles. Both the people and the advertisements on billboards indicate that the neighborhood residents are predominantly African Americans. Both Nate, a tall, thin man with graying hair and tired eyes, and Verna, a woman in her 40s with a warm smile, struggle to make ends meet; both work full-time to provide for their three sons. Martin is a handsome young man in his late teens whose interests seem to revolve around cars. He has been in and out of jobs and, as is the case for many teenagers, appears to be trying to decide what he wants his future to be. Mitchell is almost a teenager and is described by his family as "knowing people all over the city." In the evenings, he takes charge of the telephone, as most of the calls are for him. Charles (Chas), who is several years younger than Mitchell, has short-cropped hair and is not quite as tall as his brother. He, too, is friendly to the visitor entering the home and very curious, asking questions and demanding answers regarding what the visitor is doing in his house.

How Chas Henry would be further described would depend on the lens through which he was being viewed. A teacher, a social worker, a case manager, a parent, or a brother might use different words and could construct very different images of who this child is. Each description would vary in terms of the level of Chas's competence. At a young age, Chas was diagnosed as autistic, but he is an important member of this family.

Spending time with this family and observing their interactions, I as an outsider was able to see how Chas was included as just another family member rather than as a child who has been labeled autistic. Chas had a number of the typical traits used to describe children with autism, such as stereotypical movements and repetitive speech. However, he was described by his father as being well known in the community, having a "mind of his own," and having a good memory. The only description ever given that could be stretched to indicate anything out of the norm was when his father said, "Chas, he has a mind of his own and sometimes we gotta watch him." Yet this is quickly followed up with, "Yeah, both Mitchell and Chas are a handful." In none of my 12 visits with this family were the words *handicap*, *disability*, or *autism* ever used. Instead, Chas was described as being "well liked" like his brother, able to "remember everything," and "a child who falls in love with his teachers." Nate proudly said of his sons, "When I go to the store I never get out without someone comin' up to me saying, 'Ain't you Charles's daddy, or ain't you Mitchell's daddy?'"

"Taking After": The Connecting of Generations

The idea of taking after one's parents emerges strongly in this family. Nate and Verna talked about the different traits that they shared with their parents as well as similarities between their sons and themselves.

Both Nate and Verna told stories of their own experiences growing up in the South. They talked about things that they valued and were proud of: working to provide for the family, taking after their parents, and caring for those within the family and others. Nate and Verna described their background: Verna began, "When I was in high school, I worked and gave money to my mama every week." Nate added, "My mother died when I was 14 and me and my brothers still put ourselves through high school and worked too. We had to help take care of Grandmother and my sister."

Nate and Verna were proud to have overcome hardships while growing up. They saw this as the basis for traits that they passed down to their children. Nate said of his father, "He was liked by everybody and would do anything for anybody. And I'm the same way; so is Mitchell. We come well by it."

Both Nate and Verna placed their sons within the context of "taking after" either positively or negatively and in doing so appeared to accept and view what professionals might call autistic "behaviors" as merely "taking after" someone in the family. Nate explained how Chas liked to get up in the middle of the night:

> I go to bed and wake up after about 2 hours of sleep. Chas, he takes right after me. He gets up a lot, he can't sleep either, so we up together. He got that from me. I was so used to workin' two jobs and I was up all hours of the night, so I guess it really comes from me.

Not only did this offer an explanation of why Chas did something that would often be seen as needing to be changed, but within the family it was seen as being "like dad." What might be viewed as a problem behavior was instead interpreted as simply a habit that Chas got from his father. Instead of being viewed as negative, it was considered acceptable for both father and son.

The idea of taking after each other seems to be significant in terms of acceptance into the family. Although each family member has his or her individual characteristics, they are viewed as positive or negative based on the overall family rules and expectations that hold for all of its members.

For example, the oldest son, Martin, was viewed as not following the family norm. After graduating from high school, he was expected to return something to the family. Martin was never talked about in terms of how he took after his parents or grandparents. Instead, he was seen as different, although they took responsibility for his difference, blaming his irresponsibility on all that they gave him when he was young. The difference in what Nate and Martin experienced when they were young and the roles that were required of them was explained by Nate:

> I tell you the difference with Martin, where we went wrong. When he was growin' up we had money, we had good jobs. He just doesn't think he owes us nothin', that we are here to serve him. When I was his age, I was workin'.

The ideas of taking after and of giving back to the family are strongly valued and have been passed on through the generations. Failure to take after and carry on family traits may be more alienating than a disability for a member of such a family.

Caring and Commitment

Most parents face dilemmas regarding how far to go to protect their children, how much independence to allow, and where to set limits

(Featherstone, 1980). For parents of children with disabilities, this is no different. Caring and commitment can be very obscure concepts that are arbitrary at best. Their meaning can vary from family to family and from culture to culture. In the Henry family, commitment and caring were a strong part of what it meant to accept Chas, but even more so of what it meant to accept all of their children as well as people considered to be part of the family.

Because family was important, all members were valued and seen in light of their family membership. This commitment often went beyond the immediate family to their extended family. On one of my first visits, Verna talked about her aunt and uncle, whom they had brought up from Georgia to live nearby: "Though they loved their garden and their home, their kids are here and at least they are among family."

Things changed for the Henrys when they had children. This seemed to instill a deeper commitment to the success of the family as a unit versus any one member. Their social activities, for example, were set aside:

> We used to bowl, we don't do that no more, our lives changed a lot. I mean we used to do a lot of things; we would go out from time to time, but we haven't done that in years. Now all of our time is spent for our children.

The importance of commitment can also be seen in trying to prepare their children for the future. This was clear as Nate talked about moving back to Florida and how it would be better for his health but not for Chas:

> No good schools down there for Chas, we went and checked them out. He needs that; he's in a real good school here now, he has really learned a lot. He needs that 'cause he got a long life ahead of him.

Commitment to and acceptance of family members, whatever their situation, became the driving force in the Henrys' lives.

Nate expanded his idea of caring beyond his family to a young woman who rode the bus he drove and whom he described as "living in one of them group homes" and "giving everyone a hard time":

> She never gives me a hard time. I just talk with her. Once she hit herself real bad and I said, "Why do you want to hurt yourself? The Lord don't like that." She stopped. She just wanted to know someone cares.

Within a framework of caring and commitment, religion is also very important. Research has shown that religion may have a bearing on the acceptance of a child with a disability, especially in regard to helping the family get through the so-called process of grieving (Gallimore et al., 1989, p. 223; Zuk, Miller, Bartram, & Kling, 1961). Religion helped get the Henrys through whatever happened. Verna explained:

> You gotta have hope in somethin'; you gotta keep goin' on. The Lord is on our side. A few years ago Nate's knees were so bad the doctor said he would have to have surgery, so we prayed and prayed and he got better. . . . Like our minister says, all these problems give you strength to go on. The Lord is on our side.

Their faith gave them hope and accounted for some of their present social life. Weekly Bible meetings were held at the house, and weekends often involved church activities. Within the scope of their religious beliefs and involvements, the Henrys' sense of what they accepted and rejected in relation to those beliefs remained solid. At one Bible study, the young minister warned that those who do not repent will go to hell. Verna strongly rejected this belief: "Well, I ain't selfish and I ain't goin' to hell." This strong sense of identity also held true with different workers who came into the home. Although Nate and Verna listened respectfully to support workers, they also interpreted the advice they received in relationship to their daily lives, accepting some and quietly rejecting others. This was shared in frustration by one support worker: "Yeah they are nice people, but they definitely have ideas about what they want or will accept." The Henrys seemed to know what was right for their family and could accept or reject advice rather than simply abide by what they were told. They respected those who entered their lives but maintained their own sense of identity and integrity.

"Gettin' By": Family Problems versus Individual Problems

There was little sense in this family that the primary focus of their daily life was Chas and his disability. Often times the child with a disability becomes the primary focus as parents struggle with school and support issues. For the Henrys, although they had great concern for all of their children, difficulties were focused around daily struggles that appeared to change with time and the situations that the family encountered. Although it was unclear as to whether Chas's disability was a major challenge at one time, present family concerns revolved around money. The financial situation of the family has changed over time because of Verna and Nate's health problems as well as job changes. These were the looming issues with which the family struggled, trying daily to maintain the status of just "gettin' by." "I guess we can handle it 'cause we keep gettin' it," Nate said in relation to problems such as everyday bills and ongoing health needs. Only indirectly were money problems related to Chas discussed, and even then they had more to do with not understanding the system than with Chas. They were not able to count on Supplemental Security Income (SSI), because as their income fluctuated so did their benefits. Verna explained:

Yeah, we had a lot of hard times. Now we are at least able to meet our bills. And talk of SSI, we better off without it at all than this back and forth. We budget and plan what we will have with this money and then when they say we need to pay them back 'cause maybe one month I got a little overtime or somethin', we don't have any money to do it.

Phases and Changes

Families often describe their children with disabilities in terms of characteristics framed in professional jargon. The children are described as nonambulatory, as nonverbal, or as having a challenging behavior rather than as children who go through phases, moods, and changes as we all do. Over time, families may come to speak about their children in terms of predetermined categories and labels established by professionals.

As change appeared to be a normal part of life for the Henry family, they also saw Chas as changing. Verna talked about changes in her health coming with age, changes in jobs affecting their economic situation, and changes in what the kids needed and wanted as they grew. Their recognition of change was clear. If Chas's disability had been a major factor in family life in earlier years, they had moved beyond any extraordinary negative change he brought to their lives. Now they described some of Chas's actions in terms of phases. One incident that occurred in school, for which Chas would typically be described as "acting out," was described by his mother: "It seems like he actin' more bad than he was before, but he goes through phases like this." She described another incident that was more serious:

He went through a phase of wanderin' a while back. He would get outside and just want to walk . . . he loves parks. He has a good sense of direction. He just loves walking. He also loves playgrounds, so maybe he was looking for that too 'cause he remembered there was one up near his old school. One time, Chas wandered off and was gone for a long time. We called the police 'cause we was worried.

Verna and Nate voiced equal concern for Mitchell, although the circumstances were different. He had gone to his friends and stayed all day; he didn't come home or call, and consequently they were very worried: "We got real scared. You know a lot of things can happen out there. We called all around tryin' to find him."

Behaviors that could be described as stereotypical by professionals—hard shaking of the hands, rocking, jumping up and down, and repeating words—instead were viewed as excitement. On one occasion, as the family sat watching a high-speed chase scene on television, Chas jumped up and began to make a loud humming noise. He flapped his hands rapidly and paced back and forth. His mother looked at him calmly after it was over and said, "You really got excited at that Chas, didn't you?" He was not told to stop flapping his arms; rather, his mother responded naturally, seeing what might be interpreted as "autistic behavior" as a characteristic related to his likes and dislikes.

Moods, phases, and habits were the language the family used to describe things that could otherwise be viewed as negative behaviors. What might be called ritualistic behavior in a classic clinical sense were explained as follows: "He likes things to be the same—you know, kind of a habit."

CONCLUSION

This is an illustration of one family, but the lessons they offer provide insight into how families naturally focus on similarities of traits among their members rather than on their differences.

Much of family life and the interactions that occur within different families remain individual and hidden from professionals. In the field of disabilities, there is an abundance of literature based on the problems that families face in relation to their member with a disability (Dougan, Isbell, & Vyas, 1983; Greenfeld, 1986; Kaufman, 1988). This chapter does not dispute those difficulties but rather places them in a different light. The sociology of acceptance does not refute the hard times but instead offers evidence that some families either have moved beyond them or never experienced them. Such families see their child as part of a whole rather than as someone who has fragmented that whole. They tend to place disability in the context of all of their children having different needs.

They remain unfettered by professional jargon and view disability as just another characteristic of who they are in their day-to-day struggles. They become not Nate and Verna Henry who have a child with autism, but rather the Henry family.

This then becomes the challenge to professionals in their attempt to gain a deeper understanding and portrayal of individual family lives. Stories of similarities rather than differences might offer us all some insight and help to bridge the vast gulf we have created between families of children with and without disabilities. Professionals must be open to what each family has to teach, recognizing that family members are the experts on their lives. This will allow a greater understanding of what disability labels mean to families and how these labels affect their daily lives. It is helpful too for professionals to step back and be open to what emerges in families. Learning how families speak with and think about not only their child with a disability but the family in general can give valuable insight into how best to work with a particular family. Appreciating the ways families go about raising all of their children can help take the focus off of the difficulties about which so much has been written, and focus instead on the parenting styles that create the norms within each family. Such stories may have more to teach us about acceptance and family commitment than the labels by which they are defined. All families have a set of standards, values, and beliefs that they create in order to survive, to excel, and to function in society. We are only beginning to understand this kind of acceptance, although these familes have understood it all along.

REFERENCES

Bogdan, R., & Taylor, S. (1987). Toward a sociology of acceptance: The other side of the study of deviance. *Social Policy, 18*(2), 34–39.

Booth, T.A. (1978). From normal baby to handicapped child: Unravelling the idea of subnormality in families of mentally handicapped children. *Journal of the British Sociological Association, 12*, 203–221.

Breslau, N., & Davis, D.C. (1986). Chronic stress and major depression. *Archives of General Psychiatry, 43*, 309–314.

Dougan, T., Isbell, L., & Vyas, P. (Eds.). (1983). *We have been there*. Nashville: Abingdon Press.

Drotar, D., Baskiewicz, B.A., Irvin, N., Kennell, J., & Klaus, M.E. (1975). The adaptation of parents to the birth of an infant with a congenital malformation: A hypothetical model. *Pediatrics, 56*, 710–717.

Featherstone, H. (1980). *A difference in the family: Living with a disabled child*. New York: Penguin Books.

Gallimore, R., Weisner, T.S., Kaufman, S.Z., & Bernheimer, L. (1989). The social construction of ecocultural niches: Family accommodation of developmentally delayed children. *American Journal on Mental Retardation, 94*(3), 216–230.

Goffman, E. (1963). *Stigma: Notes on the management of spoiled identity*. New York: Simon and Schuster.

Goode, D. (1980). Behavioral sculpting. In J. Jacobs (Ed.), *Mental retardation: A phenomenological approach* (pp. 94–119). Springfield, IL: Charles C Thomas.

Greenfeld, J. (1986). *A client called Noah*. New York: Henry Holt.

Kaufman, S.Z. (1988). *Retarded isn't stupid, Mom!* Baltimore: Paul H. Brookes Publishing Co.

Lazarus, R., & Folkman, S. (1984). *Stress, appraisal and coping*. New York: Springer-Verlag.

Miller, N.B. (1994). *Nobody's perfect: Living and growing with children who have special needs*. Baltimore: Paul H. Brookes Publishing Co.

Pahl, J., & Quine, L. (1987). Families with mentally handicapped children. In J. Orford (Ed.), *Treating the disorder, treating the family* (pp. 39–61). Baltimore: Johns Hopkins University Press.

Pollner, M., & McDonald-Wilker, L. (1985). The social construction of unreality: A case study of a family's attribution of competence to a severely retarded child. *Family Process, 24*, 241–254.

Powell, T.H., & Gallagher, P.A. (1993). *Brothers and sisters: A special part of exceptional families* (2nd ed.). Baltimore: Paul H. Brookes Publishing Co.

Reiss, D. (1981). *The family's construction of reality.* Cambridge, MA: Harvard University Press.

Roos, P. (1985). Parents of mentally retarded children: Misunderstood and mistreated. In H.R. Turnbull III & A.P. Turnbull (Eds.), *Parents speak out, then and now* (2nd ed.) (pp. 245–257). Columbus, OH: Charles E. Merrill.

Samuelson, D. (1986, Spring). A letter to my daughter/myself on facing the collective fear of being different. *Feminist Studies, 12,* 155–167.

Seligman, M., & Darling, R.B. (1989). *Ordinary families, special children: A systems approach to childhood disability.* New York: Guilford Press.

Singer, G.H.S., & Irvin, L.K. (1989). Family caregiving, stress and support. In G.H.S. Singer & L.K. Irvin (Eds.), *Support for caregiving families: Enabling positive adaptation to disabilities* (pp. 3–25). Baltimore: Paul H. Brookes Publishing Co.

Zuk, G.H., Miller, R.L., Bartram, J.B., & Kling, F. (1961). Maternal acceptance of retarded children: A questionnaire study of attitudes and religious background. *Child Development, 32,* 525–540.

5

A "Simple" Farmer Accused of Murder

The Case of Delbert Ward

Robert Bogdan

INTRODUCTION

Morning starts early for the people of Munnsville, a small (population 499), poor, agricultural community in central New York. At approximately 5 A.M. on the morning of June 6, 1990, 59-year-old Delbert Ward came half trotting, half tripping over the road from the hilltop farm he shared with his brothers Bill (age 64), Lyman (66), and Roscoe (70). With the exception of his fast pace, Delbert looked the way he and his brothers always looked—lean body, sun-wrinkled skin, long unkempt grey-white beard and hair, baggy dirty slept-in clothes, high leather boots, and a dirty one-size-fits-all baseball hat. If he were in a city he would be taken for a street person. He hit his bony knuckle against the door of his neighbor's cabin and, with fear in his voice, yelled: "Something's wrong with Bill."

Bill was Delbert's closest companion. They were inseparable from the time their father died when Delbert was 14. They slept together in the same bed in the small ramshackle house on the top of the hill a few yards from the modest barn that housed their herd of 20 dairy cows.

A version of this chapter appeared previously in Bogdan, R. (1992). A "simple" farmer accused of murder: Community acceptance and the meaning of deviance. *Disability, Handicap & Society, 7*(4), 303–320.

There was something wrong all right. Bill was dead. That night, down at the state police barracks, surrounded by officers, Delbert signed a confession that he later withdrew. It was read to him and stated that he had held his hand over Bill's mouth and pinched his nose until Bill stopped breathing. His brother Lyman signed another statement saying that Delbert had told him he had done it. It was alleged that Delbert's motive was to end Bill's suffering. For the past few years, Bill had endured distress from accident-related ailments. He complained to his brothers about unbearable pain in his chest and head, which he said felt like a knife cutting him in two.

Delbert was arrested, charged, and tried (see Perske, 1991, Chapter 22, for a more complete description of the events). The people of Munnsville considered the Wards part of their community and reacted to the arrest and trial with a tremendous outpouring of unified support for Delbert and his brothers. Their reaction was so emphatic and pronounced that it attracted regional and national media attention (CBS/TV, 1991; Kolberg, 1990, 1991) from the day of Bill Ward's death on June 6, 1990, until the town celebration party at the conclusion of the trial on April 5, 1991.

If current professional psychological diagnostic procedures were applied to Delbert, Lyman, and Roscoe, they would be considered to have mental retardation. During the dramatic 12-day murder trial, expert testimony and evidence confirmed that judgment. Neighbors indicated that Bill had intellectual abilities that the other brothers did not. He was head of the family, could read, and was in charge of the finances. Although the details surrounding the death of Bill Ward and the subsequent trial are incredibly interesting as a mystery and human interest story, certain aspects of the drama are particularly important to individuals interested in the integration of people with developmental disabilities in the community (Bruininks, Meyers, Sigford, & Lakin, 1981; Bulmer, 1987; Taylor, Biklen, & Knoll, 1987; Taylor & Bogdan, 1989; Taylor, Bogdan, & Racino, 1991), as well as to social scientists studying "deviance" (Bogdan & Taylor, 1987, 1989; Edgerton, 1984; Langness & Levine, 1986). For the most part, community inclusion of people with developmental disabilities is seen as something that professionals and other human services workers do for clients. Seldom do we look at circumstances in which people are naturally part of a community. Similarly, social scientists in their study of deviance, especially those academics affiliated with the "labeling school," have emphasized the exclusion, not the acceptance, of people who are different (Bogdan & Taylor, 1987). This chapter focuses on the Ward brothers' acceptance in the Munnsville community both before and after the death of Bill.

METHOD AND PROCEDURES

This chapter is based on participant observation and on open-ended interviews (Bogdan & Biklen, 1991; Taylor & Bogdan, 1984) that I conducted during and after the trial (Erikson, 1976). I attended seven court sessions and interviewed people before and after each day's proceedings and during breaks. Most trial sessions were attended by a near-capacity crowd composed largely of local Ward brothers' supporters. The seating capacity of the court room was 90. At some sessions there was standing room only. Members of the media were well represented also. I sat among the town residents and heard their discussions and comments as the trial proceeded.

After the trial, I visited the town on various occasions as a participant observer and formally and informally interviewed Munnsville citizens. I visited with local residents in their homes and conducted tape-recorded interviews that were transcribed and studied. I went to the local restaurants, spent time at the local livestock auction, visited the Ward farm, and did research at the town historical library. In addition, I reviewed the substantial number of newspaper articles and television broadcasts that were generated by press coverage of the trial and related events.

The townspeople who were in the audience at the trial were predominately men and women in their late 40s and older, and those whom I interviewed were almost all in this age range. It was these people who were most active in the support and defense of Delbert Ward and his brothers. In this chapter I use such expressions as "the townspeople" and "the Munnsville residents." Strickly speaking, I mean those older people who actively backed the Ward brothers. From all I could gather, younger people were supporters as well but were not highly visible because they tended to be employed in 9-to-5 jobs and could not attend day sessions. In addition, being in a different age group, they had not grown up with the Wards and therefore were not as personally connected or emotionally involved in the trial as those who attended.

THE WARD BROTHERS AND COMMUNITY ACCEPTANCE

After sitting down at their kitchen table, I began my interview with Mr. and Mrs. Adams, a married couple in their 60s who had lived in the center of the village of Munnsville for over 40 years and who were very active in their support of Delbert Ward. Lou Adams asked how I got interested in the "Ward boys," which is the way Delbert Ward and his brothers were commonly referred to by the townspeople. I explained that I was a professor researching the acceptance of people with disabilities in the community. I added that if the brothers lived in the city they would probably be considered to have a disability, that is, mental retardation. Mrs. Adams shook her head in opposition to what I had just said and Mr. Adams commented: "Oh, we don't think of them that way. I wouldn't call them retarded. Some other people might but not here. I've never heard it." I modified my statement by adding that I advocated the inclusion of people who were different in the regular community. He said patiently: "We don't feel they are different." (See Groce, 1985, for a discussion of a community in which deafness was not seen as a disability or as a meaningful difference among residents.)

From the perspective of community *outsiders*, Delbert and his brothers were not run-of-the-mill community residents. One official from the New York State Office of Mental Retardation, recalling seeing the brothers for the first time on a television news show, said, "To me it was obvious that they were mentally retarded" (Dickinson, 1991). He made this judgment on the basis of their speech and appearance. There were also other factors that would cause others to classify them as different. With such a small milking herd, they had a very meager profit from their farm and lived far below the community standard. With the exception of Bill, whose skills were minimal, the brothers could not read or write. They dressed in a slovenly fashion and kept their property beneath the standard of other farmers in the area. The reason Delbert went to his neighbor's door on the day of his brother's death was that, unlike other farm families, the Wards did not have a telephone. Their cousin Ike lived in a dilapidated school bus that was permanently parked on the property. The Wards' equipment, techniques, and skills resulted in their accomplishing far less in a day than the average farmer. The Wards were bashful, preferring to stay by themselves rather than take part in the town's political, social, or religious activities. Lyman had such an aversion to people that he sometimes shook uncontrollably in their presence.

Although the Wards had a few friends whom they saw frequently, not many people in town interacted with them on a regular basis. But almost everyone knew them. One reason for their fame was the way they traveled. None of the brothers had a driver's license, and they did not own a car. They never left the Munnsville area, but rode their old tractor to town or to the local livestock auction. One brother would drive and the others would stand on the back, their hair and clothes blowing in the wind as they waved at people they recognized.

The appearance of the Wards, their lifestyle, and their behavior certainly made them eligible for a label such as "retard" (Bogdan & Taylor, 1982; Mercer, 1973) or "deviant" or for some other stigmatization in the community. In fact, during the trial various witnesses from outside the town referred to the Wards by such disparaging terms as "hermits," "not normal," "social outcasts," "educable mentally retarded," "mildly mentally retarded," "mentally defective," and "schizoid." Townspeople were offended by the use of such terminology in reference to the Wards.

In my research, I came to the same conclusion that Mr. Adams had posited: The Ward brothers were not labeled as deviant in Munnsville. Although they were not gregarious participants in community affairs and some might have seen them as "characters," the brothers were taken for granted, accepted, and liked in Munnsville. By accepted I mean that they had certain longstanding ongoing relationships with townspeople that were characterized by closeness and affection (Bogdan & Taylor, 1987). The differences that they displayed did not bring stigma (Goffman, 1963) or discredit. As will be elaborated upon later, their differences were not denied but neither did they bring disgrace.

I continued to question Mr. and Mrs. Adams. If they did not think of the brothers as retarded or different, how did they regard them? Mr. Adams responded:

> I think you get lots of people that are in remote areas of any town who live like the Wards. They are just accepted. They are not so different. It's just their way of life. Nobody gives much thought to it.

I asked if there were words he would use to describe them. He said: "The best words would be just *simple people*." Although not all the residents of Munnsville with whom I talked shared Mr. Adams' thoughts exactly or expressed them in the same way, for the most part his words capture the gist of how the Ward brothers were perceived by most residents in their community. One farmer, when asked if he considered the Wards retarded, said yes, but he continued by saying that he preferred the terms "simple" and "backward" when referring to them. "Simple" represented a nonpejorative way of acknowledging their uniqueness while keeping them within the social bonds of the community.

"Simple" was the most common term used to describe the Wards. Another was "backward." (A few people likened them to hillbillies.) "Simple" and "backward" were used synonymously. In discussing the meaning of these terms with townspeople, two dimensions of their definition became evident. One aspect was related to deficiency: The Wards lacked skills or competencies that most people have. For example, when I asked a middle-age farmer what he meant when he referred to the Wards as simple and backward, he explained that they did not know how to read or write, that they lacked education, and that when they bought items from the store they just handed over bills and trusted the clerk to make the right change. He went on to talk about how they always did things the hard way and had outdated, inefficient equipment. Although this deficiency dimension of the definition was pervasive, the second dimension was also present and it had positive connotations.

In discussing what he meant by "backward," the same farmer told me how the Wards were like people who lived a century ago. With a sense of pending loss he told me:

> In another 10 years, if they last that long, that'll be the end of them. There is nobody left like them. I'm glad our kids grown up knowing them.

A retired engineer who had lived in the area most of his life told me that there used to be a number of families like the Wards. "Now they're a dying breed. Simple people can't live the way they once lived. They were proud and independent."

The Wards were seen as being the salt of the earth who lived a simple life free from the frustrations of modern finance and bureaucracy. They talked directly, not in fancy abstractions, and were a counterpoint to the pretensions of our consumer-oriented society. Some inhabitants of Munnsville had this romantic view of the Wards. They represented the idealized old times, a passing way of life—something they and their children would miss.

Reasons for Acceptance

What reasons do Munnsville residents give for the Wards' acceptance in the community? What evidence is there that they were really accepted? Why weren't they defined as deviant and shunned or institutionalized?

The Ward brothers were discussed in terms of fulfilling a number of criteria that local people had for determining who belonged. The first was the length of time they and their family had lived in the area. Mr. and Mrs. Adams had lived in Munnsville for 40 years, but they told me that they did not always feel completely accepted because they had not been born there. In Munnsville there was a distinction between "insiders" and "outsiders" and that distinction roughly paralleled the status of "old timers" and "newcomers." The Ward brothers were born in the area and were old timers by any standard. As far back as could be remembered, the Ward family lived on the top of the hill overlooking the valley where Munnsville lay. Grown men and women shared early memories of going up to the Ward place as children. Those residents who had been born and raised in the community reinforced the Wards's place in the community. I met people who had gone to school with the brothers, who lived right down the road from them, who knew their parents and grandparents, and who experienced the tragedy of the father's untimely death.

Another related dimension of being accepted in Munnsville was having family in the area. Although the Wards did not have an extensive kinship group, they had cousins, nephews, nieces, and a grand-niece living nearby who maintained a relationship with the brothers and who provided another claim for the brothers being part of the community.

The Ward brothers were not just tolerated; they were actively liked and supported (Wellman & Wortley, 1990) by some community members. A strong and assertive farmer who lived down the hill from them and knew Delbert since grade school visited regularly and watched out for the brothers over the years. He told me how the Wards came to his farm one winter to buy hay. They were close to running out and needed some to feed their cows until spring. They brought a wagon that could carry about $100 worth of bailed hay but they only had $5. The neighbor filled the wagon anyway. There was another neighbor on whom the brothers could count when they had problems repairing their tractor. A farmer from across the valley dropped his bull off at the Wards to act as a stud for their herd. Neighbors let the brothers use land adjacent to theirs without charge. Townspeople helped them with their banking and other bureaucratic and financial transactions.

Shared Values

When community members discussed the "Ward boys," they often spoke about their positive qualities. According to those with whom I talked, despite some deficiencies the Wards exhibited values and beliefs that the community respected and embraced. This seemed crucial to their acceptance. Especially when discussing Delbert, community people emphasized his pride, his refusal to accept charity or welfare, his strong work ethic, his gentleness, and his honesty. One woman, a farmer in her late 40s, told me when speaking of Delbert's childhood: "He might not have lived as well as some of us, but the parents certainly instilled values in them."

The phrase "they took care of themselves—never took welfare" appeared repeatedly throughout my transcripts and field notes. Although people in the community saw themselves as helping the Wards, they did not see what they did as giving charity. According to Munnsville citizens, the Ward boys would not take charity. When the farmer who told me about the $5 hay elaborated on the incident, he emphasized that the Wards would not accept the hay if they thought it was being *given* to them. A local shop owner would give the brothers day-old bread and slightly old hamburger meat telling them that they were doing him a favor because he did not know what to do with the food, when in fact he had other uses for it. It was important to maintain the appearance of fair exchange. The brothers were always ready to help their benefactors out when needed. The summer after the farmer sold the Wards hay at bargain prices, he bought a barnlike structure located in another part of the county. He asked the boys to help him take it apart, move it to his property, and reconstruct it. They willingly joined in the project. When the farmer tried to pay them, Delbert refused saying they had helped him as a neighbor, not to get paid. Another farmer told me how his father always helped the Ward brothers: "If you needed anything they would help you just the same way."

While the Ward brothers did not accomplish a great deal during a day's work, they were referred to by community members as hard workers. Often this descriptor was linked with the assertion that they were not on welfare. The day before Bill died, he and Delbert had been clearing a field of rocks to prepare it for planting in the coming year. They were always up at 4 or 5 o'clock in the morning to do their chores: milking, cleaning the barn, feeding the calves, and putting the cows to pasture or giving them hay and grain. They did odd jobs for pay for various townspeople. Their work was their whole life. Delbert, the youngest brother, dropped out of school at the age of 14 because he was needed on the farm. In the farming community to which they belong, people who put in long days of hard labor are respected. The brothers, by taking their work seriously and by being conscientious, won respect.

In addition to their work as farmers, the Wards had had a paying job from which they retired after 20 years of service. Burton's Livestock Auction Hall in Vernon, New York, is a hub of agricultural activity every Thursday. This is the day that livestock of all kinds are brought to be auctioned. It is highly social, a meeting center for the farming community. Each Thursday the Ward brothers drove the 5 miles on their tractor from their home to Burton's where they did odd jobs, including cleaning and preparing the cattle for presentation in the auction hall. Through this job the brothers not only heightened their reputations as workers but became better known to community members than they would have if they stayed isolated on their farm. In other words, this work enhanced their presence in the community.

Especially around the time of the alleged murder, Delbert in particular, but the Wards in general, were spoken of positively as kind and gentle men. Their love of animals was brought up in interviews. One man recalled how once, when he was taking one of the brothers' herd to auction to be sold, Delbert asked if he could take a picture of the animal to remember it by. People spoke of going up to the Ward place and having the brothers bring out rabbits to show and hold. The rabbits were kept especially for their niece's enjoyment. A businessman recalled the time that Delbert could not give their cows the penicillin injection that they needed "because he was afraid of hurting the cows." The Wards were somewhat laid back, shy, passive, and polite. People mentioned that they never fought and never were seen to be in an argument. The owner of a local restaurant summarized it well when she said: "They wouldn't hurt anyone or anything."

Very important in defining the positive regard that the community had for Delbert and Bill in particular was their honesty. A waitress in the local restaurant described them by saying: "They were known for their honesty. I never heard anybody speak of them as dishonest." If they said they were going to do something they stuck to their word. Concrete examples were provided in regard to the debts they incurred. When they borrowed money from the local bank they never missed a payment. Similarly, when they bought a second-hand tractor from a local farm machinery dealer, they paid on time. You could count on the Wards. Two people told me that Bill and Delbert were possibly honest to excess in that the brothers attributed the same honesty to others, rendering them vulnerable to exploitation. In business transactions the Wards came to rely on a Munnsville businessman and a banker from a neighboring community.

In addition to considering the brothers to be independent, hard working, kind, and honest, townspeople thought of them as capable, at least in the context of the community. A number of Munnsville residents indicated that the Wards' competence and other characteristics could not be judged outside of the context of their life on the farm. That is, in the village stores or in the courtroom they appeared less intelligent and less at ease than they did in their own rural environment. As one farmer friend put it: "They don't look like they know much but get them on the farm and they are just fine." Further, the Wards were described as having the kind of sense that could not be measured on an intelligence test. As an elderly townswoman explained: "I think they have more common sense than they do the IQ thing."

In a similar vein, another aspect of the Wards' cohesion to the community was the belief by community members that outsiders could not truly understand the Ward brothers. In order to understand the Wards the way Munnsville residents did, you had to be part of the community. As one person told me: "To understand them you have to sit down on a bale of hay across from one of them and hear what they had to say." From the perspective of community members, the idea that Delbert killed his brother was outrageous, something only someone who did not know them could believe. They believed that if the lawyers and others who wore suits at the trial spent time with the Wards in the Munnsville environment, the charge of murder would be dismissed. Only three or four of the townspeople who came to the trial ever wore suits, sport jackets, or dresses. None of the jurors did. Flannel shirts, dungarees, sport shirts, and slacks were the usual attire. The lawyers, the judge, and the police officer and professionals who testified wore formal attire.

Shortcomings

Community residents talked about the Wards in terms of the values they shared with the community and their positive characteristics. This was part of having Delbert and his brothers accepted as members of the community in spite of what could be seen as their shortcomings. What about the brothers' apparent imperfections? What about the condition of their property, the junk around the yard, the filth inside the house, their appearance, their personal hygiene, and their living habits? How did their neighbors deal with their failure to live up to certain community standards?

First, it needs to be mentioned that the Wards lived at the end of a dirt road on the top of a large hill. They were secluded; people did not drive past their place. But if their house was more public, I do not think that would have made a difference. The Wards did come to town, and people did mention their shabby appearance and inordinate barn odor. However, their comments were without malice.

In my interviews, townspeople revealed a strong respect for privacy and individual rights. They reiterated that, as long as you took care of your obligations, worked hard, and did not hurt anyone, it was no one's business how you looked or lived your life. One of the Wards' neighbors became angry when I asked his opinion of the accuracy of the description of the brothers' living conditions that had been broadcast on national television. He raised his voice, not answering my question directly but rather telling me:

> Who the hell's business was it? Really! It was nobody's business! None whatsoever. They got the right to live any God damn way they want to, as long as they ain't breaking the law or harming anybody. What the hell is the difference how we live?

I asked another man about the condition of the Ward property. He said:

> The way they live is not my way to live, but its okay as long as it is not me. That's what I like about living here. People leave people alone.

A woman farmer spontaneously offered the following comment:

> Some people [outsiders] are thinking that we should have taken better care of them [the Wards]—that they weren't living right isolated in that house up there. But that is the way they wanted to live. They were happy. . . . I think that is fine.

In addition to defending the Wards' right to their own lifestyle, a number of people opposed the idea that their way of life was deviant by suggesting that it was not all that unusual. One person explained how farmers rarely dressed up and how sweaty they got, which often left them dirty and disheveled. One person told me of a woman with a college education who resided in town in a house full of cats and lived no cleaner than "the boys did." She was an active member in one of the three Munnsville churches and was referred to as eccentric. Old timers in the town referred to the Wards' living conditions and lifestyle as more reminiscent of the way some old people lived when they were growing up than of present standards.

Although people did not claim to have the same lifestyle as the Wards, some did suggest that there were specific parallels. One man, when asked if he felt bad about their living the way they did, said,

> I don't know. No. I tell you I never took a bath in a bathtub until I was married. The house that we lived in just didn't have running water. My people were poor, so I can sympathize a little bit.

A farmer in his 60s commented on how the media were making a big stink about Delbert and Bill sleeping together. He said that in his family all the kids slept together to keep warm and if someone didn't tell him otherwise he probably would still be sleeping that way.

Townspeople had a way of discussing the brothers that served to minimize any negative meaning that might be attributed to the way they lived. They expressed anger when there was testimony at Delbert's trial by expert witnesses and the police, or when comments in the media brought disapproving attention to the Wards' lifestyle or tried to link them to a pattern of perversion. During the course of the investigation, a doctor from the coroner's office performed a rape test on Bill and also stated that there might be semen on Bill's pants. Munnsville residents became hostile at what they saw as an attempt at character assassination. Embedded in the above comments is a suggestion that the people of the community felt that an attack on the Ward brothers' way of life was an attack on the way of life of other members of the community. This in fact seemed to be the case. A number of individuals commented that outsiders did not understand rural people in general, tending to group them together as uneducated and backward.

Were They Really Accepted?

Perhaps my picture of the acceptance of the Ward brothers is overdrawn. Weren't the brothers the subject of discrimination, teasing, and other forms of harassment? One farmer in his 60s who went to school with Delbert told me that Delbert was ridiculed back then. He had been held back twice and was frequently absent. The farmer had considered it his job to protect Delbert from would-be attackers, a role he continued up to the present.

I did witness one incident in the courthouse that could be interpreted as Delbert being ridiculed. As I was waiting for the trial to begin one day, a man in his late 60s came in and began talking to townspeople who were sitting in the row in front of me. He said jokingly that a neighbor had seen him on the local television news last night and told him that it was hard telling him apart from Delbert. The neighbor had been referring to Delbert's shoddy appearance. The people in front of me chuckled quietly. Although Delbert was the subject of this joke, I felt that it was not really cruel or condemning; nor did I witness anything like it again. I had frequent opportunities to see Delbert and the other Munnsville citizens interact during my data gathering effort. I spent much of the time at the celebration party for Delbert's acquittal observing him interact with the townspeople. Each day before the court proceedings and during breaks, I observed Delbert talk to the local citizens. Many approached him with greetings and conversation. I also observed him one Thursday at the Burton auction hall interacting with locals. The tone of these encounters was always cordial and positive—not condescending, mocking, or paternalistic—and indicated to me a respect for and acceptance of the man.

A few of the townspeople with whom I spoke about the Ward brothers smiled and told me humorous tales about "the boys." I developed a sense that these Ward brothers stories were part of the town's folklore. An example is one about an old tractor they owned. For a long time the tractor did not fire on all of its cylinders, which led to flooding and breakdowns every mile or so. Every time the tractor broke down the brothers took out the tools, removed a spark plug, and put in a dry one, which allowed them to travel for another mile. Another example was that Delbert and Bill were so close that Delbert followed Bill around wherever he went. Bill would stop, and Delbert, not looking where he was going, would bump into him. While in one sense these stories make fun of the brothers, they were not told in a tone of ridicule. To the contrary, I heard these as tales in the context of sharing the funny side of the Ward brothers with me. "That's just the way the Ward brothers were—if you follow what I mean?" Although my claim might be refuted, I judged the stories to be humanizing rather than dehumanizing and accepting rather than distancing. One farmer told me how he enjoyed being around the brothers. "When you get used to them they are a lot of fun."

What about the use of the term *boys* in referring to the Ward brothers? The use of demeaning or childlike imagery in connection with adults with developmental disabilities has become an important target of concern for progressive people in the field of mental retardation (Bogdan & Biklen, 1977; Wolfensberger, 1972). When I first heard the Wards referred to as boys, my immediate reaction was disdain; but as I listened further the term lost its negative connotation, at least in Munnsville. The use of "boys" was not reserved exclusively for the Ward brothers. Rather, it was typically used informally to refer to all male siblings in a given family. There were not just the Ward boys; there were also the Smith boys, the Lambright boys, and so forth. In this sense "boys" was endearing rather than demeaning.

Although the use of "boys" might not have been significant in casting the brothers in the role of children, there was some evidence to suggest that at least one neighbor may have thought of the brothers as childlike. Although I never heard them referred to in that way myself, the neighbor described them on national television as "little boys with old men's faces" (CBS/TV, 1991).

Community Reaction to the Arrest and Trial

What happened when the town heard of Bill's death and Delbert's arrest? The news traveled by word of mouth quickly. The two town restaurants and the town store were the hubs of communication, and a well-developed telephone network disbursed the news outward. The citizens of Munnsville were shocked and filled with disbelief that Delbert could have done such a thing. They immediately suspected that something was wrong—that the autopsy report of homicide by asphyxiation was a mistake and that the confession had been coerced by the alleged rough-handed tactics of the state police and Delbert's propensity to please. Outsiders were doing something to one of their own, and they reacted quickly and in unity. No one I talked to in the town was against backing Delbert Ward and his brothers. In addition, the people I talked to did not know of anyone in town, with the exception of a police officer involved in the case, who did not uphold the Wards. People varied in how active they were in their support but not in their sentiments. One informant explaining the town's position told me:

> I have seen the town at times of real controversy—when something was coming up before the school board or during elections. But the town isn't split on this. They are all one.

A few days after Bill's death, a waitress in the village restaurant drew up a petition and a local businessman who had one of the only copiers in town made multiple copies. The petition was to the Madison County Office of the District Attorney asking for a new autopsy. People went from door to door collecting signatures and spreading the news to mobilize support. Over 850 signatures were collected in a few days, and on June 12, 1990, 6 days after Bill Ward's death, the petitions were formally delivered to the county court building. Townspeople who had been active in the petition drive notified the local news media that the petitions were being delivered, resulting in extensive newspaper and television coverage.

Five days after Bill's death, a Delbert Ward defense fund was established to pay for legal and related costs. Money was collected mainly though nickel-and-dime fundraising activities. Local businesses placed donation boxes on their counters. There was a dance and a number of other community gatherings organized with admission charges, as well as raffles and numerous sales and auctions. Attendance at these community activities numbered 200–300. Over $12,400 was collected during the months surrounding the trial.

Concerned that the attorney assigned to Delbert Ward by the county was not competent enough, town residents solicited the services of a Syracuse attorney with criminal trial experience. He said he would represent Mr. Ward pro bono. (After the trial, he applied to the county for compensation for his services, a move that sparked controversy in Munnsville.) The citizens hired a private detective to help in the investigation and prepared to pay for expert defense testimony.

On the day of the bail hearing, approximately 40 Munnsville citizens were on hand. Bail was set at $10,000. The judge offered the option of putting a small amount of money down and using the Ward farm for collateral, or putting the whole amount down. One town member stood up and said that he had $1,000 to give, and another man said the same. Within a half hour the full $10,000 had been pledged, and shortly thereafter Delbert was released.

Community leaders met on a number of occasions with Delbert present to discuss several decisions to be made. They discussed, for example, the implications of having national television coverage and whether the film crews and reporters should be welcomed to town. The press got involved and various community members spoke out in public on Delbert's behalf. The outpouring of community support was so marked that it drew the attention of both local and national media. News crews from the national television programs *Face to Face with Connie Chung* and *A Current Affair* came to Munnsville to collect interviews and video footage that eventually appeared on those shows. *The New York Times* covered the story as well (Kolberg, 1990, 1991).

Community members came to the aid of the Ward brothers in small, personal ways as well. They brought them food and dropped in on them at home to make sure they were doing all right. They gave them words of encouragement and helped out on their farm. During the trial, one neighbor picked Delbert up every morning and drove him to the courthouse, providing encouragement, advice, and comfort.

The large turnout of Ward partisans at the various hearings and at the trial itself was indicative of the town's backing. The trial was held in the county court in Wampsville, a town 10 miles from Munnsville and not very convenient for the older townsfolk who attended. Those attending the various legal proceedings were so overt about their feelings for Delbert Ward that the judge regularly threatened to clear the room if people did not stop making comments and other noises showing approval and disapproval of testimony and various other aspects of the legal proceedings. The last time he warned them was on the night the jury brought in the verdict of not guilty. It was 11 P.M. and the jury had been deliberating for almost 12 hours. The townspeople were there in numbers that almost filled the court. The judge asked for quiet and no outbursts, but the crowd could not contain itself.

When I asked the people I interviewed about the tremendous outpouring of support that had occurred around the Ward brothers, the residents of Munnsville indicated that they were proud of what they and their town had done. Some said it was one of the proudest moments in their years as Munnsville residents. They talked about the spirit of unity that the trial had evoked. One resident downplayed the event by saying that the massive support for Delbert was just a magnified version of what had been shown to other residents experiencing trouble. He told me about the night that his son's barn caught fire and how the town rushed to help him save his livestock. People told me of other incidents of community support.

A picture of Munnsville as a perfect Christian community (people were overwhelmingly Christian) where everyone loves their neighbor unconditionally and acts with great benevolence to those in need is not accurate. There was back biting, pettiness, and scapegoating too. One of the first days I attended the trial I asked the person sitting next to me who the person was who had been with Delbert during the break. I was told that it was a "newly found relative." I asked for clarification and was told that the person who had been with Delbert was one of those individuals who had almost nothing to do with "the boys" before the publicity. But as soon as the television cameras rolled in, such people pretended to be close acquaintances of the Wards. One of the state police officers who was instrumental in obtaining the confession from Delbert was a Munnsville resident who was so ostracized because of his role in the case and his testimony at the trial that few people had anything to do with him anymore. It was alleged that even his relatives turned against him. Soon after the trial the police officer sold his house and left town. Community residents alleged that it was because of his lack of popularity. During the trial, Munnsville residents talked about the district attorney who served as prosecuting attorney as well as the judge who presided over the case as people whom they would oppose at reelection time. Townsfolk mellowed after the trial and grew less concerned with revenge. Whom is embraced by a community may vary from time to time. Munnsville does not embrace all of its citizens in the way it did the Ward brothers. It excludes people too.

CONCLUSION

The movement to eliminate institutionalization as a form of care for people labeled as having mental illness and mental retardation was predicated in part on our understanding of the dehumanizing nature of total institutionalization and on the process through which people are labeled and excluded from their community (Goffman, 1961). Academics developed a sophisticated sociology of exclusion. Although I do not deny the tendency of people in Western society to exclude those labeled as having mental retardation and individuals with other stigmatizing designations, we need to pay more attention to and document incidents and places where this does not happen, where people are naturally included in the community (Groce, 1985), accepted, and loved (Bogdan & Taylor, 1989). The Ward brothers are a case in point.

When Munnsville residents assert that Delbert Ward and his brothers are not retarded or different, they are not saying that there are no distinguishing features between the brothers and the other townspeople. Rather, they are saying that those distinctions, or imperfections, are not important enough to separate the Wards from the rest of the community. They are saying: "This community accepts them; they are part of us." People are not the same or different solely because of their physical or mental characteristics; it is how they are thought of that matters (Bogdan & Taylor, 1982; Mercer, 1973). The classification systems that we create manufacture the illusion that people can objectively be placed in such categories as "retard/typical" or "deviant/normal" (Braginsky & Braginsky, 1971; Sarason & Doris, 1979). The issue is not whether Delbert and his brothers are retarded, but rather the implications of labeling them so rather than choosing a more benign designation. The citizens in the Wards' town did not choose to use "retarded" or "deviant" or any other such stigmatizing label. Certainly, members of the Munnsville community have applied words like "simple" and "backward" to the brothers and others like them, but these adjectives do not carry the harsh exclusionary connotations of the words "retarded" and "deviant." "Simple" and "backward" are terms that have emerged from the community and are used to refer to people who are members. They are designations that can be applied kindly to those who belong. Some may say that this is all just a matter of semantics. But words are not neutral classifiers. What we choose to call people is tied to how we think of them and whether we consider them to be a part of ourselves.

Certainly the Wards do not conform to all local norms. However, the community chose not to dwell on the negatives but rather to identify the positives, especially those that aligned with community values. The Wards were not "integrated into the community." Integration suggests that someone who was once on the outside has now been allowed in. The Wards were never excluded. Their roots were in Munnsville, and they were recognized as being part of the history of the town. The townspeople also gave the Wards the benefit of the doubt. They chose to think of them as more competent than they might appear to outsiders (Bogdan & Taylor, 1989; Goode, 1980). They judged them in the light of the aptitudes needed to function in their own rural environment. They also chose to overlook some of their transgressions. They did not focus on their poorly kept property or the crude sanitary conditions in their house. Some would say that this was neglect, that the community should oversee its citizens more, and that the conditions the Wards lived in were below the health standards. But the townspeople did not see that as their function. Individual liberty was valued more highly than appearances and hygienic regulation. There is a tension between the individual's right to privacy and the community's responsibility to protect its citizens from disease and self-harm. Munnsville residents chose the side of the rights of the Ward men. But people knew that there were outsiders who did not share their view. I was told on a number of occasions that if Delbert was found guilty and put in prison the bureaucracy would take the other brothers and make them wards of the State.

The perspective that the Wards represent a passing way of life in rural America may be true. On the few occasions when I have given public talks and class lectures on the Ward family, members of the audience have approached me to offer descriptions of people like the Wards whom they know in their own rural communities. Inevitably such individuals were said to live more or less independently while relying on neighbors for some help. Without exception the people are described as elderly and as "the last of their kind." Although these people undoubtedly exist, the extolling of their virtues may go beyond reality and be linked instead to current problems confronting communities like Munnsville. At the time of the study and even now, the very existence of the people of Munnsville and their rural way of life was threatened by social and economic circumstances beyond their control. The area was in a serious recession, milk prices had dropped below the level that made dairy farming a viable occupation, and various social problems were at Munnsville's door. Farmers in particular, but village dwellers as well, were experiencing an assault on their identity and way of life. Especially when Delbert was arrested and accused by state officials of murder, the Wards seemed to symbolize for the people of Munnsville their community and their way of life. Although this explanation of the outpouring of support for Delbert makes logical sense and is consistent with a functionalist analysis, townspeople neither offered this explanation nor confirmed it when I brought it up in interviews.

An interesting aside is that depressed economic conditions and challenges to a community's values have been discussed in social science circles as an explanation for violence against minority group members, for the labeling of people as deviant, and for other forms of scapegoating. Historically, lynching of African Americans in the southern United States has been linked to economic downturns (Berelson & Steiner, 1964); similarly, witch hunts in Salem, Massachusetts, were related to value conflicts in Puritan society (Erikson, 1966). The Ward case suggests that acts of altruism might as easily as violence be an outcome of economic depression and conflict of values.

Bill Ward was described to me as the leader of the brothers. He was the one who ran the farm, did the shopping, handled the money, and told the others what to do. His brothers hung on his word. One farmer told me that Delbert, Lyman, and Roscoe seemed lost after Bill's death. It was spring when I listened to this established citizen speak about the Ward brothers' confusion. Above us a flock of Canadian geese was flying in V formation on their trip north. Using the geese as an analogy, he told me:

It is like when you see a flock of geese. If the lead goose is shot the others just don't know what to do. They get confused.

When I asked what would happen to the brothers, I was told that they, like the geese, would initially be confused but would adjust and a new leader emerge. As I was conducting my posttrial interviews, townspeople told me about how Delbert was changing. He was making decisions, becoming more outgoing, and emerging as the leader of the family. Bill's death was a challenge to his capacity and he was rising to the challenge. I asked a woman how she thought the Ward brothers would

take care of themselves. She said: "Oh, they can take care of themselves. They have never been on welfare. They milk a few cows, sell a
few things, buy a few things." I asked: "But won't it be difficult without Bill?" She said: "No, they have other people to help them." Delbert
will not have to do what has to be done all by himself. People will
come to his aid, the way neighbors do in Munnsville. People will help
until life regains its regularity, until the Wards get their bearing.

As this chapter has illustrated, individuals born into a community
like Munnsville—rural and tightly knit—who transgress from the
norm are not necessarily rejected. In fact, as was the case with Delbert,
the community can be highly protective of members who are vulnerable to outsiders who would cast them in deviant and stigmatizing
roles. Not only is the would-be deviant sheltered from the larger society, but the process of safeguarding the citizen creates solidarity in the
community. Perhaps by nurturing such people the community builds a
strength and integrity that sets it apart from the more impersonal sub-
urbs and cities.

We know, and the Ward case is a vivid reminder, that human vari-
ation (sometimes considered deviance or pathology) cannot be understood outside of the social context in which it exists. Outsiders came to
Munnsville and saw the Wards as legitimate recipients of the label
"mentally retarded," or deviants. The townspeople would have none
of it. The residents of Munnsville rallied around the Ward brothers not
because the latter had a disability but because they were members of
the community.

EPILOGUE

Life in Munnsville has settled back to the way it was before the trial,
but it was a hectic few years of fame for the Ward brothers before they
slipped out of the national limelight. Film makers from New York City
made a full-length documentary of their story, *My Brother's Keeper,*
which was well received by critics and movie goers alike. It won an
award at the Sundance Film Festival, and the fact that it was not nominated for an Academy Award brought angry protest from the film's
supporters. As a result, Delbert and his brothers remained in the news
and appeared on a national talk show. They traveled to New York City
and profited from their success in a minor way. Their celebrity status
provided national visibility to them and their community, and townspeople continued to look out for them as Delbert Ward emerged as the
family leader.

REFERENCES

Berelson, B., & Steiner, G. (1964). *Human behavior.* New York: Harcourt, Brace & World.

Bogdan, R. (1988). *Freak show: Exhibiting human oddities for amusement and profit.* Chicago: University of Chicago.

Bogdan, R., & Biklen, D. (1977, March/April). Handicapism. *Social Policy,* pp. 14–19.

Bogdan, R., & Biklen, S.K. (1991). *Qualitative research for education* (2nd ed.). Boston: Allyn and Bacon.

Bogdan, R., & Taylor, S.J. (1982). *Inside out: The social meaning of mental retardation.* Toronto, Ontario, Canada: University of Toronto Press.

Bogdan, R., & Taylor, S.J. (1987). Toward a sociology of acceptance: The other side of the sociology of deviance. *Social Policy, 18,* 34–39.

Bogdan, R., & Taylor, S.J. (1989). Relationships with severely disabled people: The social construction of humanness. *Social Problems, 36,* 135–148.

Braginsky, D., & Braginsky, B. (1971). *Hansels and Gretels.* New York: Holt, Rinehart & Winston.

Bruininks, R.H., Meyers, C.E., Sigford, B.B., & Lakin, K.C. (Eds.). (1981). *Deinstitutionalization and community adjustment of mentally retarded people.* Washington, DC: American Association of Mental Deficiency.

Bulmer, M. (1987). *The social basis of community care.* London: Allen & Unwin.

CBS/TV. (1991). *Face to Face with Connie Chung.* New York: Columbia Broadcasting System, February 11.

Dickinson, M. (1991). Ward trial becomes textbook case. *The Syracuse Post-Standard,* April 13.

Edgerton, R. (Ed.). (1984). *Lives in process.* Washington, DC: American Association of Mental Retardation.

Erikson, K.T. (1966). *Wayward Puritans.* New York: John Wiley & Sons.

Erikson, K.T. (1976). *Everything in its path.* New York: Simon & Schuster.

Goffman, E. (1961). *Asylums.* New York: Anchor Books.

Goffman, E. (1963). *Stigma.* Englewood Cliffs, NJ: Prentice Hall.

Goode, D.A. (1980). Behavioral sculpting. In Jacobs, J. (Ed.), *Mental retardation: A phenomenological approach* (pp. 94 –119). Springfield, IL: Charles C Thomas.

Groce, N.E. (1985). *Everyone here spoke sign language.* Cambridge, MA: Harvard University Press.

Kolberg, E. (1990). A dairy town doubts brother killed brother. *New York Times,* July 17.

Kolberg, E. (1991). Town aids a simple man in big trouble. *New York Times,* April 9.

Langness, L.L., & Levine, H.G. (Eds.). (1986). *Culture and retardation.* Dordrecht: Reidel.

Mercer, J. (1973). *Labelling the mentally retarded.* Berkeley: University of California Press.

Perske, R. (1991). *Unequal justice?* Nashville: Abingdon Press.

Sarason, S., & Doris, J. (1979). *Educational handicap, public policy and social history.* New York: Free Press.

Taylor, S.J., Biklen, D., & Knoll, J. (Eds.). (1987). *Community integration for people with severe disabilities.* New York: Teachers College Press.

Taylor, S.J., & Bogdan, R. (1984). *Introduction to qualitative research method* (2nd ed.). New York: John Wiley & Sons.

Taylor, S.J., & Bogdan, R. (1989). On accepting relationships between people with mental retardation and non-disabled people: Toward an understanding of acceptance, *Disability, Handicap & Society, 4*(1), 21–36.

Taylor, S.J., Bogdan, R., & Racino, J.A. (Eds.). (1991). *Life in the community: Case studies of organizations supporting people with disabilities.* Baltimore: Paul H. Brookes Publishing Co.

Wellman, B., & Wortley, S. (1990). Different strokes from different folks: Community ties and social support. *American Journal of Sociology, 96*(3), 558–589.

Wolfensberger, W. (1972). *Normalization.* Toronto, Ontario, Canada: National Institute on Mental Retardation.

6

Life in Mendocino

A Young Man with Down Syndrome in a Small Town in Northern California

Scott S. Andrews

Editors' Introduction

This chapter is adapted from Scott S. Andrews's doctoral dissertation, which he wrote at the Stanford University School of Education. The larger work is a detailed ethnographic case history and analysis of the life of John Mcgough, a talented young man with Down syndrome with whom Scott Andrews became acquainted while living in Mendocino, California. As part of the dissertation Scott made a highly acclaimed documentary film, *And Then Came John*. We recommend the film and his dissertation to you.

In spite of the fact that on the day of John's birth in 1957 his parents were told their son was a "mongolian idiot" who should be institutionalized, John grew up with his family in suburban Long Island, New York. In 1971 the Mcgough family moved to North Hollywood, California. John's parents divorced shortly after the move, with his mother, Lee, retaining custody of all the children. After his state-required graduation at age 21 from a segregated high school for "trainable mentally retarded students," John faced isolation, boredom, and lack of opportunity, which led to depression. The community in which he lived was not a community in the sense of being a place in which people knew and

---

supported each other. John had few contacts outside of his home and was even teased and in other ways harassed. In 1981 everything changed for John. Lee met a man at her son's wedding in Mendocino, a small town on the coast of northern California. She married and moved with her family to Mendocino. The chapter discusses Mendocino and John's acceptance in that community.

MENDOCINO: GENERAL HISTORICAL BACKGROUND

In 1852, treasure hunters in search of a wrecked Chinese junk on the California coast north of San Francisco sailed up a tidal estuary and inadvertently discovered a much grander treasure: towering redwood groves containing enough potential lumber to build booming San Francisco for the next eight decades. The men who came to harvest the giant trees, New England lumbermen and recent European immigrants, quickly replaced the Pomo Indian village on the headlands at the mouth of the river with their own burgeoning community, Mendocino.

In the 1890s, at the height of Mendocino's lumber boom, the town boasted a population of 5,000, with 24 saloons, 5 brothels, an Indiantown, a Chinatown, and a lumber mill capable of spewing out some 12 million board feet of redwood per year. The hills around the river basin were clear-cut, the air was thick with smoke from the mill, and the bay between the headlands was awash with flotsam and queues of lumber schooners.

As the 1900s wore on, the big trees were harvested further and further from the Mendocino mill, and as a consequence profitability and productivity fell rapidly. Mendocino shrank as the boom faded, and after the mill closed in 1938 the town was almost entirely emptied as people left to find work. Those who remained eked out a living by fishing or farming, or they commuted 10 miles north to work at the still operational Fort Bragg mill. By this time the Pomos had disappeared, the Chinese had left, and those who stayed on were mostly a mixture of Portuguese and northern European extraction. From the mid-1930s to the early 1960s, Mendocino passed through various stages of benign neglect. Although it never quite achieved ghost town status, the dilapidation of the physical plant was more than quaint.

But as the paint peeled and the outbuildings teetered, the natural environment gradually healed itself. Second-growth redwoods reforested the slopes, blackberries reclaimed foundation scars, and the air and water purged themselves of industrial blight. The sights and sounds of nature regained their preeminence and the stage was set for the arrival of the first of a new wave of settlers, those conscious seekers of beauty, the artists.

In 1958, the Mendocino Art Center, much later to achieve a measure of national recognition, opened on a wing and a prayer for growth in the local art community and industry. It served as a magnet for those of artistic persuasion, and Mendocino experienced a gradual yet dramatic infusion of artists, artisans, art lovers, art seekers, and the "artsy" during the succeeding 30 years.

Beginning in the mid-1960s the artists were joined by a second wave of new settlers, the urban expatriates or "back-to-the-landers." Many of these brought with them a renunciant lifestyle and philosophy self-described as "counterculture." Many had shared in the tumult and experimentation of Berkeley and Haight-Ashbury, experiencing a cathartic rush of new ideas and sensations in the exploration of free love, consciousness altered through the use of psychedelics and marijuana, acid rock, Eastern religion and philosophy, antiwar protests, and revolutionary zeal. They had also experienced a degeneration of their ideals of brotherly love and community within the ever more crowded urban centers that spawned their counterculture movement, and they had chosen to seek a simpler, cleaner, and more elemental life in their movement "back to the land."

These two major groups of new settlers came to Mendocino at a time when land and property levels were depressed, when the population and commerce of Mendocino were at low ebb, when the streets were often empty or peopled by only a few familiar faces, and when a relatively small number of new faces could make a noticeable difference in the atmosphere and balance of power in the town.

In the 10 years between 1965 and 1975 the population of Mendocino more than doubled. By far the greatest portion of this increase was composed of relatively young (late teens to early 30s), well-educated, white, middle-class men, women, and growing families who would identify themselves as part of, or at least in accord with, the counterculture movement. Until the early 1980s, these people would wield the majority of the power in the community and would identify Mendocino as "our" town.

As the population of Mendocino doubled and the national economy went into a spiral of recession and inflation, life in Mendocino became more crowded, more expensive, and more complex. The town began to acquire a reputation as a beautiful and idyllic artists' retreat, and a tourist industry of galleries, restaurants, hotels, and bed-and-breakfast inns began to renew Mendocino's potential. Land and property values skyrocketed, and a new wave of relatively older (40–70), white, upper middle-class conservatives became the third wave of new settlers.

By the early 1980s, Mendocino was once again booming, the sounds of commerce once again threatening to drown the sounds of nature. The streets were full of new cars, new shops, and new faces—most of them temporary. The balance of power weighed less and less in favor of the counterculture adherents, who ceased to identify Mendocino as "our town." Faced with the gradual loss of a cherished ideal, some chose to leave, some to stay, and some to drop the renunciant counterculture gauntlet in favor of a more integrated role in the mainstream culture of the community.

A careful reading of headline articles and letters to the editor in back issues of the local paper reveals a growing controversy and polarization on issues of land use and development from the 1970s on. Often the disputes break out along lines of growth versus nongrowth, business versus "quality-of-life" interests, and development of the commercial environment versus preservation of the natural environment. Yet almost always there is reaffirmation of a "peculiar tolerance for diversity" that is acknowledged to have sprung up in the early 1970s. This repeated reference, often reiterated in interviews with longtime residents, refers to the relatively hospitable welcome offered the new settlers by the older, more traditional blue-collar residents of Mendocino and the ongoing cooperative relationships between them through the mid-1970s.

In 1981, when the Mcgough family moved to Mendocino, there was polarization and confrontation within the community over a number of issues, but there was also a common love for the natural beauty of the area and an ongoing although "peculiar" tolerance for diversity.

LIFE IN MENDOCINO

The First Six Months

The quality of life in Mendocino did not come as a complete surprise to Lee and John. In 1978, at the insistence of John's brother, Lee had taken the family to Mendocino for a 3-week vacation. Everyone had been impressed with the beauty of the area and the openness of the people. Lee at one point had said to John, "Maybe someday you and I can make a life here," and John had replied, "That's a great idea!"

How great the idea would prove to be for John was not truly evident until after the first 6 months of living in Mendocino. It was during these months that John, and then Lee, and then the rest of the family, began to notice some striking and wonderful differences between John's life in North Hollywood and his life in Mendocino.

John started talking about the "open arms for me in this town" and at first Lee, who had feared that the move to a small community might prove harmful to John by depriving him of the cultural experiences available in North Hollywood, didn't know what he meant. But then she began to watch him more closely and was stunned by what she saw:

> We gave him a mailbox key, and one of the chores to help him orient into the new space was to go into the post office and get the mail, and he loved doing that. But sometimes I would drive him there and I would wait in the car and he'd be in the post office for 15 or 20 minutes! So, I'd look in, and I'd see that he was OK, but I'd see that people were interacting with him a little bit and I'd say "Wow—that's neat!"
>
> You know, people would stop, people with packages, and say, "How do you like it here in Mendocino, John?" He'd look around to see who they were talking to—"Oh, do you mean me—oh—Mom, do you want to tell them?" I'd say, "No, they asked you. Why don't you tell them?" John would go, "But. . . ." He had struggles with his speech—I mean his speech has improved a lot since we moved here too. And then he'd just say, "Fine," and they'd say, "Well, what do you like about it?" And he would, like, "Oh my goodness, I've gotta make a conversation!"—New thing, stranger wants a conversation. And the stranger would purposely put their package down and lean on the post office counter to show that there was no rush: "Take your time. I want to hear your thought. I'll wait till you get it out." And he would struggle and he would get it out and they would allow that viewpoint and say, "That's great! Well, it's nice to have you here!"
>
> I mean that's a lot better than any kind of therapy I ever saw, you know—He would come out looking stunned and I'd say, "What happened in there? Nice people talking to you?" And he would say, "That's right. It's amazing for me here. It's my safe and stunning new life!"

John's siblings were also amazed at his "safe and stunning" new life, and each watched closely to discern the elements that made his new life possible. One sibling especially understood the "safeness" of Mendocino for John:

> Mendocino is what John needed—it's what he never had in North Hollywood. It's safe—what he calls a "safe space." Like a lot of people in Mendocino, he's accepted for what he is, not what he isn't. And he can concentrate on what he can do, instead of being shown or being told what he can't do.

Another sibling described the freedom he found there:

> John couldn't go for a walk in LA without me being nervous about him crossing how many major streets and possibly getting hit by a car, where in Mendocino he walks down a dirt road so he can go for a walk whenever he wants. He has a lot more freedom in a small town than he ever had in a city.

John's brother, who had felt that Mendocino would be a great place for John ever since he had engineered the family's first visit in 1978, saw the move as a chance to start a new life.

> The change between Los Angeles and Mendocino was one of a rebirth as far as I can tell. It's a small community and everybody knows everybody and it's like somebody says: "Yeah, everybody's weird up here." So all of a sudden when John came to Mendocino the average person on the street would say hello and would talk to him, and all of a sudden his world began to grow again and expand again, and there were people that showed concern and care again—and he just, he just exploded! I mean he didn't just blossom, he exploded!

On August 24, 1981, after about 6 months in his new environment, John came to Lee and said,

> I feel there's a big change coming. It's all good. In a long, long time, I never had such a loving family, full of characters like this town family. I may do something different soon, but I don't know when. Maybe something, well, not so important, but a little important, but I don't know what.

New Opportunities

Shortly after moving to Mendocino, Lee found a sheltered workshop for clients with disabilities in the neighboring town of Fort Bragg. John went there for only a short while. He came home one day and said, "That's enough, I guess. Makes me feel more retarded." Lee, who was beginning to understand the great advantages of John's natural integration into the mainstream of daily Mendocino life, had to agree.

During the first couple of months in Mendocino, John found his first "regular pal" (a close friend of similar age, from outside of his family, and without a disability). He was a 24-year-old rock-and-roll drummer named Louis Demetri. They met in a local cafe, shared conversation and interests, and before long John had taken up drumming under Louis's tutelage. For Louis, the friendship was both natural and remarkable:

> We have our basic core in common: We both love music and we both believe that everybody is part of the same family—and that music and communication and understanding and eventually peace, peaceful cooperation on earth, are all our goals. And so we have that in common and that's really, for me, remarkable. I don't meet a whole lot of people that even consider such things, let alone a person like John who is totally into the movement toward life and light—that's pretty much John's main concern, which is sort of extraordinary. And besides that we just have a good time—I don't know if it looks like a roaring good time on the outside, but we like to pursue the groove. We both get great pleasure from being able to generate a groove on the drums.

For John, Louie was a person he'd been looking for all his life:

We are just the same! We are just the same! Drink together, eat together, laugh contagious together, and we go in and out of barrooms together. We been learning about what life is, about me and this guy Louie, and we been talking about bringing good things to life for people all over town.

Louie was often John's companion in the local bars where live music was played at night. Before long John had become a very familiar figure in the Mendocino night life. Five or more nights a week John could be found (and still can be found) dancing to almost any kind of music from jazz to rock to reggae to country. He was usually the first and often the only person on the dance floor—moving to the beat, applauding the musicians, and every now and then letting out a spontaneous "Wheee!" of joy.

Lee watched John's growth with bated breath, fearful that it would prove to be a short-lived mirage soon shattered by a behavior on John's part that might be viewed as outrageous or inappropriate. She found herself trying to inhibit his more extroverted acts until she was chastised by a community member who particularly admired John's uninhibited pursuit of fun and unbridled expressions of delight: "Leave him alone, Lee, he's not hurting anyone and he's the only one here who really knows how to have fun—and it's contagious!"

Lee had no idea that such acceptance, freedom, and opportunity could be possible for John, and, at the beginning at least, she met each new development with an air of skepticism:

After we'd lived in Mendocino about 9 months, John was beginning to get accustomed to the acceptance and the freedom that he found here, and he came to me one day and said, "I have something to tell you." And I said, "Really, what's that?" And he said, "Now, I will start my art."

And I was taken aback and immediately began to see all the reasons why it would be impossible. But John apparently knew somehow that now it was possible. I was taking a drawing class at the Mendocino Art Center at the time and I asked Mark Eanes, a man in the class, if he knew of anyone who would be willing to give John an art class once a week. He said, "Sure, I will."

So John started art lessons. A short time later he again came to Lee and said, "Now I will learn to sing on key!" Before Lee knew it, and with a minimum of effort, John had an individual voice lesson once a week with the local church choir director. Lee's worries about there being fewer opportunities for John in the small, rural town of Mendocino could not have been further from the truth.

As it turned out there was a lot more available in Mendocino because anything that was available was available to him, and that's a major difference. If he wanted to do music or take voice lessons, there wasn't somebody saying, "Well, you go over there to that special place in the corner and more or less stay in the background and do your voice with 'those' people over there." In-

stead they would say, "Oh, there's a voice class over there, and there's one over there, and another over here—which one would you like to try?"

By the end of John's first year in Mendocino he was holding down two part-time jobs (sweeping in front of the local general stores on Saturdays, and sweeping and cleaning at a local cafe on Fridays); taking weekly voice, art, and guitar lessons; attending aerobics classes five mornings a week; occasionally reading stories to kids at the local preschool; helping his mother teach a class in self-esteem to a group of troubled adolescents; making daily visiting "rounds" in the community; and going out to dance or listen to music at least five nights a week. He had numerous friends and acquaintances, and he was daily becoming more verbal and more assertive.

John wanted to somehow repay his "town family" for all the caring, acceptance, and opportunities they had given him. In November 1982 he had his first opportunity to do so on a grand scale.

John's First Art Show

Just after John's first art lesson, John and Lee had gone to an art show opening in Mendocino. John had looked around with great interest and then said to Lee, " 'Splain this to me, what you call this?" Lee explained that is was called an "opening" and that it was kind of a celebration that took place when an artist showed his work to the public for the first time. John said, "Oh, I get it, I do that too soon, but I don't know when." Lee's first internal response was

> Wait a minute—you just started art, and you gotta be more professional to have a show. It takes this and it takes that, and it takes agreement, and there's a lot of artists in this town would say, "Great! John's gonna have a show, we'll come see his work," and not "<u>John's</u> gonna have a show?"
>
> But I was starting to learn that a lot of things were now possible for John, and so I took his cue and tried to see the goal rather than the barriers. I told him, "OK, when the time's right I guess you will!"—thinking that perhaps in 10 years he might be ready for a show.

As it turned out, after about 9 months of weekly art lessons with Mark Eanes, painting and making collages while listening to classical music, Mark felt that John was ready:

> After about 9 months of doing these paintings, I said to Lee, "You know, I think he has a really strong body of work right now—we've got lots and lots of paintings and I think it would be fun for him to have an art show in town." She was a little surprised and taken back, and said, "Well, I don't know—are you serious?" and I said, "Sure. I think he's got some great works here, I think we should share them with the community."

So they matted the paintings, found a gallery that would showcase John's work, and advertised the opening. In Mark Eanes's words (personal communication, December, 1982),

> It was an enormous success on many levels. There were a lot of people there, and we were selling the paintings for from $15 to $45 depending on the size, and I think all but about 3 or 4 of the 28 paintings sold, which is some kind of a record for any gallery! And what delighted me was that I knew there were going to be a lot of people who knew John who'd be coming to the show who would pat John on the back and say, "These are great!" regardless of what they saw when they came in because they knew John and thought this was a great thing. But when they saw what was there and the quality of what was there, they were truly surprised and delighted and taken aback. I felt that a tourist coming into the gallery without knowing John would still say, "These are very nice!"
>
> And that's what a lot of people did and said—and so you had a lot of people buying the works partly because they knew John, but you also had a lot of people buying the works because they're great works of art!

For John, his art show was his "love flow for the whole town," his first opportunity to return something to the community on a grand scale. It was also his first ever opportunity to enjoy widely acclaimed success. He basked in the attention and when interviewed by a newspaper reporter said: "Now I finally know the feeling of being a hero, a star, and a genius!"

Art Show Aftermath

As a result of John's art show and a local newspaper article, John became known and recognized by an even greater proportion of Mendocino coast residents than before. He was perhaps the best known citizen in the town of Mendocino. Outside of the local area, the newspaper article also attracted my attention and that of my partner. We went to Mendocino to meet John and his family and to discuss the possibility of a documentary film about John Mcgough, the artist. We were disappointed when John told us that he wasn't particularly interested in mounting another art show, but we were intrigued by his self-possessed manner and the knowledge, supplied by his mother, Lee, that he had not been so assured—or an artist at all—prior to moving to Mendocino from Los Angeles 2 years earlier. When Lee called us a month later to suggest that John's upcoming 26th birthday party might be a good event to film, we decided to go and see for ourselves.

John's 26th Birthday Party

About 3 weeks before he was to turn 26, John announced his birthday wish to Lee:

I know what I want to do for my birthday. I don't want any presents. I just want to have a great big party for all my friends and pals from the whole town—come, have a great fun time, pop out of the drama, remember who they are, and enjoy.

Lee: Oh, OK. . .

John: Lots of music and dancing.

Lee (to herself): Well, that lets out the living room, maybe I can get a building in the state park. . . .

John (with assertiveness): "One more thing I want. I want to wear my heart's desire—what do you call the black suit with the ruffled shirt and the thing in back and the hat?

Lee: You mean top hat and tails?

John: Yes, that's it.

At first Lee was dubious that all this could or should be done for a birthday, so she discussed it with friends. Before long one person had volunteered a tailed tuxedo jacket, another a top hat, and the manager of the Mendocino Hotel a large room for the party. By then it was obvious to Lee that the party was "meant to be":

The only problem we had was how to invite; you cannot send a written invitation to the whole town. We didn't really want to put up a poster because we have an awful lot of people passing through this town who are not part of the town or our life, and the town was enough to handle! So we just started word-of-mouthing it, and that's how it happened.

And so, on a Tuesday night in March of 1983, somewhere between 150 and 200 townspeople arrived to help John celebrate his 26th birthday. Some had received the word-of-mouth invitation that included the direction to come "dressed as your heart's desire," and they had dressed accordingly. John greeted all of his guests, danced with them to the live rock music provided by Louie Demetri's band, played the flute, sang, and played drums with the band for half a dozen songs.

Despite the presence of movie lights, camera crew, and loud music, there was a constant hubbub of laughter and conversation. Everyone seemed to be having a great time. Mark Eanes, John's art teacher, commented on the diversity of the crowd:

All the friends I talked to said, "This is great! It's a great party and there's such a diverse cross-section of people." You know, there's a lot of people who you wouldn't normally expect to see in the same room and having fun.

When it was time to cut the cake there was a universal appeal for John to make a speech. Lee handed John the microphone and John spoke:

I just want you to know, thanks a lot . . . and hoping for happiness through beautiful times . . . and thanks for all your crowds . . . and I feel my love, deep in me, for the people who I see right now, and of course, especially my mom. (applause) Have a fun time, have a fun time and enjoy it! (applause) Oh man! I like it, thank you a lot! (applause, cries of "More! More!") First I cut the cake, and I hope you have a decent sleep when you get home! (cheers and laughter) Amen and thank you! ("Thank you, John!")

Birthday Party Aftermath

After the party, life went back to normal for John. He carried on with all his regular activities and even added a few. He joined the Presbyterian church choir, singing regularly in choir practice and in church on Sundays under the wing of a fellow choir member. He had weekly meetings with a skills counselor provided by the state for ongoing training in independent living. He was a frequent caregiver to his grandmother, who had come to live with the family when Alzheimer's disease made it impossible for her to live on her own. He added the Mendocino Deli as a regular stop on his daily rounds around town and took every opportunity to show the videotape of his birthday party to friends and visitors.

After a few weekend return visits it became obvious to me that my key to understanding and capturing John's relationship with the town would be to become both a member of the community and more intimate with John.

In August 1984, I moved to Mendocino. Over the next 3 years I became a part of John's routine—observing, interviewing, and filming my way to *And Then Came John*.

John's Teacher Status in the Mendocino Community

The video *And Then Came John* gives a rich visual and aural description of John's life after his 26th birthday party. It includes material from interviews with John's friends and family, but in the interests of brevity it excludes material that is included here to give a fuller and deeper understanding of his relationship with his Mendocino "town family."

A very significant question, asked by an outsider after John's birthday party, was "Why were there so many people there? Most people would be overwhelmed if 20 people showed up for their birthday party, let alone 200! What exactly is their relationship with John Mcgough?"

Elicited answers to these questions, culled from a broad sample of friends and neighbors, revealed information not only on how Mendocino has affected John but on how John has affected those around him.

A prominent theme of these interviews was invariably John's role as a teacher.

One friend worked as a waitress in a local cafe where John cleaned and swept up on Fridays. Often during the slow times she and John would talk:

John has taught me how to be a better listener. First of all because what he's saying is hard to understand, but also because what he's saying is not necessarily your basic everyday conversation. Coming from his mouth would be these great concepts, and I'd turn around and I'd go "What?" Because I didn't expect it from him and he would catch me off guard. I think because John has had to work harder to get his feelings across and had to overcome a lot of obstacles in terms of people's prejudices, he's thought more about what he wants to say. And so when you stop and listen to him, you learn a lot.

It makes me realize that no matter what obstacles you have in your life, you can overcome them—if you just reach out. And I think John does that and I think this is a community that responds to it. He's given a lot more to this community than many people realize.

Another friend lives about half-way between the Mcgough house and the town of Mendocino. John frequently walked to town and sometimes stopped by his house to say hi or to chat. This friend was also surprised by the profound direction that their conversations sometimes took:

He has a lot more depth, a lot more understanding of things, a lot more clarity than I certainly would have thought. He sees everything that he does as being for all mankind. He uses that phrase quite frequently. He feels that his ability to be spiritually strong without being physically strong is a lesson that he's learning and his expectation is that the lesson will be of value to everyone—for all mankind. The most impressive part of that was that it felt original—it felt like John was speaking from his soul, from his own experience, from his own observations. He has taught me, in a very subtle, quiet, nonabstract, nondogmatic way, the value of just being who you are. Just being. And trusting that what you do has value and will make a difference in the bigger picture.

John's skills counselor was the sound person during the videotaping of interviews and interactions with John. For 8 years she had been a special education teacher. When she first learned that there was to be an art show in town by a man with Down syndrome, she was skeptical. She felt sure that he was being exploited and doubted that he had any talent that would stand up in comparison to artists without disabilities. When she finally saw some of John's work she was amazed by its quality. Since then, her ongoing relationship with John has continued to inform her understanding of the inappropriateness of forming preconceived notions of others:

I think the main thing that I've learned from John is the value of unconditional love. I can see with his relations with everybody that he's open and he loves everybody. He gives everybody a fair share, a fair chance. He doesn't put conditions on anybody. He has helped me see that I too can be a loving person by being open and loving and not putting conditions on people—not laying on any of my preconceived notions about different kinds of people by the way they look, or by the way they dress, and just accepting them for who they are.

Another friend was John's guitar teacher for a year and a half. Often during their sessions and sometimes just as friends hanging around town together, their conversation would start with music and lead elsewhere:

Spending time with John has been real helpful in altering my basic attitude toward life. Once I picked him up from the movies where he had just seen a Walt Disney double feature, and I asked him, "Well, John, which one did you like better?" And he just looked at me like he had no concept of what better meant. It was like, "They're both wonderful and what's this 'better'?" And so I had to ask myself, "Why am I doing this comparative thing? Something doesn't have to be better to make it valid." And I was able to apply that in other ways I looked at the world too.

John's first skills counselor when he came to Mendocino was also a friend. Besides developing a close relationship with her and her children, John also gave this friend cause to consider the validity of what she was supposed to be teaching him:

One of the assignments required by the organization I was working for was to teach him certain skills that they considered important. We had these exercises where he had to figure out: "What takes longer: cooking a meal or going shopping for the meal, or shaving or talking on the phone?"

He'd just shrug his shoulders and say "I don't know," and he didn't know—it just made it seem like a very stupid question. It made me realize how our society is very crazy making. How there's a lot more wisdom in the so-called retarded people—I mean just the exercise of "what takes more time?" When you're involved in a task that you love, it's outside of time, and to require someone to be able to put it into a slot so it could be categorized to a clock, just seems so unnecessary.

And money—John did so well in town in being fair with people. If he didn't have enough money he would just tell them that he would bring it back and he would. He just conducted his own business with the people in town with so much heart that for me to require him to be able to count by fives and twenties and quarters it was like, "Maybe the world needs to operate more on John's level instead of on this system that we've all been raised under." It just made my own foundation a little shakier on what I had accepted as the way it had to be.

John's aerobics class teacher was, along with her husband, part of a singing duo that sometimes invited John on stage to perform. For her, John was a constant reminder of her own prejudice:

He's made me look at myself and the fact that just because someone may not look "normal," according to the way we look at normality, or think "normally" or speak "normally," I think that's not okay—I judge that. He's taught me that about myself. I feel that many people in town have become aware of the fact that just because someone's different doesn't mean that they're not on purpose or that they can't be a tremendous influence on others for good, or . . . or a teacher. He is so well known and he is so loved and appreciated that I feel he has had that impact on Mendocino.

John's hairstylist for his first 5 years in Mendocino, had a relationship with John that went beyond her shop—"just like most relationships in small towns." But sometimes, especially when feeling depressed, she actively sought out John:

I've been in bad shape and I've really gone and intentionally connected up with John because he's a good, light, wonderful hug—it's just wonderful to have someone who's so delighted to see you. And I think John does this for all of us who think we have struggles. You know, John is supposed to be a Down syndrome person, which has all these implications, societal implications. And here's this person who offers all of us probably a lot more than we offer him—you know, those of us who think that we are so together and we have all the things we're supposed to have but we get down and have these grumpy moods—and then here comes John. . .

Another friend moved to Mendocino shortly after John and Lee and the rest of the family had arrived on the scene. One of her most vivid and characteristic images of life in Mendocino involved John:

I remember seeing John, actually for the first time, at the Sea Gull Bar when he was "directing" the band. I was captured by his total lack of inhibition—he was having a wonderful time, oblivious to creating any kind of a sensation, which in a sense he was doing. I loved watching someone who had such a sense of himself. Later I was his art teacher for a short while—and John showed me more about myself than anyone I have ever dealt with. He has a sort of serenity, which sounds very bizarre because he can be the biggest goof in the world, too, and a lot of people see him that way, but his serenity has something to do with knowing who you are, and having a center, and acting from that place in yourself—and somehow John was able to show me that part of myself.

A local ceramic artist got to know John through his role as John's mentor in the Presbyterian church choir. To this friend, who is also a liturgical lecturer, John is a profound teacher:

John's whole being, his sense of presence, is a way of teaching. In fact, I think it's the most profound way of teaching that there really is—let's say it's a nondidactic way of teaching because he's teaching by example. What John illustrates is that there is only one truly fine dimension to art—that the highest point of art that we can reach is the art of human relationships—that transcends the making of physical stuff. And John is a supreme artist in that sense. The relationships he builds are a model for all of us.

For John, who was stunned by his acceptance into the Mendocino town family and so desirous of giving to the community through his art show and birthday party, his individual relationships with members of the Mendocino community have been and remain ongoing opportunities to give and help in return. Despite the early labeling and expectations of John as uneducable, his relationships with his Mendocino neighbors have shown him to be not only educable but an educator. And despite the fact that John's friends quoted above were the first people outside of his family to acknowledge and appreciate his influence as a teacher, according to Lee, John himself has been aware of his teaching role for some time:

> John uses this expression, "popping out," and he has for a long time. His feeling is like, we can handle anything when we're "popped out" of the attitudes or the dramas that we create. I think that's what he feels his role is best accomplished by, because he does that when he goes out in public. People will "pop out" . . . people will look at John and expect a certain thing to happen, and that thing won't happen. Something else will happen that does not fit their preconceived notions of what John should be doing or being, and then they'll be, in effect, popped out.

In John's words:

> Some people gotta pop out of some attitudes and problems. I want to let them know who they really are. What I'm saying is, "I want to let the whole world know who they really are, what they are about themselves . . . and enjoy themselves." That's all. That's all I know.

CONCLUSION

It is obvious that both John and Mendocino are unique. However, it is not too far-fetched to believe society could undergo a revolution in thought and attitude that would allow a view of fellow humans as unique individuals rather than as types. Such a resolution would herald a broader definition of intelligence and usefulness, one that includes such qualities as intuition, artistic and musical sensitivity, spirituality, and the ability to love unconditionally. In such a society the lot and life of people formerly labeled as abnormal and deviant solely because of a disability would be greatly improved.

Mendocino was such a place for John. It allowed him to be himself and valued him for it. A critic might say, "But Mendocino is a very special place, at a very special time. How could what happened to John be duplicated elsewhere?" It is true that Mendocino has a unique history; the influx of counterculture, new settlers, and the openness with which they were received by the old settlers did create a "peculiar tolerance for diversity." But Mendocino is far from perfect. It has its "small-town" feuds and polarizations, its misanthropes, its divisions between rich and poor. Moreover, there are many other small, tightly knit communities, both in the country and the city, that value friendliness, openness, and interdependence. If there is a lesson to be learned from Mendocino, it is just that the quality of openness and acceptance seems more developed there than in most other places.

No doubt other communities can learn and incorporate the value of this lesson. As John's brother put it,

> John, and his acceptance in this town, has a lesson to offer to any town because it's just a matter of where you live and where you're at—taking a look at the guy who walks around the corner or the lady who sits on her stoop all day long, and not looking at them as a handicapped man or an old senile lady, but looking at them as a part of your town. And if any community allows its members to be individuals, then someone like John, or someone like you or me is going to be loved and accepted.

EPILOGUE

At one point, a well-meaning member of the Mendocino community approached Lee to say that she didn't think John was progressing quickly enough in becoming a fully independent person. The woman offered to help Lee in making that happen. When Lee asked the woman if she had approached John on the matter to find out what he wanted, the woman said she hadn't. When asked, John replied that he was comfortable and fully enjoying his life with Lee. If he felt he needed a change he would let her know.

About 6 months later John received a letter from the organizing chairman of the Fourth International Down Syndrome Convention in Tel Aviv, Israel, asking him to come and speak about his experiences in Mendocino. Without hesitation, John firmly but politely declined. He did not want to leave Mendocino, nor did he wish to do anything that might set him apart from the mainstream. He had labored for too long under the Down syndrome label, and now that he had escaped it he had no intention of reconfirming it. He told Lee, "You go—that's your thing, not mine."

John leaves no room for doubt. He recognizes and cherishes his life as an integral part of the Mendocino "town family," and, if a change in his life is needed, he'll be the first to know.

7

Baking Bread Together

A Study of
Membership and Inclusion

Zana Marie Lutfiyya

This chapter describes the Allelujah Bakery, a place where people with different backgrounds and experiences work together. The metaphor of yeast rising in dough is often used at the bakery to refer to the potential of individual action within a community: The story of the bakery is that of many individuals all of whom contribute an important ingredient to the "dough" of their joint work life; together they create a "loaf" that is more than the sum of its parts. The Allelujah Bakery represents the combined experiences of several individuals conducting a joint enterprise. There an individual is not "integrated" into the ongoing activity; rather, each member is held responsible for facilitating the involvement of everyone else. That is, at the bakery there are no paid staff people who are solely responsible for the involvement and participation of people with disabilities.

Typically, the range of personal relationships and connections between people with and without disabilities is one indicator of "personal social integration" (Wolfensberger & Glenn, 1973). Researchers have demonstrated that such relationships do exist, although most people with developmental disabilities still have few such connections (Lutfiyya, 1990, 1991a). It has also been suggested that some individuals without disabilities are more accepting of individuals who are seen as different. The reasons for this orientation to acceptance may include familial ties, religious commitment, humanitarian sentiments, or feelings of friendship (Bogdan & Taylor, 1987, 1990; Taylor & Bogdan, 1989).

More recently, researchers have begun to look at settings in the community where people with disabilities are accepted and included (Chapter 8). *Inclusive settings* are those in which individuals with and without disabilities participate together as equal members. The term was first used in educational circles (see, for instance, Jorgensen, 1992; Stainback & Stainback, 1992). These activities may or may not be tied to a particular geographic location. Such environments may include an ongoing activity, such as a community choir (Chapter 9); an intentionally formed group of like-minded people who choose to live together (Lutfiyya, 1991b; Racino, 1993); or a town whose members accept and rally around individuals who need assistance, including those with disabilities (Groce, 1985; Chapter 5).

There are differences across the environments, including the composition of the groups, the activities in which the members take part, and the presence of intentionality or an ethos that supports the inclusion of individuals with disabilities. Despite these differences, individuals with disabilities are accepted and involved in all of these settings. Systematic study of such settings will enable researchers to determine the factors that account for the involvement of people with disabilities. The Allelujah Bakery is one such setting.

THE BAKERY

The Allelujah Bakery was founded by two priests involved in the Catholic Worker movement.[1] The bakery was initially established to promote and support opportunities for social justice. Consistent with the movement's perspective, the bakery was not opened to "help" poor or disabled people. Rather, it was meant to offer "wealthy" people the chance to be part of a larger and more representative community.

The bakery fulfills more than one function in the lives of the people who work there. It is a place of work and meaningful occupation and a place where people find companionship. The bakery brings together individuals from different backgrounds and experiences (e.g., activists in the peace and social justice movement; local parishioners;

---

[1]Founded by Dorothy Day and Peter Maurin in 1933, the *Catholic Worker* began as a monthly newspaper. Meant as a Catholic response to the *Communist Daily Worker*, the paper promoted pacifism, voluntary poverty, anarchism, and agrarianism. In addition, Day, Maurin, and others began to offer food and shelter to homeless people. Over time, bread lines, soup kitchens, and "houses of hospitality" were opened. In 1994, the *Catholic Worker* is still being published and worker houses operate in over 60 U.S. cities (Day, 1959; Murray, 1990).

those who have faced difficulties such as incarceration, excessive use of drugs and alcohol, poverty, homelessness, and unemployment). There is a tension between the efforts to create and support a small community of people who work together and support each other on the one hand and to maintain a high enough level of production to provide work for all of the members on the other. This is a dilemma that members of the bakery acknowledge, struggle with, and accept as inevitable.

THE WORKERS

One of the founders, Father Bryan, still works at the bakery, where he delivers bread, keeps the books, and takes part in weekly decision-making meetings. The other "core members" are four women who have worked at the bakery for years. They have the responsibility of running the bakery and participate in the decision-making meetings. Liza is the bakery manager and Olivia is her assistant. Despite their titles, both spend most of their working time as bakers. Everyone else at the bakery is referred to as a baker or a member of the baking crew. Tony has been designated as a "jack-of-all-trades," a recognition that he could perform all of the daily nonadministrative tasks.

During my observations, there were approximately 20 members of the baking crew. There were six core members. These included a man and a woman, both in their late 80s, who have worked at the bakery since it opened. Danny was the youngest of the regular baking crew. A quiet man who keeps to himself, he lives in a large shelter for men and is said to sniff glue; he occasionally misses work. When he doesn't come in, Father Bryan seeks him out to make sure that he is okay. During the course of the study, the baking crew expanded to include two cousins, men from Central America who entered the United States illegally as economic refugees. Given sanctuary in the area, they were given jobs at the bakery until they got their official papers and could move on to better paying jobs. The composition of the baking crew highlights the bakery's ties to the Catholic Worker tradition. It is a place of needed and meaningful work where individuals who might be rejected from other places of employment will be hired, welcomed, and encouraged.

VOLUNTEERS AND VISITORS

Some individuals have volunteered their services at the bakery for a number of years, as do most of the drivers who deliver the bread to parish centers, soup kitchens, and offices around town. In addition to these regular workers, the bakery serves as host to many visitors. Most visitors are schoolchildren who take a field trip to spend the day, but a few are adults who are friends or relatives of a regular worker. This flexibility in personnel at the bakery made it easier for me to be a participant observer. I took an active role at the bakery, participating in all aspects of the bread production including preparing dough, making loaves, running the ovens, packaging the bread, and cleaning. I helped prepare meals that the bakers shared and joined them on meal and coffee breaks. In addition, on invitation I took part in special events such as birthday parties and holiday celebrations. I also worked a few extra days, such as on Sundays before major holidays (Thanksgiving, Christmas, and Easter) when the bakery was open for 12 hours to fill special orders. On two occasions I delivered bread orders.

The Allelujah Bakery is an inclusive and open setting. Two main factors account for this: 1) the ethos of a diverse working community, which is rooted in a particular set of beliefs and values; and 2) the specific and planned actions on the part of some individuals to ensure that all of the workers from a variety of backgrounds are welcomed as members.

TONY SANTI

Tony Santi is one man whose personal story is now a part of the lives of the others who work at the Bakery (Lutfiyya, 1992). Tony was placed into a state institution for the mentally retarded as a child and was discharged as a young man. He spent several years off and on the streets, working at part-time jobs and engaging in petty theft for which he served two jail terms. During this time he met Father Bryan. The two became friends, and Father Bryan visited Tony regularly when he was incarcerated. After completing his second jail term, Tony worked with Father Bryan delivering bread and eventually got a job at the bakery. I include a vignette of Tony as a way of picking up one thread that is woven into the fabric that is the Allelujah Bakery. Tony's experiences as a working member of the bakery demonstrate one way that we can think about social integration.

It is a hot, hazy afternoon. About a dozen people have gathered in the backyard of a two-story house. They are seated around four card tables that have been placed end-to-end. The tables are set with plates, cups, bowls of salad, platters of hot dogs and hamburgers, and a large chocolate cake. A cooler containing beer and soda sits on the grass. The laughing and chatter stop as everyone turns to face the short, smiling man sitting at the end of a table. He formally welcomes everybody to his home. In return, they raise their drinks and salute him.

The host of this picnic is Tony Santi. The others are his coworkers from the Allelujah Bakery where he has worked for over 10 years. There is nothing remarkable in this typical summer scene unless one knows something about Tony Santi, his guests, and their commitment to each other.

BAKING BREAD: BUILDING CONNECTIONS

At the bakery, the act of baking bread is a means of building personal connections. The important work of the bakery is not simply the baking of bread; it relates more to how this activity is structured and how the bakers are involved in the work. Baking bread is one way to establish and maintain a small community of people bound by a common purpose. All of the members of the baking crew have valid and valuable roles in this work, and everyone's contribution is necessary. The bread is baked by individuals who could not do their work without the cooperation of the others.

Involving everyone in the baking crew in a meaningful way is a real challenge. Many of the workers would not generally be viewed as highly skilled or capable on the open job market. In this section, I examine the three ways that everyone at the bakery—regulars and visitors alike—are enabled to make valued contributions to the ongoing work. While these processes are applied for everyone at the bakery, and by people for each other, the examples will highlight Tony Santi's experiences.

FACILITATION

The baking of bread is structured to help bring individuals together in pleasant or constructive interactions. In some instances, the act of facilitating interactions is conscious and planned; in others, it is spontaneous. But the purpose remains the same: to make particular interactions or relationships succeed. Although Liza, the manager, maintains that her main concern is in running the bakery as a business, she carefully orchestrates the work and involvement of all of the workers, with or without disabilities. Several other members of the baking crew follow her lead by engaging in this activity.

Sometimes opportunities are created for different people to work with each other and so complete the task at hand. Thus, the older members of the baking crew are regularly paired with a younger person who can help with certain tasks such as heavy lifting. Facilitation is used to smooth over or resolve the problems that may arise between individuals. At one point, Tony had left the bakery for 2 months after a heated dispute with Liza. During this time, Olivia, her husband, and Father Bryan intervened with both individuals to pave the way for a reconciliation and Tony's return to his job. Finally, an individual may be coached to make a particular response in a difficult situation. For instance, one woman, Tina, found it hard to work with Tony because he did not always follow her directions. Liza, the manager, encouraged Tina to reframe her directions to Tony as advice and suggestions. Liza pointed out that most people don't like to be given curt orders and that Tony was no exception. Liza went so far as to have Tina practice repeating some phrases that she might say to Tony.

Facilitation is not confined only to the bakery and working hours. Both Liza and Olivia try continually to involve Tony in a number of "wholesome" social activities within the parish where he lives, such as monthly potluck suppers, religious mass, and other special events.

INTERPRETATION

The workers at the bakery, in particular Liza and Olivia, interpret the behavior of the members of the baking crew positively to each other and visitors. This effort has two results: First, the person is validated and recognized in some way; and second, further positive interactions are promoted. As she works, Olivia often tells stories about other members of the baking crew, and she also gets them to share their experiences with the others. She highlights the extraordinary moments of people's lives, but also acknowledges the mundane ones.

One morning during a coffee break, Tony was being teased about his haircut. Olivia gently interrupted and asked me if I had heard about how Tony had saved the life of his neighbor, paving the way for Tony to tell the story. Tony had discovered a fire in the next apartment, called the fire department, and alerted the caretaker. Together they broke the door down and rescued the unconscious inhabitant. As Tony was telling this story, Olivia prompted him not to forget certain details. Instead of being the butt of teasing and jokes, Tony now received praise from his coworkers about his efforts in the rescue.

ACCOMMODATION

Accommodation refers to any actual changes in the physical or social environment that make it easier to involve a person within the setting. A common example of accommodation is making an environment physically accessible by adding a ramp. At the bakery, changes were made in the structure of the work day in order to enable someone to take a more active role. Thus, no bread was delivered or picked up until after 2 P.M. so that the woman who packed the orders would not have to come to work until noon.

Sometimes the accommodation that was arranged extended past standard working hours. A good example of this occurred when Liza arranged a part-time job for Tony. He needed more income and was looking for other jobs to replace his bakery position. The church where the bakery is located needed someone to clean up after monthly community suppers. Olivia and Liza thought that Tony would be an excellent choice for the position. From the perspective of these two women, this job provided Tony with extra cash but did not interfere with his job at the bakery. Since the suppers didn't end until 9 P.M., the two women suggested that Tony come in first thing the next morning to do the cleaning. Tony refused the job regretfully, as he did not want to be in the church on the one morning a week when he would be forced to encounter someone he really did not like and whom he avoided.

In response to this, Liza suggested that Tony come in the evening of the supper, eat with the people, and clean up afterward. Although it would be late, he lived only a few blocks from the church hall. Tony agreed to this if he could come in toward the end of the meal and not be required to socialize with everybody. The organizers of the community suppers did not want to entrust Tony with a key to the hall, as only two people were allowed to have a key. Liza then arranged for someone to lock up immediately after the supper, with Tony leaving through a door that would remain locked even if someone exited through it.

Liza reasoned with the organizers of the community suppers that this change in schedule would suit Tony, and it might serve as one way to encourage his participation in parish activities and provide him with a decent meal. In response to her efforts, the organizers and Tony agreed to this arrangement.

CONCLUSION

The experiences of the workers at the Allelujah Bakery offer many lessons for those of us interested in encouraging the social integration of people with disabilities. First, they provide us with a different frame of reference that comes with its own language: that of meaningful and valid work, membership, and the connection between the two. Membership is earned by working at the bakery and by the way the baking crew tries to work with each other. Every member of the crew is expected to perform the physical work of baking as well as the less visible task of facilitating the involvement of coworkers.

It is crucial that we see the bakery for exactly what it is. The founders believed that authentic and valued work opportunities in a congenial and supportive environment are important for all people. The bakery is a modest attempt to create such a workplace. It is not a work placement nor a supported employment program. Rather, it is a group of people struggling to manage the physical work while building community with each other. This effort, while largely unrecognized, is both important and instructive. It is these associations of ordinary citizens that will help to bring about the real inclusion of individuals with disabilities into community life.

How can professionals support and encourage these efforts? This is, of course, a question that begs an answer. Perhaps the issue is not the roles that professionals should play, but rather the roles that professionals might abandon. What would happen if we chose to have a personal involvement in a community group in our own neighborhood? What would happen if we tried to establish one small place where another would be welcomed? What would we learn if we made this effort with other people and not alone?

I do not suggest that people forego paid supports or professional assistance. Nor do I hold to a romantic ideal of "the community" as a place where only good things can happen to people. Rather, I suggest that the lessons to be learned from the people of the Allelujah Bakery make personal, and not professional, sense. The founders and the workers of the Allelujah Bakery subscribe to a particular set of values and traditions that inspire and motivate them, and they try to live these out in the company of like-minded others. Perhaps we might try to do the same.

REFERENCES

Bogdan, R., & Taylor, S.J. (1987). Toward a sociology of acceptance. *Social Policy, 18*(2), 34–39.
Bogdan, R., & Taylor, S.J. (1990). Relationships with severely disabled people: The social construction of humanness. *Social Problems, 36*(2), 135–146.
Day, D. (1959). *The long loneliness*. Garden City, NY: Image Books.
Groce, N.E. (1985). *Everyone here spoke sign language: Hereditary deafness on Martha's Vineyard*. Cambridge, MA: Harvard University Press.
Jorgensen, C.M. (1992). Natural supports in inclusive schools: Curricular and teaching strategies. In J. Nisbet (Ed.) *Natural supports in school, at work and in the community for people with severe disabilities* (pp. 179–215). Baltimore: Paul H. Brookes Publishing Co.
Lutfiyya, Z.M. (1990). *Affectionate bonds: What we can learn by listening to friends*. Syracuse, NY: The Center on Human Policy.

Lutfiyya, Z.M. (1991a). "A feeling of being connected": Friendships between people with and without learning difficulties. *Disability, Handicap & Society,* *6*(3), 233–245.

Lutfiyya, Z.M. (1991b). "Mighty prophets of the future": The Orion Community. In S.J. Taylor, R. Bogdan, & J.A. Racino (Eds.), *Life in the community: Case studies of organizations supporting people with disabilities* (pp. 227–241). Baltimore: Paul H. Brookes Publishing Co.

Lutfiyya, Z.M. (1992). *Facilitating personal networks and social relationships.* Syracuse, NY: The Center on Human Policy.

Murray, H. (1990). *Do not neglect hospitality: The Catholic Worker and the homeless.* Philadelphia: Temple University Press.

Racino, J. (1993). The Madison Mutual Housing Association and Cooperative: "People and housing building community." In J.A. Racino, P. Walker, S. O'Connor, & S.J. Taylor (Eds.), *Housing, support, and community: Choices and strategies for adults with disabilities* (pp. 253–280). Baltimore: Paul H. Brookes Publishing Co.

Stainback, S., & Stainback, W. (Eds.). (1992). *Curriculum considerations in inclusive classrooms: Facilitating learning for all students.* Baltimore: Paul H. Brookes Publishing Co.

Strully, J.L., & Strully, C. (1992). The struggle toward inclusion and the fulfilment of friendship. In J. Nisbet (Ed.), *Natural supports in school, at work, and in the community for people with severe disabilities* (pp. 165–177). Baltimore: Paul H. Brookes Publishing Co.

Taylor, S.J., & Bogdan, R. (1984). *Introduction to qualitative research methods: The search for meanings* (2nd ed.). New York: John Wiley & Sons.

Taylor, S.J., & Bogdan, R. (1989). On accepting relationships between people with mental retardation and non-disabled people: Towards an understanding of acceptance. *Disability, Handicap & Society,* *4*(1), 21–36.

Wolfensberger, W., & Glenn, L. (1973). *PASS 3: Program analysis of service systems.* Toronto, Ontario, Canada: National Institute on Mental Retardation.

8

A Temporary Place to Belong

Inclusion in a Public Speaking and Personal Relations Course

Ellen S. Fisher

Since the 1980s, the field of disabilities has devoted increased attention to social relationships and the full participation of people with disabilities in community life. Various researchers and commentators have focused on how people become involved in and maintain personal relationships (Bogdan & Taylor, 1987; Lutfiyya, 1990, 1991; O'Brien & Lyle O'Brien, 1992; Taylor & Bogdan, 1989; Traustadottir, 1991); how people participate in groups and organizations (Chapters 7 and 9); and how people are included in communities (Groce, 1985; Chapter 5). Yet to date few insights have been proffered regarding the characteristics of inclusive community associations and organizations that make them places that effectively foster acceptance.

This chapter examines the experiences of two people with disabilities who were accepted as full members in a 14-week course in public speaking and personal relations. It represents an effort to: 1) learn about an association in which, with the assistance of ordinary community members, people with disabilities are welcomed as members; 2) identify the specific characteristics of that organization that make it an inclusive community place; and 3) generate from the data some ideas that can provide guidance to practitioners who assist people with disabilities to make and maintain connections.

TWO PARTICIPANTS/TWO PERSPECTIVES ON THE THOMAS HUGHES COURSE

It's like a big support group. And you'll find that the camaraderie between people just gets stronger and stronger. I mean [you] . . . go in as strangers. . . .

And, as the course proceeds, . . . you share things with each other that you never intended to share. . . . And it really enables you to do a lot of soul searching, and finding out who you really are.

I have gotten a lot out of this class. I have gained a lot of self-confidence. At the beginning, I was really afraid to get up and talk in front of all of you. Now, it's not so hard. . . . I have also met a lot of great people in this course, and I think that we have all learned a lot together.

These words are expressions of two different people with disabilities about the Thomas Hughes Course in Effective Speaking and Human Relations in which they participated.

The first quotation comes from an interview conducted with Arlene Sumner, a diminutive, assertive, 40-year-old disabilities advocate who uses a wheelchair. Arlene took the Hughes course in order to improve her public speaking abilities and in order to grow personally. But the course exceeded her expectations in that it also enabled her to make some new connections and to associate with people who, for a short time, became involved with each other in a unique way.

The second quote is part of a 2-minute talk given by Robert Baker at his Thomas Hughes graduation. Robert is a creative, 38-year-old man who has a visual impairment and a seizure disorder. The circumstances surrounding Robert's talk, as much as the words themselves, reflect some of the qualities of the course that promote the full inclusion of all participants.

Robert stood in the front of the room facing his audience. When he was done speaking, the class responded with a big round of applause. Then a large man approached from the wings and took Robert's arm; together, they walked back to Robert's seat. When Robert was seated, the course instructor said, "Well, Robert, you have really grown in this class. You are certainly going to be successful at whatever you do from here."

Robert took the Hughes course in order to increase his potential at a telephone sales job. When, 2 weeks into the course, Robert lost his job, he continued with the course, and it became an important factor in his life for the next 3 months. Instead of increasing his sales potential, the class offered Robert a chance to meet people and to become a full-fledged member of a community association, for a limited period, with others who shared the experience.

THE THOMAS HUGHES COURSE: HISTORY AND FORMAT

Thomas Hughes courses emphasize personal relations rather than speaking ability. Public speaking has come to be viewed by Hughes instructors merely as a means to an end, a way of learning to get along with others and, ultimately, a conduit to success in life.

The classes are generally populated by 30–40 students, a class instructor, and 5–8 graduate assistants. The latter are former students who have returned to help teach the course; they introduce the instructor at the beginning of the class, give sample talks illustrating each assignment, and handle the paperwork for the course. Less tangible duties include bringing extra enthusiasm (a key ingredient in the Hughes formula) to the class, encouraging students to do their best, and assisting students in whatever way is needed.

Support occurs both during class time and beyond it. During class time, assistants make constructive comments to all of the students and assist with particular problems. Outside of class, each assistant is assigned a specific list of students to telephone once a week, in order to go over the week's assignments and determine what help they need.

The particular course in which Robert Baker and Arlene Sumner became enrolled was held in a business park on the edge of a medium-size city. Class sessions took place every Wednesday night for 14 weeks from 6:30 P.M. to 10 P.M. The cost of the course was high—$850—and was paid on Arlene's behalf by her employer. In Robert's case, the fee was paid out of his Supplemental Security PASS.[1]

Arlene and Robert were in the same group for many of the sessions. When Arlene had surgery and could not finish with Robert's class, she returned several months later to finish the course with a subsequent group of students.

I personally became enrolled in the course with Arlene during her second round of classes. My experiences in the class contributed greatly to my understanding of the Hughes course and how people are included in it. (Participant observations of the classes, as well as eight interviews, constitute the data on which I have based my analysis. The interviews were of Robert, Arlene, Larry Wall, a Hughes graduate assistant, and Karen Carson, a Hughes sales representative.)

Each class session that Robert, Arlene, or I attended began with a graduate assistant giving a sample talk. Afterward, students were called up one by one to give 1- to 2-minute talks which they had prepared. When everyone was finished with the first round of talks, the class voted for the person who in their opinion had given the best presentation as well as for the person who had displayed the most personal growth. Winners were announced and were called up to the front

---

[1]Supplemental Security Income (SSI) PASS Plans arise out of an SSI regulation that allows SSI recipients to set aside funds, which would otherwise by considered as available to meet their needs, to be committed to a plan to achieve self-support, resulting in eligibility for SSI.

of the room to receive awards—usually pens or books—and to give acceptance speeches. Following a 10-minute break, class reconvened and the entire process was repeated. Assigned talks were on a range of subjects, but often were concerned with various Hughes principles that encouraged both personal growth and the practical and emotional support of other people.

USING COOPERATION AND ACCEPTANCE AS TOOLS FOR SUCCESS

Role of Philosophy

The Hughes course is similar to the community choir described in Chapter 9 in that it is firmly rooted in a philosophy that highly values the inclusion of all types of people. Thus, it can be inferred that a philosophy that consciously fosters inclusion and acceptance is one factor that may make a community association a plausible place for people with disabilities to become full members.

The Hughes course is based on a definitive and pervasive philosophy that stresses the importance of personal growth and of learning to get along with others, both within the class and outside of it. Getting along with others means learning to understand and accept all people, including those who may be perceived as different from oneself. It means learning to value rather than shun diversity. Thus, the philosophical outlook that propels the Hughes course is in many ways ideal for promoting the full inclusion of people with disabilities.

The Hughes philosophy is partially expressed in nine lists of principles. These principles make specific prescriptions about how students should conduct their lives. Posters explaining these principles line the classroom walls, and another copy of them is available in the Course Guide. Throughout the course, students are asked to utilize the principles with regard to their classmates. They are also asked to choose principles from each of the lists and to choose people in their outside lives with whom to try them out. They are then required to act on each choice and to report back to the class on the results.

For example, Arlene Sumner chose the principle "Become genuinely interested in other people" from the "Become a Friendlier Person" list, with the aim of making an effort to become closer with an old friend from whom she had grown apart. Arlene reestablished contact with her friend, who several years earlier married a man whom Arlene did not like. Arlene tried to become interested in her friend's new life with this man. As a result, she and her friend reestablished some of their former closeness, even though Arlene continued to dislike the husband. This experience then became the topic of Arlene's 2-minute talk in the seventh class session, when people reported on the results of their application of a principle from the "Become a Friendlier Person" list.

All of the Hughes principles are viewed by Hughes people as outgrowths of human relations. Larry Wall (the graduate assistant who was assigned to telephone both Robert Baker and Arlene Sumner) explained it this way:

> The way the course works is that you have to make an active effort . . . to improve your life in terms of human relations. And you are given one or two challenges every single week, [in order to] . . . develop better relationships with people, as far as friends, family, and strangers too. And we all become a part of the class. And, although we all have different goals, we are all moving in the same direction. The goals are usually pretty similar.

Thus, the philosophy into which students are indoctrinated mandates support of others in the group, as well as the development of better relationships with people outside of the group. And having such a philosophy in common strengthens students' sense of membership with others.

In addition to helping all students in the course to become members in the sense used by O'Brien and Lyle O'Brien (1992), this philosophy can specifically enhance the full participation of people with disabilities in the course. For example, in the second session of Robert's class, the course instructor announced that Robert was taking taxicabs to and from the class. In response, two men immediately volunteered to help; for the remaining 12 weeks, one man picked Robert up on the way to class each week and the other dropped him off on the way home. Commenting about the ease with which Robert was able to secure assistance in solving his transportation problem, Larry Wall explained that giving a classmate a ride "just sort of naturally fits in with the Hughes philosophy."

The notion of challenging oneself is also an important part of the Hughes ethic. It means that students are expected to do things that they previously considered beyond their capabilities. Arlene Sumner told me that she viewed challenging oneself as an important part of the course. She felt that "if you take the challenge, Thomas Hughes takes you, in the beginning, from where you are, [and helps you] to grow and achieve."

Like the philosophy of support, the notion of challenge does more than foster personal growth in all students. It can also directly enhance the participation of people with disabilities in the course. One example of how this principle looks when used in connection with a participant with disabilities is Larry Wall's story about how he became Robert Baker's graduate assistant.

According to Larry, before the beginning of the spring session, he and the other prospective graduate assistants met with the instructor to decide which students would be assigned to which assistant. Normally, the list is simply divided up between the graduate assistants without much thought. However, on this occasion, the instructor explained to the assistants that someone would be joining the class who had a visual impairment and seizure disorder and who would require some special supports.

Larry responded to this announcement by volunteering to have Robert on his list of students because he viewed assisting Robert as a special opportunity to "challenge myself" and to "grow." Thus, Robert's special needs were interpreted by Larry as something that made becoming his assistant more rather than less attractive.

The overarching notion of positive thinking is another important part of the Hughes philosophy. Participants in the course are advised to substitute positive thoughts for negative ones. The idea is that thinking positively may actually reverse a negative situation. For example, one of my classmates, a department head at a large insurance company, told a story about what happened when she was told by her director that she was going to be laid off and that her department was being abolished. She thought to herself, "I'll use this as an opportunity." So, trying not to panic, she brainstormed with other people in her department until they came up with an innovative idea about how the department could serve a different function. Then she approached the director with the plan. To her amazement, the director approved it, saving her job and the jobs of all the others.

As is the case with support and challenge, positive thinking makes a particular contribution with regard to the participation of people with disabilities in the course: It encourages students to frame their thinking about people with disabilities in terms of their contributions rather than in terms of their deficits.

A specific example of this positive framing is Larry Wall's reaction to Robert's frequent telephone calls to his house. Robert is a person who has many assets; but, like everyone else, he is not perfect. A quirk of his is that he sometimes telephones people quite often; at times, this has annoyed his friends and acquaintances. Yet Robert's frequent telephone calls to Larry's house were interpreted by Larry as a positive sign. He explained to me that "Robert wants to know everything, which is good."

Role of Structure and Organization

The Thomas Hughes course is specifically designed in a manner that maximizes the support that participants can provide each other. As is the case with organizational philosophy, it can be inferred that a structure that encourages cooperation and support is one factor that can make a community group more likely to fully include people with disabilities.

The structure and organization of the Hughes course positively influence the level of support and acceptance exchanged among members of the group. Everyone in the group is affected; in addition, there are specific repercussions with regard to the participation of people with disabilities. The course utilizes a general format, certain specific forms, and an overall organization aimed at encouraging students to cooperate with and support each other.

First, the basic class format encourages active participation by students. Karen Carson (the sales associate who was interviewed during the course of the study) explained:

> [We] . . . do not . . . have an instructor stand up in front and lecture for three hours. [Rather], we have a lot of group interaction, because people can learn from each other's situations. In that sense, the course is not, in essence, education. It's training in how to interact with people.

Thus, interaction and interdependence of class members is purposefully structured into the format.

Second, some of the forms that are utilized resemble those used in cooperative learning. For example, in my class, students often worked in pairs in order to practice their talks before addressing the whole class. This practice made individuals more comfortable about giving their talks; it also helped them to get to know their classmates. During one session, I was paired with David Ramsey, a short, athletic-looking man of about 40. After practicing our talks, we had a few minutes to chat; he explained to me that he had been a golf pro but had recently had a hip replacement and had to give up golf. So he became the manager of a golf club. I thus learned—as I did at other times in the course—that there were people in the course who had hidden disabilities. After that, David and I talked together quite a bit during breaks and before and after class.

Another example of the utilization of cooperative forms is that on several occasions students sat in horseshoe formations, in clusters of six to eight. The small groups were given a task to work on together and were then asked to report back to the larger group. People in the horseshoes got to talk together more than they normally would and also learned to work together as a team. At the end of these exercises, the entire class voted on the best team. So a sort of competitive team spirit was fostered in each group.

Last, the overall organization of the course builds in support. For example, having graduate assistants available in addition to the instructor ensures that there are five to eight people who are involved in the course whose main job is to assist students to fully take part.

This existence of supports makes it easier to structure in special assistance for participants with disabilities. Thus, Larry Wall was willing to adapt the level of support he typically gave students to Robert Baker's special needs because of the Hughes philosophy. And Larry was able to do so because of the structure. So Larry talked with Robert every week because it was part of his job to make sure that students assigned to him were prepared for class. He talked with Robert more frequently, and for longer periods of time, because he perceived that Robert needed this extra support in order to be prepared.

Also, during class time Larry's job was to assist all students. Assisting Robert to the front of the room to give his talk, waiting to one side while he spoke, and then assisting him back to his seat was a relatively simple adaptation of this generalized support.

Development of a Group Ethos of Support

Students in the Hughes course engage in a group process whereby they become more and more interdependent. Judging from the evidence presented by the course, it can be inferred that, in organizations where people engage in a process that opens them to others emotionally and causes them to be accepting of all members of the group, the growing sense of community within the group may ensure that people with disabilities are fully included.

During the 14 weeks that the class members come together, they share stories and support on ever-deepening levels until a strong emotional tie forms between them. According to Karen Carson, "there are a lot of similarities to group therapy." Arlene Sumner said,

> This course just forces you into listening to what other people are saying. And you listen deeply, and with such intent—I did, anyway—that, what the other person is experiencing, you feel inside. It gets to that point.

During the early sessions, the group begins to learn mutual trust. Arlene explained that, going into the course, she felt very nervous. But she soon felt enveloped in the atmosphere of sharing:

> People end up talking about issues in their personal lives, about their successes, their failures in their marriage or their career, and maybe about a bad relationship with a parent or sibling. . . . And, as the course goes on, you form a real connection with the other people.

So, as the class proceeds, people are expected to listen carefully, to share their feelings about important matters in their lives, and to form a bond with other members of the group. These are actual rules of the group. And there are others, both stated and unstated. For instance, individuals are expected to keep things within the group. Arlene said, "You could share whatever you wanted to, with the understanding that it wouldn't go outside to public knowledge."

In order to really belong to the group, people are asked to accept others within it almost unconditionally. When I asked Arlene how the class might react if someone gave a poor speech, she replied that she didn't know because that had never happened. All of the speeches were always good. She also explained, "By the time the training is over, you feel like a family."

People are rewarded for understanding and following the group rules and are penalized—or, at least, viewed with disdain—for ignoring them. Thus, when Larry Wall talked about Robert's participation in the class, he said that "Robert caught on . . . right away" to giving constructive feedback to other speakers and to responding to the positive feedback of others with regard to his own talks. Larry listed this savvy about the rules as one of the reasons Robert "won" multiple pens and books (for giving the best talk in several sessions).

Arlene said, with reference to class participation and personal growth outside of the classroom, "If you don't put a lot into it, you don't get a lot of out of it." She described one student—a very quiet lawyer who came to the class to learn to be more outgoing, and with whom she and some other class members had gotten together outside of class—as "not really participat(ing) with his whole self. . . . For one thing, he acted one way in class and another way outside of it. He was kind of a sham." Karen Carson (the sales associate) also said that what people get out of the course "depends on the person, on the effort that they put in." Larry Wall said,

> It depends on what people are willing and able to accomplish. Some people, early on in the course, will aim for their one objective—of developing a better relationship with a certain person, for example—and hate everybody else.

The growing interdependence of class members, as they engage in the prescribed group process, brings them (insofar as they are willing and able to participate) into a unique relationship with others for the short period of time that the course runs. For 14 weeks, people have a new group of kin with whom to share their innermost feelings, their trials and tribulations.

Arlene Sumner experienced her participation in the course as a great benefit. And, for Robert Baker, it filled several needs that were not being filled anywhere else in his life: to be listened to and treated with respect by a group of people in the community and to become a full member of a group that included people both with and without disabilities.

CONCLUSION: SOME LESSONS FOR THE FIELD

This course in public speaking and personal relations displays certain attributes as an organization that make it an accepting, inclusive place to be. These include a philosophy centered around personal growth and based on learning to understand and accept diverse others; activities that are structured so as to be conducive to the provision of that support; and the conscious development of an ethos of support between members of the group.

Associations that display these characteristics may represent fertile ground for inclusion of all people. Expanding on the specific example of this course, some general principles that may be drawn from the study are as follows:

1. Organizational philosophy is a key element that may make a community group more or less accepting of people with disabilities. When an organization or association has a philosophy that consciously fosters inclusion and acceptance in general, people's differences may be accepted as a natural application of that philosophy.
2. The way that activities are structured in a group may greatly affect the level of support and acceptance between members of the group. This will affect everyone in the group, including people with disabilities. A structure that includes small group work, partners work, and other exercises that bring people closer together, combined with built-in positive feedback between members of the group, is particularly conducive to full inclusion of all group members.
3. The level of emotional closeness or distance between members of a group, and whether or not some level of group spirit is fostered, will affect how effectively people with disabilities are included. In associations or organizations where people are encouraged to form an emotional bond and to meld as a group, those with disabilities may be naturally supported from within the organization by other members of the group.

Belonging to local organizations is an important way that people participate fully in the life of their communities. The fragmented nature of modern society may make this truer today than it was several generations ago. As described by O'Brien and Lyle O'Brien (1992), people now have different memberships [which] occur in widely separated locations. They know little of other's history beyond the particular circumstances of their meeting. Their social networks include many people who would be strangers to one another if they happened to meet. (p. 19)

In a world where such "dispersed memberships" have for many taken the place of being known in the cohesive, whole community of yesteryear, it is of particular importance that the diverse places and situations in which connections between people are made be accessible for those with disabilities.

The importance of fostering links has recently been recognized in the area of supported employment and incorporated into the employment specialist's work. Hence, in the job development phase, emphasis has been placed on the location of jobs most likely to produce satisfying bonds between people. Then, once a job has been found, the importance of utilizing the natural supports available in workplaces, not only to provide assistance in work tasks but to foster mutually enriching relationships between people with and without disabilities, has been understood and acted upon (Hagner, 1989, 1992; Hagner, Cotton, Goodall, & Nisbet, 1992; Hagner, Rogan, & Murphy, 1992; O'Brien & Lyle O'Brien, 1992). Thus, viewed from another angle, it has been acknowledged by supported employment practitioners that the function of a good job is not only to provide meaningful work but to provide a forum for making connections.

Leisure pursuits have received less attention than work as a way of helping people to connect. Yet places where people engage in leisure activities together may be just as significant as workplaces as locales for forging new alliances (Walker & Edinger, 1988).

Until we learn more about how support takes place in community groups, people with disabilities who could participate in the great variety of associations that exist may be denied these opportunities. It is therefore imperative that, when human services workers attempt to promote connections between people with disabilities and other citizens in their local communities, they recognize the value of community organizations as settings for the forging of new and valuable connections.

Furthermore, when searching out local associations, people seeking to foster links between others with and without disabilities should look for those groups that have some of the characteristics inherent in the Hughes course. Just as it is vital to investigate the "workplace culture" when developing jobs—looking for worksites that are conducive to the forming of positive relationships between workers (Hagner, 1989, 1992; Hagner, Rogan, & Murphy, 1992)—it is equally important, when investigating group recreational opportunities, to look at the "associational culture" of community organizations, with the idea that those organizations that have the specific attributes that make places accepting will be more likely than those that do not to successfully absorb new and diverse people into their midsts.

Despite its advantages, the Hughes course is not a perfect venue for including people with disabilities. The major drawback of the Hughes course is its short duration. The course provides full and somewhat consuming membership for 14 weeks. When the time is up, those who have been welcomed as members no longer have the opportunity to meet. Their situation may be slightly different from the way it was when they began, but both of the Hughes associates interviewed (Karen Carson and Larry Wall) admitted that there is a good deal of "slideback" in the personal growth that students achieve in the course and that often people come to feel as disconnected as they did before.

For Arlene Sumner, the fact that the course had a beginning, a middle, and an end was acceptable. She explained,

> I feel that I met a lot of good people. And I may not ever see them again. But at least I know that, when we were together, we shared a common bond, and we shared something special with each other. And, for me, it's okay to let go.

For Robert Baker, however, the end of the course meant that he went back to his life of little stimulation, spending his days at the adult care home, waiting for the supported work program to call him about a job opportunity.

Last, it should never be forgotten that any sort of life planning must begin and end with the person. Thus, the most inclusive association is the wrong place for someone who has no interest in the organization's mission. Both Robert Baker and Arlene Sumner had a strong interest in attending the Hughes course. Someone else might not have such an interest.

If professionals seeking to make connections start by looking at the person with disabilities in terms of his or her priorities and interests, and then look for organizations where the associational culture promotes the making of connections (and, ideally, where membership is ongoing rather than time-limited), they will have the best chance of assisting the person with whom they are planning to begin a successful group membership by participating in a fruitful new venue for people with similar interests and talents to meet one another.

REFERENCES

Bogdan, R., & Taylor, S.J. (1987). Toward a sociology of acceptance: The other side of the study of deviance. *Social Policy, 18*(2), 34–39.

Groce, N. (1985). *Everyone here spoke sign language.* Cambridge, MA: Harvard University Press.

Hagner, D. (1989). *The social integration of supported employees: A qualitative study.* Syracuse, NY: The Center on Human Policy.

Hagner, D. (1992). The social interactions and job supports of supported employees. In J. Nisbet (Ed.), *Natural supports in school, at work, and in the community for people with severe disabilities* (pp. 217–239). Baltimore: Paul H. Brookes Publishing Co.

Hagner, D., Cotton, P., Goodall, S., & Nisbet, J. (1992). The perspectives of supportive coworkers: Nothing special. In J. Nisbet (Ed.), *Natural supports in school, at work, and in the community for people with severe disabilities* (pp. 241–256). Baltimore: Paul H. Brookes Publishing Co.

Hagner, D., Rogan, P., & Murphy, S. (1992). Facilitating natural supports in the workplace: Strategies for support consultants. *Journal of Rehabilitation, 58*(1), 29–34.

Lutfiyya, Z.M. (1990). *Affectionate bonds: What we can learn by listening to friends.* Syracuse, NY: The Center on Human Policy.

Lutfiyya, Z.M. (Ed.). (1991). *Personal relationships and social networks: Facilitating the participation of individuals with disabilities in community life.* Syracuse, NY: The Center on Human Policy.

O'Brien, J., & Lyle O'Brien, C. (1992). Members of each other: Perspectives on social support for people with severe disabilities. In J. Nisbet (Ed.), *Natural supports in school, at work, and in the community for people with severe disabilities* (pp. 17–63). Baltimore: Paul H. Brookes Publishing Co.

Taylor, S.J., & Bogdan, R. (1989). On accepting relationships between people with mental retardation and nondisabled people: Towards an understanding of acceptance. *Disability, Handicap & Society, 4*(1), 21–36.

Traustadottir, R. (1991, August). *Supports for community living: A case study.* Syracuse, NY: The Center on Human Policy.

Walker, P., & Edinger, B. (1988). The kid from Cabin 17. *Camping Magazine,* May 18–21.

9

Singing for an Inclusive Society

The Community Choir

Compiled and Introduced by Robert Bogdan

INTRODUCTION

There is a movement afoot to change the fact that all too often human services agencies dominate the lives of people with developmental disabilities. Typically, integration is something professionals and staff do for "clients." However, there are many places in the community other than human services facilities where people who have been labeled developmentally disabled spend time. In such places, individuals with disabilities may be there not because of the intervention and support of human services workers but as a result of natural or ordinary social process. In such places people with developmental disabilities are included by ordinary people who are involved in their lives. Often such inclusion and acceptance is taken for granted rather than considered to be a special accomplishment. We, the research team at The Center on Human Policy, call these places *natural environments.*

Our team is studying natural environments in order to better understand inclusion and acceptance (Bogdan & Taylor, 1987; Taylor & Bogdan, 1989) of individuals with developmental disabilities. Sites become known to us serendipitously; we come across them in our daily lives, someone tells us about one, or a site becomes evident through our other studies of community integration (Lutfiyya, 1991; Taylor, Bogdan, & Racino, 1991). We have visited restaurants, bakeries, recre-

A version of this chapter appeared previously in Bogdan, R. (1992). The community choir: Singing for an inclusive society. *TASH Newsletter, 18*(4), 11; *18*(5), 14–15; *18*(6), 6.

ational centers, and so forth in urban neighborhoods and small towns, in order to observe and talk to people who are in a position to make these environments naturally inclusive. Occasionally we encounter someone who plays a particularly important role in creating and maintaining a natural environment with an atmosphere that is supportive of integration. We have met thoughtful citizens who have valuable insights about how community integration comes about. This chapter presents the edited tape-recorded transcripts from a series of interviews I conducted with such a person, Karen Mihalyi, who is director of the Syracuse Community Choir.

The Community Choir is a singing group that Karen founded in 1985. It counts among its 70 members a wide spectrum of people, including a few labeled severely developmentally disabled. Karen and many of the choir members live in a section of Syracuse known as the Westcott Street area. The choir also practices and finds many of its strongest supporters there. In the 1960s and 1970s, that section of the city first became known as the Westcott Nation; "Nation" designated that the people who lived there were a different breed—a generation not tied to middle-class conventions and aspirations. On the outskirts of Syracuse University, this section of the city has maintained that reputation and some of that character. It has always been racially, culturally, and ethnically diverse. African Americans, international students, old timers, graduate students and their children, people who attended the university but never quite finished or left, artists and intellectuals, lesbians and gays, and others live there in relative harmony. There you will find a new-age shop, a women's center, a used book store, a framing shop, a movie theater that shows recent films for $2, an incompletely stocked small-chain supermarket, a Middle Eastern deli, an Ethiopian restaurant, three pizzerias, a vintage clothing store, a laundromat, a mom-and-pop Greek fast food store, a bakery, a food co-op, and a bar.

Karen is 40 years old and has lived in the Westcott area for almost 20 years. She has spent those years working on projects aimed at increasing peace and justice in the world. She lives what might be called an alternative lifestyle, in the sense that she has never been employed full time in a regular job but rather has been active in political organizing and community building. She earns her living through a variety of activities including feminist counseling, conducting workshops, and consulting. She is paid the token amount of $50 per week for serving as the choir's director. She lives simply. She owns a small house that she shares with two other people and drives a 1983 Honda. Karen is vibrant with enthusiasm and commitment.

KAREN'S OWN WORDS

The choir started in 1985. It is an outgrowth of many themes in my life. Before it began I went to Nicaragua. I had been working in the women's movement almost full time for over 10 years. In Nicaragua we attended incredible meetings where I saw people, everyday people, all kinds of people doing theater and music. They really made an effort to have something for everybody, not just the "talented" or the young or the old or the rich. Organizers were going back to these tiny towns and creating theaters, poetry workshops, and dance. I sensed what an incredible process it is to create something this way. I believe the world is for everyone. We need to make a place for everyone. That is what I have tried to create with the choir.

I decided to do a choir with no tryouts. Everybody, no matter what, would have a place in the choir. There is a place for everyone in the world. That was really the idea, that the world is for all of us. I also wanted to create good music—progressive pieces that talked about real people's stories, and struggles for liberation—music you don't get a chance to hear much on the local radio.

It was in January of that year when I got back from Nicaragua that I thought, "That's what I'm going to do." It just came to me. There was a peace event—a rally and parade—planned, and someone had asked if there could be singing. I started asking people. I'd had some contact with disability issues. I worked for the College for Living (a program located at the local community college that offers classes and other activities for people who have been labeled developmentally disabled) and did women's groups at DASH (a local advocacy, re-source, and service agency for people with disabilities). But when I thought about the choir I didn't think about consciously recruiting people with disabilities.

I contacted someone I knew who used a wheelchair, Molly, and I asked her if she wanted to be a part of the choir. I drove over with her to the park where we were to sing to see if the site was accessible. She drove me on her battery-driven vehicle, which was like a golf cart. I re-member what a different view of the world I got being taken by her. The site wasn't accessible. We tried to do something about that. At first, the choir consisted mostly of my friends and those whom we had found by word of mouth. Then I purposely recruited for diversity.

I don't really screen people, but I intentionally seek out kinds of people who might not be represented well in the choir. I'll ask people, Would you like to join? I mean, I'll ask anybody, but I give more atten-tion to people who aren't white and able-bodied.

We started to rehearse for another concert, an alternative Fourth of July celebration. We held the celebration in the Baptist church, which was not accessible. At that point I wasn't as aware of accessibility as I am now, and Molly didn't push it. We said, "Okay, we'll just carry Molly up the steps." It was a beautiful concert in the main hall. Downstairs we had booths, all kinds of peace booths—like a fair. It was packed with people; 350–400 people came. Then we decided to continue.

We had some mailings that I organized. I had a committee of people, but I am the one who got it started. We did a lot of recruiting, put out notices everywhere: "This is a choir for everyone. You can say you don't know how to sing, but try out. There is a place for you in the choir."

I had some background thinking about inclusion. The women's movement more than any other movement that grew out of the 1960s began to address the issues of inclusiveness. It was painful. People were confronted by each other: by the whiteness of the movement, by its middle classness, by the lack of sisters who were disabled. The movement inspired my intention to do something about class, race, disability, gender, and homophobia issues.

My relationships with people with disabilities goes way back. When I was in the ninth grade I was hired to be a summer baby sitter for a family up in Old Forge. The son, who was 3 at the time, had cerebral palsy and was blind and legally deaf. I had brothers and sisters, so I knew a lot about kids. His parents were treating him like he wasn't normal, and I didn't think that was right. I remember saying to them, "If he is going to have a tantrum, and you are going to pick him up all the time, he will just keep doing it." He couldn't talk, but I remember I played my guitar and he would put his teeth on it and feel the vibrations. He could hear with his teeth. I was so young but so clear about him. What a gift that experience was for me.

I grew up in a very small community in upstate New York. My grandmother was a teacher in the same school at which my parents taught. Our family was very egalitarian. I had great parents. They taught us that every person is okay. Everybody in the town was connected. A number of town people would be considered developmentally disabled today. One of them was Ernie. He was in our church, and he rang the church bell. I can see my father standing in front of church shaking hands with Ernie. The other person was a really good friend, Christine. She was considered to be retarded. Up until the eighth grade we were all in the same beautiful school, and she was in my class. There were only 20 or so kids per grade. I loved it, that sense of community. In our town, it was clear that you took care of each other.

Christine couldn't read, but we dismissed that. We were just with her. I remember going to her house, her coming to my house, and hanging out at the school and laughing and playing together. Then when we went to the consolidated high school, there was a special class; she was put there. I hardly ever saw her after that. That's very painful. I knew then that special classes separated people who ought to be together.

There was an African American man who moved to our town and was my music teacher. He and my grandmother really taught me everything I know about music. I adored him. My parents invited him to our house. He left town and I remember he and my father saying good bye. They hugged and there were tears in their eyes. I learned from my father by example. My dad just loved Mr. Thomas. I realized only recently where my intolerance for racism comes from. I thank these two men, Mr. Thomas and my father, for teaching me so well.

We lived in a small town, but I was very political. It was a very political time. I started Syracuse University but got too involved in antiwar protests and working with poor people. I just didn't know what I was doing in school. I went back to school to study social work. I was organizing for welfare rights on the west side of Syracuse and becoming increasingly involved in that community.

I moved in over here by the University to the Westcott area. We started the Women's Center, and I was involved in that and other things until about 1982. During this time, a group of us were living collectively. We are still together, live in the same area, and are close friends.

Somewhere along here I met Holly Near, a well-known folk singer and writer. She stayed at the house a lot and I was part of the production team for her concerts. I always wanted to do music and drama but felt that wasn't important. I thought I should do political work or social change work—i.e., organizing. She felt that the movement needed music, and that music was an important part of social change. It was about creating or shaping culture for peace and justice.

There is one Holly Near song in particular that touches the spirit of community of which I am part: "It Could Have Been Me." There is one verse about a student shot at Kent State and another about a Vietnamese farmer who was killed. It moved me a lot. She gave our generation energy. I use a lot of Holly's songs in the choir to sustain me and give focus to issues. I remember her singing at a rally we had. She sang a song about a 70-year-old woman with dignity. There was a verse about a woman in a wheelchair and another about a woman signing. It was Holly who started doing interpretation at concerts to reach the deaf community. Susan Fruenlich was her interpreter. All Community Choir concerts are signed.

When I was active in the Women's Center I also started working at DASH. They called me because they knew my work and wanted a leader for a women's group. I had to pick through my own stuff and straighten myself out about disability. We all have problems around it, such as not slowing down enough to listen to a person or not letting people finish sentences. I try to be very sensitive to the fears of women with disabilities. More ought to be done around issues of sexual abuse and rape. Sexual abuse and rape is part of so many of the experiences of those people. In the groups that I led at DASH, so many of the women were abused.

When we had the first blind people in the choir, I asked members who could see to help with the words. Then I read something that had been written by a woman who was blind. She pointed out that every place she went in the seeing world there was never braille. At that moment I decided that every number we do would also be offered in braille. People in the community volunteered to do it. Recently we applied for a grant to get a computer brailler so we can do it easier.

The choir is a hodgepodge. There is a high percentage of people with disabilities, many of whom have hidden disabilities, and some of whom have been institutionalized in psychiatric hospitals. There are children and a few older people, but these groups are underrepresented. There are Native Americans, African Americans, Hispanics, European Americans, lesbians, gays, poor people, rich people—you name it.

We did quite a few concerts last year. There was one for Jowonio (an integrated preschool) and another one for the Onondaga Indian Nation. There was the tea in January. And for African American history month we did a show. We did the tea to raise money. It was fun. It was a real tea with china cups. We did an International Women's Day concert; we sang at an AIDS Survivors benefit; we sang at a Peace Child celebration; we sang at Earth Day and then at the Imagination Celebration. What else? We sang once, sometimes twice a month. We charge for some but a lot are free. At some concerts we charge $3–$10 at the door on a sliding scale. That is what we charge at the winter solstice concert. At that concert we make a particular effort to represent different religions and cultural groups equally, such as Native Americans, Jews, and Africans. It is not your typical Christmas show.

One day shortly after the choir had begun, we were at rehearsal and there arrived a bus load of individuals from a group home for people with mental retardation. One of them was Margaret and one was Rhea Meyers, both of whom are still in the choir and are very valued members. But when I saw the group I just freaked. I said, "This is going to be too much for me." We started receiving calls from group homes: "Well, we hear you've got a place to drop our people off for an activity." One person in the choir who had experience in group homes said: "No, this is not going to be a dumping place." But it is hard to walk the fine line between being open and being able to say no. People have to really want to sing to be in the choir. Margaret has cerebral palsy, is blind, has been labeled retarded, and can't talk very clearly. She sings and is welcome. A number of people who have been in the choir since the beginning are from group homes.

Let me tell you about Margaret. She is 48 years old, and she lives in a group home and sings tenor. She was institutionalized for many years in a developmental center. I think she is considered to have severe mental retardation. I don't even know labels. I don't want to know them. She came to makeup rehearsal and sat at the piano. We were singing a song that had Spanish in it, and she knew every single word in the song. She said, "I learned." This was a very difficult song and she sang totally on key. Jane, who does a lot of work with HELP (an agency that operates community housing for people with disabilities), says that Margaret's vocabulary has really improved as a direct result of her being in the choir.

The reality is that Margaret gets very little attention from anybody outside of the choir. When she comes to choir, she gets attention and you can see her grow. The work she does all day at the sheltered workshop is tedious; in contrast, the choir is her lifeline. But that is true for other people in the choir as well, and not all of them are labeled.

It has been difficult, there is no question about it. For a while, the tenor section included three people who needed a lot of attention. When Margaret sings her face lights up with joy. She is very much loved. She knows people. She greets them and they are friendly to her. She's affectionate and loving, and she has grown a lot in the choir. Some people are close to Margaret, but she needs a lot of attention, which is not always available. She has to go to the bathroom. She has her period. It means that the tenors, the people around her, have to take that responsibility. I really want to talk about it, because many people in the tenor section need a lot of attention. A number of people dropped out because of that last year. They couldn't deal with coming to the choir wanting to sing and having to take care of someone's toilet and other problems. They didn't feel joyful. It felt like a burden. I don't want anybody with a disability to feel like or be considered a burden. That is the crux of oppression.

It was very hard to understand her last night. We were doing appreciations (when members of the choir say supportive things to other members). I told them that I was going to take a break from the choir. People were saying all these great things about choir and Margaret started talking. No one could understand her. And then she said, "I'll miss you." Margaret is a very important part of the choir.

One of our most difficult problems has been the issue of transportation for people with disabilities. So we made a decision. We were going to provide transportation for people who couldn't obtain their own. That meant that if you joined the choir you were required to pick up people, some of whom had wheelchairs. Some of the wheelchairs were very heavy and dragging them into a car took a long time. Some individuals got burned out and left the choir because they couldn't deal with all of that. So this year we tried to get Call-A-Bus (public bus service that comes to the door and is wheelchair-accessible) to at least give us one sure way. Now Margaret and Rhea have staff from their group homes bring them. It is really difficult to work out these problems with no money and no staff and still have people love each other. It is very hard.

This choir is not concerned about musical perfection, but we need to have enough people who are musical to be good. I don't worry that the choir's quality is compromised by the inclusion of people with disabilities. Some people have asked, "What if you had too many disabled people in the choir?" I don't think that could ever be a problem. Singing doesn't have anything to do with disability. I have been worried about having so many people who need attention that we won't be able to do music together. I do worry if I don't have enough good singers. Some good singers have disabilities; some don't. We have people who are "singing-disabled" in the choir. I have given some of them singing lessons to help them along.

We are trying to create community and make music too. The choir is about singing and it is about community. The two things go together. By being together and creating a sense of doing something together community begins to form. It is also what the audience feels when it is with us—community. We do a lot of community building in our concerts. Singalongs and other stuff. We sing about oppression. One thing I was thinking about was how to do more of that with people with disabilities. We can't single out people because of their disabilities. You think about them too much and they wind up being clients.

We had a party after rehearsal last night. It was a great party for hugging and talking. There were blind people, people in wheelchairs, African Americans, old and young people, and so forth. Rhea and Margaret were shaking hands with everybody at the end of the evening. It is wonderful. It is my dream come true. That is what I believe, and that's what people see when they see the choir. People ask, "Can Margaret really sing?" I say, "Yeah. One of the best." It is really worth it. This idea of inclusion is certainly beautiful. As I stood in front of the choir last rehearsal and looked for a while at the people there, I just wept. This is my family.

There are great stories in this choir. One time one of the basses was involuntarily committed to the psychiatric center. A bunch of us went to see him every day. Even sang a little. He was so pleased. Last night a member with cancer stood up and said she was undergoing chemotherapy. She wanted people to know this, and she talked about what it was going to be like and what she needed. We care for each other. Every time Diane Murphy, a professor of social work, sees the choir, she tells me I am the best social worker she knows. Carol Green is an African American woman who has cerebral palsy and also doesn't hear very well. She has incredible energy. There are several people in the choir with whom she has become close. She has been invited by choir members for dinner a number of times. She and a certain woman go out regularly, which has been wonderful for both of them.

Integration can be confusing and disruptive. It doesn't always work to just plop people together. People have a lot of issues that come up. We did a workshop on disability last spring. People without disabilities went upstairs and those with disabilities stayed downstairs. The group without disabilities answered this question: "What is hard about being with people with disabilities?" Someone started by saying, "I'm afraid I'm going to be asked to do more than I can." Another said, "I can't figure out what they are thinking." People laughed. They got to say things that they had been too embarrassed to say before the fuller audience, like "I am scared of Margaret." Then they talked about what they appreciate about people with disabilities. Downstairs the people with disabilities talked about the kinds of things they hated. One person said, "I never want to hear again from another person, 'oh my brother was crippled, so I know what it is like.'" Then the two groups came together and talked. That was very powerful; people really felt connected. We need to do such activities around racism and homophobia too. We need to deal with how to create community. The people with disabilities wanted us to do it again.

There hasn't been as much personal mixing between the people with disabilities and those without as I would have hoped for. Isolation is still a problem. When there is a break from practice people get up and socialize, but not everyone is included. There is some tendency for people with disabilities to be left out. We have talked about it. People are more aware, but harping on it makes them self-conscious.

Our philosophy is that we only give our concerts in a place where all members of the choir will feel comfortable. If you are a person of color and are in the choir, and you go to a place to sing and see nothing but white middle-class faces, you might not feel right. With disability we started to think about accessibility. We wanted to use sites that would be as accessible as possible. We could not be strict because there are very few sites that have accessible bathrooms and accessible performing areas. We find it too difficult to do our concerts in places that are not accessible. They can't move from their chair onto the toilet. We have done such things as use portable potties. We were asked to do a concert up at Clayton at the old opera house. It was a really big deal, but the opera house was totally inaccessible. We made a decision as a choir to do it anyway, but they provided makeshift ramps to get up on the beautiful old opera house stage. There were no bathrooms so we had to make a little room furnished with portable potties. It was awful, but we did it. I don't know if we would do it again. It would be a decision the choir would make—if the people with disabilities wanted to do it.

We sang at Central City Psychiatric Hospital. They asked us to sing at a coffee house there. I wouldn't do it again. There were a number of people in our choir who had been institutionalized at Central and had hated the experience. Performing there now was awful for them and for the rest of us too. Singing there just perpetuates the system. It pretends to be community-oriented but isn't. They have this beautiful auditorium; it is free; it is accessible. I don't want to keep promoting this idea that Central is a community-based facility. The coffee house was just very strange. Practically the only people who came were the aides and the therapists. We don't want to support institutions like that.

There is one person in the choir, Mildred, who has cerebral palsy who is a solid member of the choir. She is there all the time. She is in a wheelchair and has difficulty moving. Mildred has an aide who goes home at 8:30 in the evening. However, sometimes choir practice goes until 10 or 10:30. There is trouble with the Call-A-Bus service at that time of night. Mildred has trouble undressing without her aide when she gets home. Yet she is so determined to be in the choir. She is on the board; her number is the number to call for information. What has been happening is that certain people who take her home also undress her and help her get to the toilet and to bed, which takes about 40 minutes. So you know if I take her home I am done at 9:45 and by the time I get back it is almost 11:30. I'm exhausted. I try to feel joyful about it. It's hard. I try to think how she must feel. The transportation and the aide problem is so huge, but we have to respond or we would lose a person we want there, someone who is loyal and a good singer.

Disability—it's difficult at first when you are not familiar with a group you have a stereotype about. If you are not used to relating to a person with disabilities, you are not sure how to. You don't want to make a mistake or do something to offend the person. So you hold back. Now I dive right in and hope it is understood that I am trying my hardest. I am really losing my self-consciousness around people with disabilities. At first I think I mostly listened. I listened to people and read some—mainly by people who had disabilities. But my ease mostly came by getting close with people, hearing their stories, and loving them.

We had a guy named Ned in the choir who had multiple sclerosis. He was in a wheelchair. Before one concert I remember seeing Josh Cameron, who was about 6 at the time, leaning on Ned's chair talking. It was so natural. I looked over and I thought, "Well Josh, disability won't be a problem for you." They hardly knew each other. That was a very powerful moment for me. Actually I have had a lot of those moments with the choir. I often get goosebumps when we are giving a concert and the audience is hearing our message. It even happens at rehearsal. I hope it is empowering to those who hear us. It is empowering to me and to the other members of the choir.

When the choir began, I started to see the possibility of what participation might do for members. Most important, people would become more relaxed around those who were different. There would be arguments between people, because that is a natural part of friendship. Sometimes it is difficult to let friendships develop naturally. It's hard because sometimes the person without the disability is patronizing, patting the other on the head and so forth. Also, it is difficult for people with disabilities not to project at me the anger they have at the world for the way they are treated. One disabled person made me a tape complaining about how I was treating her. She is blind. In the tape she said I wasn't sensitive to people with disabilities. I hadn't worked hard enough on the transportation. I didn't answer the tape for a long time. For her it was really important. She was angry because I tried to talk to her about her taking some responsibility for her own needs, not waiting for someone else to do it. Arranging for her own transport. In a way it is really a great thing that this woman sent me that tape, but it was hard for me. I just couldn't hear it. I work so hard to make it right for everybody, it's hard to field the complaints. That is one of the things that gets to me.

The conflicts we have in the choir often center around diversity, which is good. Some people with disability were scared because we had been asked by the Gay Alliance to sing at a rally. So we had a meeting to talk about it. Our piano player, Andy, who is blind, said he didn't want to go. He said, "I don't want to be seen there; somebody might think I'm queer." Some very eloquent people talked about what it was like for them to be gay or lesbian. Of course, people thought that everyone knew that there were people with diverse sexual preferences in the choir. Andy came back and made a speech. He said, "I've been thinking about this. As a blind person I always feel left out. I think this world should be okay for everybody. I decided I'm going to play. I don't know much about gay and lesbian people, but I guess I will find out." It was a great speech.

I read about Jews who survived in northern Europe during the war. Almost all of the Jews who survived knew non-Jews. They had allies. They had friends, and when you are friends with a Jew you are not going to let him or her be killed. If we stay isolated, we don't build allies, don't know people who are different from ourselves, don't love them, can't think about them as family. Having relationships with people is what makes community work. What happened to me is that I had experiences that helped me to understand the power of inclusion. I am trying to create an opportunity for that to happen to others, both people in the choir and those in the audience.

I am no longer living in a collective, although our collective family feels very close. We feel connected to each other and the community around us. I want to live in a community where people care for each other. I want there to be a sense of caring for each other, like our little town in Glenfield, my roots, where I grew up. I want to know people from the time they are born until they die. I want to be around to see kids grow up, to have lifelong relationships with people in which we evolve and help each other. I have that. Some of these people I have known for the last 22 years. I have been at births and have sung at Toni Tavarone's, Lillian Reiner's, and Dan Rubenstein's funerals. (These were people from the community who were proactive for peace and justice issues.)

People look at the choir and they say it's because of Karen, because she is unusual. It is not true that people can't do what I do. I don't want it to be, "Karen does all these great things"; I want it to be other people too. Yeah, Karen's amazing but so are you and so is Margaret and so is everybody. How do we as teachers, as facilitators, as leaders, as friends, create those spaces to allow people to do what is in them to do? I have found my space.

After about 23 years of creating community, I need a little break. I have decided to take a 6-month leave from the choir. I am burned out to a level I have never felt before. I know the sense of the community that we have created will go on whether the choir continues or not. I know that community was created with diversity. I felt it. I watched how people with disabilities, whites, African Americans, Native Americans, old people, young people, lesbians, gays, heterosexuals, working class people, and more were all brought together to sing. I needed to know because I needed to end this chapter of the choir with a feeling that it happened. I am totally in love with the choir. I can't stop thinking about them. But something has to change. I hope that in the next 6 months there will be enough people to take over some of the jobs, so that I feel supported and that there are other people who are thinking about the choir enough to make it work. We are having a community meeting in March to talk about it. We are putting it to the community to consider what we need to do to keep the choir. I don't think the choir is going to fold.

CONCLUSION

People get involved in the lives of people with developmental disabilities by different routes. Perhaps the most common avenues are via family ties and human services connections, but, as Karen's story suggests, the range of paths is much broader than we generally realize. There are belief systems and lifestyles in the community that are compatible with the inclusion of people with developmental disabilities. Not only can people with developmental disabilities be included in a community choir, but, as our research reveals, they can and do become part of churches, work groups, neighborhoods, small towns, and recreational clubs. This involvement can come about naturally. Through their contacts with ordinary people in natural settings, individuals with developmental disabilities can be part of the community. We need to learn from those who are involved in such efforts how it is accomplished and what obstacles they face so we might be their allies.

Karen's advocacy for people with developmental disabilities has its roots in her early experiences in a small town in rural New York, but it has come to fruition through her lifelong commitment to seeking equality for people of color, the poor, women, gays, lesbians, and those with alternative lifestyles. Her decision to include people with developmental disabilities in the choir was compatible with her larger understanding of the inclusive society she wants to live in and work toward. Seldom do people in the field of disabilities manifest a richer embodiment of the struggles in which they are involved. Especially now, with the heightened interest in diversity and multiculturalism, people working in fields related to disability need to build coalitions with others who are working to abate prejudice and discrimination in other arenas and learn to see their work as part of a larger effort of building a just, appreciative, and accepting society for all people.

The sharing of Karen's thoughts and experiences with you is not to suggest that her political and social orientation is the only one compatible with the natural inclusion of people with developmental disabilities in the community. Although some will find her approach to life compelling, as she advises, everyone need not be like Karen. We have met other people who are just as articulate and just as dedicated to inclusion as Karen but with very different values and politics (e.g., a conservative business owner). As there is room for everyone in the choir, there is a place for everyone in working toward the natural acceptance of people with disabilities into our communities.

As Karen's words reveal, there can be great joy in inclusion and working toward diversity. We need more people to speak out about the personal side of relationships with people with developmental disabilities. We need to share what it feels like to enjoy the companionship of others and the sense of community that can be created around mutual commitment. Karen also points out the difficulties and the pain involved. As with all meaningful relationships, relationships involving people with disabilities take work and commitment. To have people with developmental disabilities involved in relationships helps them immensely. But Karen does not include people with disabilities in the choir to help them. She includes them for herself, for her own joy. She wants to make music, and they want to sing.

REFERENCES

Bogdan, R., & Taylor, S.J. (1987). Toward a sociology of acceptance: The other side of the study of deviance. *Social Policy, 18*(2), 34–39.

Lutfiyya, Z. (1991). *Personal relationships and social networks.* Syracuse, NY: The Center on Human Policy.

Taylor, S.J., & Bogdan, R. (1989). On accepting relations between people with mental retardation and nondisabled people. *Disability, Handicap & Society, 4*(1).

Taylor, S.J., Bogdan, R., & Racino, J. (Eds.). (1991). *Life in the community: Case studies of organizations supporting people with disabilities.* Baltimore: Paul H. Brookes Publishing Co.

10

"My Heart Chose Freedom"

The Story of Lucy Rider's
Second Life

Bonnie Shoultz

INTRODUCTION

Lucy Rider is a 43-year-old woman who lives alone in an apartment in East Salt City, a town not far from Salt City. She has her own furniture, including a television set and a VCR, and a cat. Her walls are decorated with her own drawings and paintings as well as with artwork that other people have given her. She works 3 hours a day, 4 days a week, as a hostess in a fast food restaurant, where she greets customers, brings them refills on their drinks and other items, and cleans the tables. She has many friends, including a man named Jim who helps her with transportation and payment of bills, and is close to her mother, who lives in Salt City. For a number of years she has supported an international foster child through the Save the Children Foundation, even when she has had little for herself. Lucy is a friendly, outgoing, trusting woman who has been on her own for less than 2 years. She has made friends in her apartment building, at church, and among members of the lesbian and gay communities in Salt City.

I met Lucy in 1987 at a gay pride workshop entitled "Being Gay and Disabled." Roy, a gay man whom Lucy had met through her family's retail business, organized the workshop and asked me to attend because he hoped that I, as a lesbian working in the disability field, could contribute to the discussion. At least partly because I had not been "out" for a long time myself, the issues the workshop participants presented were new to me. Isolation was a main topic of discussion. The participants said that because they were typically dependent on heterosexual, or "straight," people—boarding home operators, home health aides, agency staff members, parents, and other family members—for their survival, it was difficult to be open about their sexual preference. They feared rejection, withdrawal of support, eviction from a residence or boarding home, or active attempts to coerce them to change their sexuality (through psychiatric hospitalization, for example). One man, who had been open with some of his home health aides, found that information about his sexual orientation had been placed in agency records and shared with new people who came to work with him. Even though his support was not withdrawn, he felt that his privacy had been invaded, and he worried about whether the quality of care he received would be affected.

The other type of isolation participants discussed was that from gay people without disabilities, whom they perceived as unaccepting of those with disabilities, especially as lovers, and who often did not understand the special transportation and support issues involved. The participants found this isolation to be especially painful because the gay community, especially the lesbian community, viewed itself as valuing inclusiveness and accommodation. However, these men and women felt that they could not easily develop relationships within that community (see Corbett, 1994, for further discussion on this issue). They had difficulty traveling to events, making friends, and dating. They were rarely involved in the "inner spaces" of the community, such as parties in private homes, brunches, and small working groups dealing with specific social or political issues. The church serving gay men and lesbians was an exception. Lucy, for example, was a regular attendee at the church, thanks to Roy's willingness to drive her there and back each week. A few other church members had disabilities as well.

Lucy had been invited to this workshop by Roy, and she told her story of extreme loneliness and isolation. She said she spent most of each day alone or with her mother and sister and only left the house to go to church and work. In the 16 years since her accident, she had met only a few other gay people, and none had stayed in her life except Roy. She had no lesbian friends. I became interested in befriending her, and when I invited her out she accepted. We spent our time together for the first few months just getting to know each other. We often went out for lunch or dinner, to concerts, and to the women's bar. As time went on, she and I became friends, and we have attended some community events together. On other occasions, I've seen and spent time with her at events I have attended with my partner.

In 1991 I asked her if she would like to write about herself. She agreed enthusiastically and over the next few months produced a 52-page autobiography that we edited together. In 1992 I asked if she would let me write about her. I explained that I would take extensive notes every time I talked to or was with her and that this would be a research study. After she agreed, I compiled field notes for 6 months, during which I saw or spoke with her at least twice a week. Most of this chapter is based on the data collected during this period, from July through December 1992, and on the autobiography she wrote earlier.

Doing research with and about a friend is a sensitive task. As a friend, I tend to take Lucy's point of view rather than analyze it or to take my own point of view when what she does affects me. Also, I care about her and do not want to write anything that might hurt or upset her. Our friendship has changed both of our lives. It changed Lucy's life in dramatic ways, even while I was doing research with her. Therefore, writing about Lucy necessarily means writing about myself, as I have been both participant and observer. Finally, I am aware, as she is, of how much she could lose if her story were to be misused or misconstrued. Nevertheless, we decided to proceed and to read and revise the material together upon its completion. Lucy gave her approval but likes her autobiography far better.

This chapter focuses on lesbian identity, family relationships, religious faith, isolation and confinement, abuse and control, friendship, and angels, because these are the important themes in Lucy's life. The discussion tends to be more thematic than chronological. For clarity, I have included a chronological chart (Figure 1) of Lucy's history.

AFTER THE INJURY: LIFE CONFINED

Lucy Rider was severely injured in a car accident in 1971, when she was 18 years old. She was told that a rod had penetrated her brain and that she had been in a coma for several months before awakening in the hospital. When she regained consciousness, she had permanently lost all memory of her life before the accident or of anything she had known before. Eating, talking, using the bathroom, and walking were among the skills she had to relearn. She says that she was "like a baby" when she came out of the coma—except that it was like being born into the body of an adult woman.

Lucy's injury and the hospitalizations that followed altered her life in many ways. The injury left her with a large depression in her skull in addition to some permanent disabilities, including problems with short-term memory, word finding, and spelling. She has paralysis on her right side; her hand is curled, her arm hangs at her side, and she

Lucy Rider's Life History

1952 **Born**

1971 **Accident/Closed Head Injury**

1971–1973 **Hospitals and Rehabilitation Center**
Rediscovers a loving family
Discovers sexual preference
Creates Miriam, her angel
Behavior leads to decision to institutionalize

1973–1974 **Admitted to State Psychiatric Facility**
"Worst Nightmare—Hell on Earth"

1974 **Goes Home with Family**

1974–1985 **Life Revolves around Grandmother**
Grandmother is best friend during the day
Miriam with her during the night
Works in grandmother's diner

1985 **Grandmother Dies**

1985–1987 **Life without Grandmother**
Suicide attempt, admission to psychiatric hospital
Short-lived relationship with a woman patient
Return home
Move to apartments above sister's store
Six months in adult basic skills classes
Attempts to connect with Christians
Aborted attempt to leave home and enter women's shelter

1987–1990 **Gays and Lesbians**
Met Roy, began going to church serving the gay/lesbian community
Attended Gay Pride workshop where we met
Started going out 1-2 times a month with me
Became acquainted with other lesbians
Attended some community events

1990 **Gave up Miriam**

1990–1991 **Sheila—First Lover**
Visiting Sheila, staying overnight
Going out into neighborhood with Sheila
Meeting Sheila's family and friends
Conflicts over being "out"
Breakup

1991–1992 **Freedom and Connections**
Family situation deteriorates
Lucy makes other lesbian friends—Joan and Sandy
Lucy enters shelter (May 1992)
Sheila & Lucy rent apartments (June 1992)
Intersecting support networks form around Lucy (June-Oct. 1992)
    Lucy's mother's ex-husband
    Sheila's family and friends
    Joan, Susan and I
    Services (VR, Protection & Advocacy, family support agency, Housing services)
Lucy "makes it" in her own place
Sheila moves; Lucy begins search for better place (November 1992)
Supported work agency begins to support Lucy in job search (December 1992)

1993 **Toward Independence**
Sheila finds Lucy a new apartment (January)
Lucy moves to East Salt City (February)
Lucy makes and learns from mistakes, with help
Lucy meets and plans with Carrie
Services slowly build around Lucy
Supported employment job
Medicaid waiver proposal and case manager
Home health aide for household work
Rent subsidy comes through
Miriam reappears

1994 **Lucy firmly established in her new life, planning for a good future**

Figure 1. Chronological outline of Lucy Rider's life.

cannot bend her right knee voluntarily, although she can walk with a limp. Because she sometimes has difficulty understanding what she is told or given to read, and because she often acts impulsively she needs support in making decisions and help in correcting mistakes.

When Lucy first awoke from her coma, she pulled out her catheter repeatedly. This damaged her urethra, and she never regained full control of her bladder. At some point during her hospitalizations all of her teeth were pulled, and she has never obtained dentures. Preferring toothlessness to the inconvenience of dentures, she has so far refused to consider the idea of using them. She learned to smoke cigarettes in the hospital, a habit she has not broken. Today she smokes two packs a day and has a chronic cough. She was a patient in two hospitals, then in a rehabilitation center, and was finally sent to a custodial psychiatric center because of "uncontrolled behaviors (explosive anger, sexually inappropriate behavior)," according to one psychiatrist's report.

Several very important themes in Lucy's life originated in the hospitals and the rehabilitation center. One was that she became aware very early that she had strong sexual feelings that were aroused when she looked at female, not male, nurses, custodians, attendants, and doctors. A second was that she learned that she had a family who loved her, especially her mother and grandmother. Third, she was reintroduced to Christianity and the Bible, at which time she was "born again into the Lord." Fourth, she created an imaginary "angel," Miriam, who visited her from heaven and has been her lover, on and off, for over 20 years. A fifth and overriding set of themes has to do with Lucy's strong and often expressed anger about the control and abuse she experienced after her car accident within confined settings from which she could not escape. The institutional experiences resulting from the accident represented both the beginning of Lucy's remembered life and the beginning of 21 years of confinement.

Lucy's Coming Out

Lucy "came out" as a lesbian years ago, after awakening in a hospital after the car accident. Although the literature on sexuality of people with developmental and other disabilities often includes general discussions of sexual orientation and a recognition that some people may be homosexual (Monat-Haller, 1992; Sobsey, Gray, Wells, Pyper, & Reimer-Heck, 1990), the discussion is typically presented from a heterosexual perspective and often focuses primarily on problems allegedly associated with homosexuality. It is particularly difficult to find research on particular lesbians or gay men with disabilities (but see Appleby, 1994). Nevertheless, this salient feature of a person's identity merits recognition. Lucy has embraced and expressed that identity, believing that anyone who seeks to understand her must know about and accept that aspect of who she is.

For a gay man or lesbian, coming out has many levels of meaning, all related to the assumption of a personal and social identity (Abbot & Love, 1972; Faderman, 1981; Klaich, 1974). According to one definition, "coming out is the process whereby a gay man or lesbian comes to accept a gay or lesbian identity as his or her own identity" (Dworkin & Gutierrez, 1992). In my experience, however, "coming out" is a blanket term that is used by gay men and lesbians in various ways. It can refer to the time when a person first realizes that he or she has a sexual/affectional preference for people of the same sex and that such feelings run counter to what is generally accepted in the society. These realizations may not occur simultaneously, but coming out to oneself does not really happen until one acknowledges both one's preference and society's rejection of it.

Coming out can also refer to the time when there is a first lesbian or gay relationship, which may or may not occur at the same time one comes out to himself or herself. Coming out to others occurs every time a person reveals his or her sexual orientation to another person, and it is usually done in an attempt to get closer to others and/or to reject the social pressure to stay "in the closet." Coming out also refers to the state and degree of openness about one's orientation. For example, one may say that he or she is "out to my family," "out at work," or "out" in general, or even publicly out to anyone and everyone who reads a newspaper, watches television news programs, or attends public events at which sexual orientation might be acknowledged.

A person can be in the closet to the world at large but out to the gay community, with a fair degree of assurance that the secret will be kept. One can even be out without knowing it, if acquaintances (usually heterosexual people, including well-meaning individuals who are not aware of the person's reasons for wanting to hide his or her sexual orientation) have spread the word behind his or her back. Coming out may happen just a few times in one's life (e.g., if one is closeted) or repeatedly, as one enters different social environments and wants different people to know. There are also different degrees of being in the closet. Some feel that the closet is an instrument of control by a society that wishes to maintain the prevailing relations of power (Heyward, 1989), in which any form of sexual orientation deviating from heterosexuality is treated as abnormal and is punished, ignored, or otherwise suppressed (Rich, 1983).

Lucy has experienced disapproval, acceptance, liberation, and love because of her lesbian identity. In the early years, disapproval and attempts to control or keep her from expressing that identity were most common. Lucy believes that she has always been a lesbian, and her belief was recently confirmed when she was told by a former class-mate that she was a lesbian before her accident. As long as I have known her, she has wanted to be very public about her identity, stating that she tried to be open about it from the time she became aware of her sexual feelings for women. Her coming out, however, was often a problem for the professionals whom she encountered, for church peo-ple, and for her family, who had difficulty accepting her lesbianism. As is true for most lesbians, she felt pressured to identify herself as hetero-sexual (Rich, 1983) or, if she couldn't do that, to keep her sexual orien-tation to herself.

Lucy's first memories are of her sexual feelings. In her autobiogra-phy, she writes:

> Now, I'm going to start with the things I remember of my new life. I woke up in the hospital 19 years ago. I was 18 years old, going on 19, and all I could think of was sex. All the patients were too old, but the nurses were hot stuff!

At this point, she had no name for these feelings and no awareness that a person is expected to be sexually oriented to the opposite sex. She soon learned that sexual behavior by patients was discouraged and that same-sex romance was strongly disapproved of. When she tried to kiss a female patient, a nurse told her, "What are you doing? Two ladies don't kiss. Only a girl and a boy can kiss."

However, she had strong urges and tried in many ways to act on them, unaware that there were strict social expectations that she was failing to meet and that her disability made her especially vulnerable to restrictive repercussions, such as placement in a psychiatric hospital. It was not uncommon at the time of Lucy's accident for young lesbians without disabilities to be hospitalized in an attempt to "treat" their ho-mosexuality (Faderman, 1981; Klaich, 1974). Lucy's disability meant that she was surrounded by professionals in settings where her behav-ior, although natural to her, would come under close scrutiny and could possibly result in her punishment and institutionalization. The psychiatrist's report cited earlier implies that this may have been a ma-jor reason for her admission to the psychiatric hospital.

Later, when she came out to her family, they told her, "You *can't* be a lesbian!" This was her first exposure to the label that refers to her sex-ual preference for women. Over the years and through many argu-ments, she was insistent about who she was, and she believes that her family has come to accept what she calls "my lesbian ways." In 1987, she met Roy at her family's store, where he came to shop for the spe-cialty items sold there. They came out to each other, he invited her to the gay community church, and her life began to change. He introduced her to other lesbians, and in 1990 she met Sheila, who became her lover. Her friendships with other lesbians finally led to her move away from her family home.

The Family Lucy Rediscovered

Lucy's family, people of whom she had no memory when she emerged from her coma, were factory workers, mechanics, and owners of small businesses that served the working class community of northern Salt City. Her devoted grandmother, along with her mother, worked to bring her home from the psychiatric institution where she was placed after the rehabilitation experience. Lucy's half-brothers and half-sister were living with her mother and grandmother in Salt City, and in the mid-1970s the family bought a house to which Lucy could come home. Her grandmother owned a small diner where Lucy's mother worked. She wrote about the years after coming home:

> My best friend during the day was my gramma. . . . On weekends, in the summertime, we would have cookouts in our backyard. Saturdays, me and gram would go shopping to get groceries. Still I had a hunger, not for food but in my soul. Yes, I had friends but they were hand-me-downs, gramma's friend first and momma's friend first, you know what I mean? It was a long time before I met someone who could tell me what friendship means, really means!

In 1985, Lucy's grandmother died of cancer; shortly after, Lucy tried to kill herself by ingesting a massive dose of aspirin. She was sent to a psychiatric hospital for a short time and then returned home to live with her mother and sister. When I met her in 1987, they were living above a store built and owned by her sister. Each person had her own apartment on the second floor and shared the shower and laundry room. Lucy's two-room apartment comprised a small bedroom, with an open toilet in the corner, and a small kitchen.

Lucy's family believed that she had no sense of direction and that if she fell she would not be able to get up by herself, so she was never allowed to leave the building by herself. She relied on family members and friends to take her places, but her mother had acquired severe physical disabilities and her sister was very busy with her business. Lucy rarely left the building except to visit the doctor or go out with a friend. I took her out once or twice a month, and Roy took her once a week to the church services. For the first 3 years of our friendship, those were virtually the only times she left home. For the rest of the time, she stayed in her apartment or joined her family downstairs for an hour or two on the business floor. She was very lonely.

Reborn into the Lord

Another important part of Lucy's identity is her strong and abiding Christian faith. She has found ways to resolve conflicts between her sexual and religious orientations despite the condemnation of homosexuality by many religious denominations. While Lucy was in the hospital, she was reintroduced to Christianity by her grandmother. She said in her autobiography:

> My gramma always talked about God, but I had no need for religion. Little did I know that my gramma planted a seed inside my heart.

Later, she said, a Christian volunteer came to the hospital and gave paperback Bibles to each patient. When she told her she could not read, the volunteer, using the Bible and other religious materials, taught her. She learned many passages of Scripture and quotes them in her writings. Several passages have special meaning to her. In the first years of our friendship, Lucy practiced her religious beliefs devoutly, saying prayers before meals and at other times of the day and quoting Scripture to me. She tried frequently to convince me to believe as she did, and we finally agreed to disagree about religion rather than lose our friendship.

Religious institutions have been problematic for Lucy, however. When a woman who had been a paid companion to Lucy invited her to church one day, Lucy enjoyed the experience and arranged to have the church bus pick her up for services regularly. She wrote:

> I kept quiet about my lesbian lifestyle. Then something in my heart said, "Tell the pastor you're gay." The next Sunday I told the pastor after service I would like to talk to him. I went in his office and sat down and told him I was a lesbian. He got up and in a loud voice said, "God doesn't love gays, get the hell out!" You know what? I did!

A year later she discovered a Christian radio station and began to telephone the station every day. One woman who talked to her regularly claimed to be a friend, even after Lucy told her about being a lesbian. However, the woman told her that being a lesbian was a sin, and they argued about it for weeks. Lucy wrote, "Finally, I broke! I lost my faith in what I believed in. I believed in her Lord, not mine." However, based on what Lucy was saying about her life at home, the woman helped her make plans to leave home and go instead to a shelter for abused women. Lucy's family found out about the plans from someone else at the station and removed the telephone from her room. (When I met Lucy, she was only allowed to use the telephone in the store, which closed at 6 P.M.) Lucy decided that she had made a serious mistake, and she came back to her belief in "her" Lord. This event also served to heighten her family's suspicion of people who became involved with Lucy. However, they still permitted her to go out with people she met later, such as Roy and me.

When she began to attend the services of the Metropolitan Community Church in Salt City with Roy, she felt as though she had come home. When he first invited her, she was suspicious. She wrote, "I said to myself, 'Oh god, not another one who is trying to change me.' But something inside of me said, 'Go for it! This time you might catch the bronze ring!'" This church teaches that the Bible does not forbid homosexuality and gives alternative interpretations for biblical passages that seem to condemn it. Lucy loved this church and felt that its message matched her own faith. Through this church, she met other gays and lesbians for the first time since her accident 15 years previously. Eventually she met the woman who would become her first "flesh-and-blood" lover.

"The Angel Beneath My Wings"

While Lucy was in the hospital, an "angel" came to her in response to her prayers for a true friend. This angel, Miriam, became her lover after a few weeks. Lucy explained it this way in her autobiography:

> You may think I was crazy to believe in an angel who falls in love with a human. Well, maybe I was, but it beats being alone and talking to yourself. It beats sleeping alone and it beats . . . masturbation.

Miriam has been with her on and off ever since. Many of the people in Lucy's life have resisted this idea. In my discussions with people, concern and pity were common responses to hearing about Miriam. However, those who have stayed close to her have come to accept Miriam as a part of Lucy's life.

Lucy described how her family reacted after she decided to tell them about her angel lover:

> We (Lucy and Miriam) waited until after supper to tell them. I told them and [. . .] they said, "Do you want people to think you are crazy?" I yelled, [. . .] "She is in my heart and nobody is going to take my angel out!"

Years later, Lucy's mother came to accept a limited amount of talk about Miriam. When she was still living at home, her family asked her not to talk about Miriam when she was downstairs in the store and Lucy tried to comply with that request. However, whenever she developed a new friendship, she told the friend about Miriam and asked for understanding.

Miriam was absent from Lucy's life during several periods, depending on what was occurring in the rest of her life. Three years after I met her, Lucy decided it was time to give Miriam up for good. She was still living at home but was feeling more a part of the world outside, and she concluded that if she wanted a flesh-and-blood woman to love she would have to stop spending her time with her angel. Her autobiography describes their leave-taking:

> I didn't want to say goodbye to my angel. But I knew it was time for me to grow up. I had to live life to its fullest. . . . I whispered, "Baby, you don't have to go," and she said, "Sweetheart, yes I do. Dear, it's time to grow up . . . it's time for you to wake up."

A month later she met and fell in love with Sheila.

During most of Lucy's life after her injury, she had been extremely lonely and isolated. Even though there always were people nearby, she felt alone. She yearned for friends who were lesbians and for a lover but knew no way to satisfy these longings. I believe that the hospital personnel, and later her family, viewed her disability as severe and primary to her identity. Thus, they kept her in confinement out of fear of the harm they imagined would come to her if she were set free. At the same time, they were unable or unwilling to help her enter into social environments where she would have felt less lonely. Her angel was her outlet and her escape. Unable to leave her physical surroundings and unable to spend her days with other lesbians, she created Miriam as an ideal being to love and talk to, to make love with and to dream with. With Miriam she could be everything she couldn't be in real life. The creation of Miriam may have saved her sanity and therefore may be interpreted as a healthy adaptation under the circumstances. Surely, it gave her the strength to endure the years in which she spent so much time alone.

Abuse, Control, and Anger

Lucy recounts many incidents that could now be labeled sexual and institutional abuse as well as others that related to her then lack of control over her own life. For example, she learned the difference between herself and a man, and about male sexuality, when a hospital janitor came into her room and asked her to fondle his genitals. She did not enjoy it but was curious, and she was surprised when he was fired because of what he had done. She also had several unwanted sexual encounters with men in the community, to which she agreed because she lacked experience and the knowledge that she could or should refuse. The abuse reinforced the lessons she was being taught, which was that her life was under the control of other people and that expressing her anger about that could result in further abuse, restriction, or isolation.

She described the state psychiatric facility to which she was admitted from the rehabilitation center as a "hell on earth." She wrote:

> It was a hospital for mental patients, criminals, and old people with mental problems. It was horrible! First, they checked me for lice. They spread my legs

apart and searched me and checked me for disease! Oh God, it hurt! They told me to take a shower and they left. I was heavy and handicapped. . . . I was afraid I would slip. I was bare except for my shoes. Then it was bedtime and they said, "Go to bed!" You know what? Instead of having a room for each bed, they had one big, large room for all the patients. I said, "Oh, my God!" There must have been 200 beds. The nurse said, "Pick one," and she shut the door.

Her grandmother visited her very often and was working to get her out of the facility, but Lucy was extremely unhappy. She wrote:

Miriam and Jesus Christ disappeared because I thought this was hell on earth! Oh God, let me tell you something, there were straightchairs. These were like highchairs that babies use. If you were bad, real bad, the nurses would take all of your clothes off and put you in the straightchair and put you in the closet.

Her grandmother came to take her home in 1974.

At home, Lucy was under the control of her family. As long as her grandmother was alive Lucy could accept that control, but living with just her mother and sister was more difficult. She was often angry with them and they with her. I often sensed that her anger made them even more reluctant to trust her or to give her the freedom she wanted. I also often worried that they would refuse to let her see me if I tried to intervene.

Experiences of abuse and control are common for people with disabilities (Morris, 1992), and anger is a common but frequently discounted response. Indeed, as I was writing this chapter, I realized that originally I had not named these as key issues but had framed my recounting of Lucy's story as though other issues had more importance. However, I came to see that control by others was a major thread running through the other themes, that abuse had to be acknowledged, and that Lucy often responded angrily when she encountered either. I believe that there is an interplay between these and other issues in her life; for example, it is very likely that people exerted even stronger control because she was a woman with disabilities who insisted on speaking of Miriam and of being a lesbian and that her anger both brought punishment and kept her from succumbing to loneliness and depression.

FRIENDSHIPS AND FREEDOM

Lucy's life began to change when she met Roy and me. Because of her mother's medical condition, Lucy was unable to leave the store without great difficulty, and more of the responsibility for Lucy was placed on Lucy's younger half-sister. This sister was expected to become Lucy's guardian when her mother died. Although her mother understood that Lucy needed to go out, she remembered the time Lucy was was almost taken to an abused women's shelter, and she was afraid. I tried to gain her mother's trust, but for several years I did little else to change Lucy's situation but be her friend.

The changes in Lucy's life accelerated after she met Sheila. Roy had introduced Sheila and another woman to Lucy, and Lucy followed up after learning that the two women were just friends. She called Sheila, who invited her to her apartment, and they became lovers that evening. Their romantic relationship lasted 3 years, on and off, and they are still friends. Sheila had known Lucy's mother for years, and Lucy's mother trusted Sheila. However, Sheila did not view herself as a lesbian and insisted that the nature of their relationship be kept secret from everyone except for a few gay men and lesbians. She and Lucy frequently argued over this, with Lucy asserting that she wanted the whole world to know the truth about their relationship and Sheila insisting that they hide it from Sheila's family and friends. Sheila always won these arguments, but Lucy was very unhappy about this. Finally, the two broke up over this issue.

In 1991, Lucy met Joan and Sandy, two lesbians who were to become important friends to her. With her mother's permission, I had helped Lucy to register for and get to Joan's community college course for women with disabilities, the first course Lucy had taken for years. Joan asked Lucy to cofacilitate the next session's course, and they became friends as they met to plan and teach the course. Lucy met Sandy, who frequently took her out to eat or shop, through her church.

Escape and a New Home

During that fall and the following winter, the conflicts between Lucy and another family member escalated. Joan, Sandy, and I often talked among ourselves about Lucy's situation, and, when Lucy began to beg us to help her move out, we agreed to do so. One morning in April, Joan, Sandy, and I took her to Adult Protective Services. After hearing her story, the intake worker agreed to help and placed her in a shelter temporarily. We called her family and told them she was safe, and, although they were very upset, her mother finally agreed that Lucy could go. She said to me, "As long as she calls me every day to let me know she is safe, I will trust you." Lucy was more than willing to make these calls and did so faithfully.

A few days later, I left town for a week. When I came back much had changed. The staff at the shelter had begun to help Lucy search for a place to live and apply for services through various agencies, and they were planning to teach her some basic community skills such as riding the bus. At the same time, her mother invited her to come back home, promising that things would be better. Lucy sought the advice of a shelter volunteer, who told her to pray about it. Lucy did pray, and, as she told me later, "My heart chose freedom. I decided I had to make a life for myself." She also said, "I thought Mama would be mad when I told her, but she said, 'Okay. I just want you to know that there is a place for you if you ever change your mind.' I was so surprised!"

Lucy had also called Sheila, who worried because the shelter was in a bad neighborhood. They renewed their romantic relationship, and Sheila convinced Lucy that they should rent two apartments in the same house in a neighborhood not far from Lucy's mother. I returned home after the security deposit had been paid and just before Lucy was ready to move. Sheila moved in downstairs and Lucy upstairs, and Sheila helped Lucy with her money and other practical aspects of living on her own. Sheila's friends and family members, and even Lucy's mother's ex-husband, all helped Lucy with various tasks such as grocery shopping, furniture moving, snow shoveling, cleaning, and so forth. Jim, a man who attended their church, began to help Sheila and Lucy with transportation to school, church, and other places they wanted to go.

Making New Friends and Keeping the Old

After Lucy moved, Sheila, Joan, and I began to help her obtain services she needed. For example, she wanted to know whether she had a guardian, as she had always been told, so we contacted the protection and advocacy agency. They checked with the courts in the three counties in which guardianship could have been awarded and found that she did not have a guardian. This meant that, contrary to what she had always been told, she could make all of her own decisions. She needed adaptive equipment in her home, and another agency became involved. The case manager from this agency became an important source of support for Lucy, helping her to get medical care that had long been needed, including physical therapy and gynecological examinations. Lucy was placed on a waiting list for the Department of Housing and Urban Development's Section 8 program, which would ultimately provide her with a rent subsidy. She also wanted to go to school and eventually to work, so the vocational rehabilitation office was contacted. They paid for her to go to an adult education program twice a week with Sheila, who was also one of their clients, and put her on a waiting list for a supported work program in Salt City.

There were frequent conflicts between Lucy, Sheila, and others in her closest support network, which consisted mostly of Sheila's friends and family members. For example, Lucy's rent and utilities accounted for most of her Supplemental Security Income (SSI) check, so she had little left to spend on things she needed or wanted. She had never handled much money and tended to spend whatever she had on what she wanted at the moment; everyone (including Lucy) agreed that she needed help with it. Still, she often argued with Sheila about money to the point that Sheila frequently asked me to get Lucy a representative payee. Sheila, who was also an SSI recipient, had a rental subsidy to help with her own expenses, but she was impatient with Lucy's frustration over having next to nothing. Other conflicts occurred over another friend, who was known within their network as "not quite right" and who sometimes became violent. Sometimes Lucy would invite this woman to stay overnight, and they would be very friendly; at other times the woman would threaten to report Lucy to the authorities or to hurt her.

The relationship between Lucy and Sheila was complicated. Lucy rarely spoke up when Sheila was with us, and Sheila was often bossy toward Lucy. She told me that Lucy had not been taught basic skills of daily living, including how to get along in society, and she spoke of her role with Lucy as that of a teacher. Sheila, who had been a special education student, was very streetwise even though she had difficulty reading and doing arithmetic. She knew how to get benefits and services, and she accompanied Lucy to appointments at numerous agencies. She also had definite opinions about what was acceptable in society. She often told me that Lucy was very smart but either didn't know how or refused to do things the "right" way. Lucy usually complied with Sheila's strong suggestions; however, privately she told me that, while she didn't always agree, she went along because she was afraid of losing Sheila's love.

Lucy's middle-class lesbian friends and agency workers often questioned Sheila's or Lucy's opinions about what Lucy should do. For example, we were very concerned about her spending so much of her SSI check on rent, and we worried that Sheila had too much control over Lucy. In spite of these concerns, Sheila and her network intersected fairly well with the other networks around Lucy—her middle-class lesbian friends, her mother and her mother's ex-husband, the agency workers, and her church friends—so that whenever a crisis arose, someone was able to deal with it. Sheila, a very talkative woman, kept everyone informed about Lucy's problems and needs. Lucy was able to stay out of the residential services system and to develop skills for living independently and getting along in the community because of the support she received from all of these networks. None of her friends had the time or energy to give her all the support she needed; however, somehow she, Sheila, or someone else found people who would meet a particular need, such as a ride to the grocery store, a railing for the steps, money for school, help carrying the laundry upstairs, help with the garbage, and so on. With all of this, and because she was learning more about taking care of herself, Lucy's circumstances improved.

Sheila Moves and Lucy Follows

Six months after they moved in, Sheila announced that she was moving out. It was clear to me and others by this time that, although Lucy felt that they were lovers, Sheila no longer did. However, she said that she was moving because she needed better accessibility. She had severe arthritis and had believed when they rented the apartment that a ramp to her door could be constructed. After they moved in she learned that the house could not be ramped because the front yard was too small and had too steep a slope. She was concerned about the winter, so she convinced the landlord to let her out of her lease, and she moved to East Salt City.

Lucy had to stay where she was, with much less support, but she managed in spite of the harsh Salt City winter, which deposited dangerous amounts of ice and snow on her steps and sidewalk. Three months later, while we were trying to find her a more suitable apartment, Sheila intervened again. She helped her get out of her lease and move into her (Sheila's) new apartment complex, which is where she still lives, a year and several months later. Sheila and Lucy are friends, except for the periods when they are angry at each other, but Lucy has assumed much more control over her own life. Lucy no longer spends time with members of Sheila's family.

While Sheila became less important to Lucy, Lucy was meeting service workers and other people who have since formed a growing network supporting her. Late in 1992, a supported employment agency looked through their waiting list and selected her for one of their programs. An administrator at this agency, also a lesbian, became another friend and advocate for her within the agency. Through her, Lucy was introduced to a woman with developmental and psychiatric disabilities who lives in an institution. Lucy views this woman, Carrie, as someone she can give to. She said, "All my life people have been taking care of me. But Carrie needs me to take care of her."

A case manager has helped Lucy and Carrie to apply for funding to support them, each in her own apartment but in the same building. Carrie has a paid roommate, and both get assistance with their apartments (including their budgets) and with community involvement during the day. Her service coordinator, who is heterosexual, has tried to find lesbians to work with the two women and to involve them both in selecting the people who will work with them. For example, Lucy had problems dealing with a male job coach and, upon her request, was given a female coach. As she has attained more control in her life, she has demonstrated much less anger.

Lucy's Life Today

During the 3 years in which Lucy was with Sheila and for some time after they broke up, Miriam was not in the picture. Lucy had a few other sexual relationships, all short-lived. However, feeling that her lovers had disappointed her repeatedly, she brought Miriam back last year at a time when she was feeling lonely and wanted a lover she could count on. She has been calmer and happier since then, and she attributes it to her relationship with Miriam. She is careful about when to refer to or talk to Miriam, and as a result no one who knows about Miriam has created trouble for Lucy. She does not talk about Miriam at work, with people she doesn't know well, with psychologists and others in similar positions, or with her landlord or neighbors.

Today Lucy's life is one of activity and many relationships. For example, she now sees her mother several times a month and talks to her by telephone every day. She sees friends and service workers, goes to church and bingo, works, and has leisure time activities. There are four major types of social networks, all intersecting, that support and connect to Lucy and each other. These are her family (including her father and a half-brother who have not seen her since her accident but have contacted her since her move), her lesbian and gay friends, community people such as neighbors and those with whom she works, and a growing number of service workers. These intersecting networks made it possible for Lucy to maintain her own apartment and avoid living in a group residential setting, and they helped her to go to school and find her present job.

LEARNING FROM LUCY

Lucy's life story holds many messages for service providers, family members, and friends. I hope that it can also be helpful to people with disabilities, even though it is filtered through the lens of my experience. The primary implications of Lucy's story have to do with the necessity of understanding the person's perspective, of listening to and respecting the person's choices, strengths, and needs. In Lucy's case, this means being open to what her identity as a lesbian means to her, appreciating her sociable nature and other people's attraction to her, being willing to accept Miriam as a necessary part of her life, being aware of her history of abuse and control, problem solving for ways to demarginalize and build on her status as a lesbian with disabilities, and supporting the family relationships she values in spite of serious problems in the past.

Lucy's lesbian identity is central to her concept of who she is as a woman. She is a proud lesbian. She has not internalized the social disapproval and rejection of homosexuality that was prevalent when she came out and that still exists in our culture (Chauncey, Duberman, & Vicinus, 1983; McAllan & Ditillo, 1994), and her loyalty to that identity has served her well. Today she lives a fuller life because of the gay men and lesbians, within and outside of the service system, who helped her gain and sustain her freedom. In today's more accepting climate, it is possible for gay and lesbian service workers to give direct support to gay men and lesbians with disabilities in ways that were not possible previously, and Lucy has benefited. Gay and lesbian workers have come out to Lucy, drawn in their friends to support her, and made sure she received services that conform to her preferences and needs.

Lucy's freedom was attained and supported by heterosexual people as well, because of her ability to attract people who want to help her when she needs it. She is a likable woman who gets people to laugh, and her openness about her sexual orientation forces them to decide whether or not they are on her side. Many heterosexual family members and service workers have decided in favor of Lucy and have learned to view her lesbian ways from her perspective as well as from their own. This has also meant accepting and working with the other gay people in Lucy's life and, in her mother's case (because Lucy used to tell her mother everything), permitting Lucy to leave the house with her gay friends.

Another lesson in Lucy's story has to do with what to make of Miriam. Writing about Lucy's angel has meant that I have had to reflect on my own and others' attitudes about Lucy's belief in Miriam. I have talked about Miriam with the service providers who are now in Lucy's life and have concluded that for them, as for me, Miriam is accepted as having a meaningful function for Lucy. One provider overheard a person in her office say to another, "Lucy won't work on Mondays because Monday is for her and Miriam." Neither treated the idea of Miriam as a delusion or as pathological, but as a fact of life in working with Lucy. Because Lucy has carved out a place for Miriam that gives time and space for other people, they can accept Miriam on Lucy's terms.

Finally, it has been critical for those of us who have a professional background and who care about Lucy to acknowledge and work with her family and friendship relationships, regardless of how we might view them. These relationships are as much a part of Lucy as her lesbianism, and we have followed her lead in regard to them. It would be easy to give these relationships a variety of labels and to interfere in such a way that she would leave them behind. However, this would mean replacing one form of control with another rather than supporting Lucy to engage with people, even those who once dominated her, on her own terms and from a position of equality. A major lesson we have learned is that, given support, Lucy has moved into a position of mastery over her life.

Finally, the concept of intersecting networks of support may be useful as the human services field moves toward creating individual supports for people with disabilities. For some people, we may need to respect and support existing networks, whereas other people may need help in creating informal networks of support. We must also recognize that people with disabilities, even when we perceive them as recipients sitting at the center of a number of intersecting networks of support, are also givers of support to others. Lucy, for example, gives a great deal to other people: She gives love, encouragement, money, presents, and practical assistance. It is Lucy who keeps her support networks alive and working for her.

REFERENCES

Abbot, S., & Love, B. (1972). *Sappho was a right-on woman: A liberated view of lesbianism.* New York: Stein and Day.

Appleby, Y. (1994). Out in the margins. *Disability, Handicap & Society, 9*(1), 19–32.

Chauncey, G., Jr., Duberman, M.B., & Vicinus, M. (1983). Introduction. In M.B. Duberman, M. Vicinus, & G. Chauncey, Jr. (Eds.), *Hidden from history: Reclaiming the gay and lesbian past* (pp. 1–13). New York: Penguin Books.

Corbett, J. (1994). A proud label: Exploring the relationship between disability politics and gay pride. *Disability & Society, 9*(3), 343–357.

Dworkin, S.H., & Gutierrez, F.J. (Eds.). (1992). *Counseling gay men and lesbians: Journey to the end of the rainbow.* Alexandria, VA: American Association for Counseling and Development.

Faderman, L. (1981). *Surpassing the love of men: Romantic friendship and love between women from the Renaissance to the present.* New York: William Morrow and Co.

Heyward, C. (1989). *Coming out and relational empowerment: A lesbian feminist theological perspective.* Wellesley, MA: Stone Center.

Klaich, D. (1974). *Woman + woman: Attitudes toward lesbianism.* New York: William Morrow and Co.

McAllan, L.C., & Ditillo, D. (1994). Addressing the needs of lesbian and gay clients with disabilities. *Journal of Rehabilitation Counseling, 25*(1), 26–35.

Monat-Haller, R.K. (1992). *Understanding and expressing sexuality: Responsible choices for individuals with developmental disabilities.* Baltimore: Paul H. Brookes Publishing Co.

Morris, J. (1992). Personal and political: A feminist perspective on researching physical disability. *Disability, Handicap & Society, 7*, 157–166.

Rich, A. (1983). Compulsory heterosexuality and lesbian existence. In A. Snitow, C. Stansell, & S. Thompson (Eds.), *Powers of desire: The politics of sexuality* (pp. 177–205). New York: Monthly Review Press.

Sobsey, D., Gray, S., Wells, D., Pyper, D., & Reimer-Heck, B. (1990). *Sexuality, disability, and abuse: An annotated bibliography.* Baltimore: Paul H. Brookes Publishing Co.

11

Community Based
Is Not Community

The Social Geography
of Disability

Pam Walker

This chapter explores issues related to the social geography of people with mental retardation. The term *social geography* is used to describe the interaction of the "personal geography" of people's lives (the places they go) and their social networks (relationships with kin, friends, and acquaintances). The focus is on the connection between social geography and community membership.

The deinstitutionalization movement and the current emphasis on community integration have had a significant impact on the social geography of many people with developmental disabilities. Yet, to a large extent it is still limited by a variety of factors and circumstances. Nowadays, people with disabilities spend much more time in the community, but in many ways they are not part of the community (Bercovici, 1983; Bogdan & Taylor, 1987; Edgerton, 1967). A more in-depth understanding of why this is so can be gained from looking at the places where people spend time in the community and the social interactions and relationships they have in these places.

In the disability field, there has been a lot of discussion about the importance of community integration and community membership for people with developmental disabilities. At the same time, there has been little analysis of what is meant by *community*. In the social sciences literature, there has been extensive dialogue about the meaning of that term. Traditionally, many definitions have linked community with "place" (Bell & Newby, 1974; Wellman & Leighton, 1979). For example, Wellman and Leighton (1979) note that most definitions of community tend to include three components: networks of interpersonal ties, common locality, and solidarity sentiments and activities.

Urbanization and industrialization have significantly affected both where people live and with whom they maintain relationships. For many individuals, the sense of community is derived not so much within a purely geographic-political context, such as a small town or village, but rather within their social networks, which may be linked to place (e.g., neighborhood), work, religion, leisure interests, kinship, social class, and the like (Macionis, 1978; Minar & Greer, 1968). Although place may not play the role it once did in defining community, particularly in urban areas, it is still an important factor having an impact on people's social relationships and networks (Agnew & Duncan, 1989; Fischer, 1982; Minar & Greer, 1968).

In order to understand the experience of community in the lives of people with disabilities, it is important to look at the places they go, their social networks, and the connections between them. Terms such as *social context* (Fischer, 1982) have been used to describe that which incorporates both the social and physical environment. Social contexts are shaped by the social relationships and interactions that take place within them (Blumer, 1969; Fischer, 1982; Gusfield, 1975). It is the purpose of this chapter to explore the social construction of space as it relates to the idea of community membership for people with developmental disabilities.

The first part of this chapter offers a description and analysis of the personal geographies of three people's lives, looking at the types of places they go. The second section focuses on people's social connections and networks in relation to community places. The final section comments on the social meaning of place and community.

INFORMANTS

This chapter is based on participant observation and in-depth interviews with three people with mental retardation. The research involved spending time with these informants in their homes and in their neighborhoods and communities. This included taking walks; going to church, to bingo, and to malls; having dinner at home with family members or group home residents; eating out at favorite restaurants; going to the library; taking the bus; going to a bowling alley, a bookstore, an ice cream shop, a baseball game, the zoo, or places of work; and so forth. It also involved interviewing family members and staff members to gain further insight into the life of each person. Each informant is described briefly below.

Judy Edwards is 25 years old and lives with her mother and sister in subsidized housing in a residential section of a medium-sized city. They have lived in this apartment for about 8 years. Judy has mild mental retardation, and her sister, Carrie, has moderate mental retardation. Since Judy finished high school 4 years ago, she has had some job training and several jobs, some through supported employment agencies, others on her own. Most recently, she got a job in food service at a thruway rest area, but was laid off. Judy spends her free time with her family, by herself, and with her friend Nancy, who also has a disability and to whom she was introduced by their mutual case manager. She also takes part in some recreational activities for people with developmental disabilities sponsored by a human services agency.

Charlie Henderson is 28 years old and lives with his parents in the house he grew up in with three older siblings. He has Down syndrome and moderate mental retardation. Since he finished high school, he has had a few different jobs. His most recent job was as a housekeeper at a motel. On the advice of the supported employment agency, Charlie resigned from this job because of pressures from the new manager that would likely have resulted in his being fired eventually. Outside of work, Charlie spends most of his time with his parents; he is also in frequent contact with a brother and a sister who live nearby.

Ellen Goodman is 46 years old and lives in a group home with seven other people with disabilities. All of the people in this residence have both a visual impairment and a mental retardation label. Ellen does not have a job but likes to get out of her house during the day, so she spends time at the main office of the agency that operates her group home. Outside of her home and the office, Ellen spends most of her time in the community with agency staff. She loves music, and a staff person accompanies her to an arts school for piano lessons and to a nursing home where she plays piano for the residents once a week.

PERSONAL GEOGRAPHY AND DISABILITY

The sociological literature has documented the significance of various places in people's lives, ranging from urban bars, to neighborhoods, street corners, coffee houses, and the like (Gans, 1962; Katovich & Reese, 1987; Liebow, 1967; Nathe, 1976; Whyte, 1955). From the places people go, within the context of their interactions, they can potentially derive a sense of membership, belonging, and identity. However, the opportunities for this to happen depend to an extent on the types of places people go and the types of interactions that take place within those places.

All three people in this study go to a wide range of places in the community—stores, restaurants, bars, workplaces, banks, neighborhood centers, homes of friends and relatives, churches, social service agencies, and many more. In order to explore the role of these places in people's lives, some of the characteristics of these places will be examined. These include homogeneity versus heterogeneity; public versus private places; places characterized by social anonymity versus those characterized by social interaction/friendship; places where people share common interests as opposed to a diversity of interests; and neighborhood and community places.

Places with Homogeneous Versus Heterogeneous Groups of People

One way to meet others and develop social networks is to spend time in places frequented by people who share common interests or characteristics (Gorman, 1979). Our society contains various places with homogeneous populations based on differing characteristics such as gender, race/ethnicity, religion, age, interest, socioeconomic status, and disability, to name a few. Some are places to which people go by choice (e.g., churches, clubs), and some are places to which people generally are sent against their will or based on another person's choice (e.g., institutions for people with mental retardation). Also, some are socially valued places (private health clubs), whereas others are devalued (nursing homes, public housing).

All three people in this study spend or have spent significant amounts of time in places that are homogeneous based on disability. These include special schools, separate classrooms in regular schools, segregated workplaces, segregated residential settings, segregated continuing education activities, and segregated recreation activities. Some of these environments involve small groups of people who have an opportunity to get to know one another and develop friendships. All three people have also gone to places that are homogeneous based on some other dimension, such as religion (churches), interest (music, cars), and social class (social service agencies). These environments predominantly involve large groups of people and/or are not conducive to sustained social interaction.

Judy lives with her family in the community, a family that relies primarily on public assistance. She attended separate classes in regular schools, and she participates in some recreational activities for groups of people with disabilities. For a few years, she took part in recreational activities at a neighborhood center that included some people with disabilities among many others without disabilities. Judy also spends time in various social service offices both because of her disability and because of her need for financial assistance.

Charlie, who lives with his parents, a middle-income family, first went to a Montessori school for children with disabilities followed by an elementary school also for children with disabilities. His parents felt comfortable with the arrangement. As his mother put it, "That was good, because they had all the same kind of kids, and everyone knew about them." He later went to school in a special education class within a regular school.

Since he finished high school, Charlie has been in a few supported employment jobs. His parents object to certain aspects of sheltered workshops and therefore refuse to allow him to go to one. His mother commented:

> We said if he got sent to a workshop, we'd keep him home. Do you know the Thomas boy? He goes to one of those workshops, and his mother told me he only makes something like $15 a week. That doesn't even pay for transportation. They send some of them around the city digging ditches and things. . . . I don't think Charlie could do that and keep up.

Neither would his family members place him in a group home. His sister feels that he might be "content but not happy" in a group home. She and his two brothers are all willing to have him live in their homes eventually.

Ellen lives in a group home with seven other people with developmental disabilities. She currently does not have a job, although efforts are being made to help her find one. She spends a portion of every weekday at a human services office, as a break from being home. She sometimes visits friends at an activities center for people with disabilities located next to her group home, and she plays piano weekly at a local nursing home.

Judy, Charlie, and Ellen also go to places that contain heterogeneous groups of people, which are primarily places of their own or their family's choosing. However, such places tend to be large and public, such as malls or restaurants: not the types of settings where one meets others and has sustained social interactions.

In effect, all three people, based on the places where they have spent time, have been given ample opportunity to develop both an identity based on disability and an affiliation and relationships with others who have disabilities. However, the types of places that they have gone that include people without disabilities, outside of family, have given them little opportunity to develop social connections with others based on shared personal characteristics.

Public Places Versus Private Places

Another distinction in the types of places people go is public versus private. There is an increasing trend toward privatization of people's lives—a tendency to spend more time and conduct one's relationships in private spheres versus public ones (Bulmer, 1987). Often, particularly in cities as opposed to small villages, there is public estrangement, not familiarity. However, even when people come to know each other in public, these relationships of public familiarity are usually distinct from people's private, more intimate relationships (Fischer, 1982). It follows, then, that to the degree that people are cut off from private settings, they are also excluded from the social worlds that revolve around these private settings.

The places to which Judy and Ellen go in the community are predominantly public, such as stores and restaurants. The private places to which they go tend to be large community environments or smaller environments for people with disabilities. For Judy, exceptions include a friend's apartment, her father's apartment, a neighborhood center, church, and various recreational settings sponsored by a human service agency. For Ellen, these include the Arts Place, where she takes piano lessons, the activities center next to her house, church, the nursing home, and her sister's house in another city. Charlie has more of a balance between public and private places because he visits a variety of public places as well as a variety of private places, such as the homes of family members and relatives as well as the home of a friend with a disability.

Overall, Judy and Ellen have little access to private social worlds, whereas Charlie has significantly more through his family connections. All of the informants have limited participation in the private worlds of people with disabilities. However, none of the informants participates in the private social worlds of peers without disabilities.

Places Characterized by Social Anonymity Versus Social Interaction/Friendship

In their free time, all three informants go to places predominantly characterized by social anonymity as opposed to social interaction and friendship. For example, they spend significant amounts of time in such places as malls, restaurants, movie theaters, and other large public or private areas. Some places to which they go, such as churches, offer both the possibility of relative social anonymity and that of extensive social involvement. However, within these environments, they tend to maintain social anonymity rather than involvement and interaction. For example, both Judy and Ellen attend church, but have not become involved in smaller groups there such as committees or the choir; neither have they developed relationships with people at church. Judy went to a neighborhood center, where she enjoyed the activities and developed a relationship with a key staff person, but did not develop relationships with peers without disabilities. At these activities, Judy was often nearly the only white person (the others were Asian and African American) and the only one in her early 20s (the others were primarily in the mid-teenage years), both of which, in addition to her disability, may have made her stand out as "different." Judy stopped going to the neighborhood center after the staff person to whom she was attached left. She explained that she felt she was "getting too old" to go there.

Exceptions to this pattern of participation in places of social anonymity include time with family members and relatives, attendance at small gatherings of people with disabilities (e.g., continuing education courses, recreational activities), and visits to the homes of friends with disabilities or to certain local businesses.

Of the three individuals, Charlie spends the most time with family members and extended family members. He occasionally participates in social activities with groups of people with disabilities, such as Special Olympics or continuing education classes. In his neighborhood, he used to frequent a small ice cream shop, resulting in his acquaintance with a young woman who works there. Judy spends a significant amount of time with her family, but almost none with relatives. She engages in some social activities, both organized and informal, with groups of people with disabilities. These include such activities as bowling and exercise, as well as evening get-togethers at a friend's house. Finally, Ellen socializes with groups of people with disabilities at her own house as well as at the activities center next door. All three people spend almost no time in places that provide opportunities for social interaction with peers without disabilities.

Places Where People Share Common Interests Versus Diverse Interests

Participation in places where people share common interests gives people an opportunity to make connections and form relationships based on these interests. Such participation can contribute to helping a person with disabilities acquire an identity based on interests rather than just on disability (McGill, 1987).

The individuals in this study go to few locales where people share common interests. Such locales tend to be either 1) large public or private places (e.g., car shows, arts school, zoo) characterized by social anonymity; or 2) places comprising people with disabilities who share a common interest (e.g., continuing education, recreation). For example, based on her interests, Judy goes by herself or with family members to such places as the zoo or church, or to places with groups of people with disabilities such as bowling, exercise class, or a whale watch trip. Charlie goes to places such as car shows and movies or takes part in sports programs or other recreational/continuing education activities specifically created for people with disabilities. Based on her interests, Ellen goes to church, takes music lessons, and plays the piano for singalongs in nursing homes. None of the three participates in small formal or informal groups of people without disabilities based on interest.

Neighborhood and Community Places

The traditional notion of neighborhood is one of a setting that includes a variety of places or locales (cafes, street corners, bars) in which social interaction takes place. As urban design has changed and people's mobility increased, research has suggested a decline in people's orientation to neighborhood as a geographic entity and an increase in their use of more geographically dispersed settings for activities and relationships (Macionis, 1978; Minar & Greer, 1968). There is still strong evidence that use of and identification with neighborhood places is significant for many people (Bell & Boat, 1970; Bulmer, 1987; Keller, 1968). However, studies indicate that this varies depending on various characteristics or circumstances, such as race/ethnicity, social class, age, and mobility (Bell & Boat, 1970; Bulmer, 1987; Keller, 1968).

All of the informants in this research utilize places within their neighborhood as well as those in the wider community to varying degrees. Judy, who does the most independent travel in the community, often by foot, spends the most time in neighborhood places. Although Charlie and Ellen sometimes go to neighborhood places with family members or staff, they often go outside the neighborhood traveling by car with family members or group home staff. Judy likes walking around her neighborhood, where she feels safe and enjoys the quiet. She often shops at stores within the neighborhood, and she used to participate at a neighborhood center. Charlie, who does not independently use most neighborhood places, used to regularly patronize an ice cream shop in his neighborhood on his way home from work. Also, on occasion, he and his father and brother go out to drink and eat at a neighborhood tavern.

In general, the three people in this study are drawn to neighborhood places because of convenience or familiarity, but not because of social connections with others in these places. Likewise, their use of broader community places is based on interest or familiarity versus personal social connection. Regular use of certain places has in a few instances led to familiarity and in some cases to acquaintanceship with people without disabilities, but not to close social relations.

Summary

Overall, Judy, Charlie, and Ellen go predominantly to large public or private places in the community. These places are characterized by social anonymity in contrast with social interaction and connection. Outside of family homes, they have little or no access to the homes of friends or neighbors, particularly those without disabilities. In addition, they spend almost no time in environments composed of small groupings of people who come together on the basis of social relationship, common interest, shared identity, and the like, with the exception of groupings of people who have disabilities.

The geography of their lives is largely determined by others, not themselves. For Charlie, it is largely determined by his family as well as by the disability services system; for Ellen, it is largely determined by the system. The personal geography of Judy's life is significantly less controlled by the system or the family than Charlie's or Ellen's. Nevertheless, it is limited by her lack of social connectedness beyond the family and with others without disabilities, her lack of financial resources, and her lack of support from the disabilities services system in terms of her going to a wider variety of places.

For all three individuals, significant factors that seem to affect the geography of their lives include the following:

1. *A person's income level affects his or her access to various community places.* For example, Judy goes to a wider variety of community places with greater frequency, when she has a job and therefore has money for bus tokens and other items (food, arts and crafts materials, admission to movie theaters, etc.). However, this does not necessarily have a significant impact on the types of places she goes or the potential for social interaction.
2. *A person's degree of independence in getting around the community, or the availability and accessibility of transportation, affects his or her ability to go to a greater number of community places.* Judy, who is much more independent in terms of mobility than Charlie or Ellen, goes to many more places of her own choosing in the community. But again, independent access does not necessarily lead to greater social interactions and more diverse environments.
3. *The extent to which family members or service providers play a protective or restrictive role as opposed to a facilitative role can make a significant difference in the number and types of places a person spends time.* Judy's mother facilitates her attendance at a variety of public places to

which she cannot travel on her own (because they are not on bus routes, are too far to walk, etc.). Judy's social worker has helped her gain access to recreational group activities with others who have disabilities. However, neither her mother nor her social worker assists her in participating in smaller, socially oriented settings with people without disabilities. Charlie's family facilitates his participation at a variety of public places as well as in the private social worlds of relatives and family friends. However, they do not assist him in participating in private social worlds of peers without disabilities or in situations characterized by social interaction with others without disabilities. Human services workers have facilitated his participation in work settings alongside coworkers without disabilities and in recreational activities with others who have disabilities. However, they have not assisted him in developing sustained social contact with people without disabilities. In Ellen's case, human services workers assist her in attending a variety of large public and private places, including some that are composed only of people with disabilities and staff, or people who are elderly and staff. They do not help her to spend time in places where she might have significant social interaction with people without disabilities.

4. *A person's interests play a role in determining which community places he or she visits.* Ellen, Charlie, and Judy all go to some places in the community based on interest. However, they do not go to places in which they have much opportunity to get to know and form social relationships with people without disabilities on the basis of interest.

5. *A person's social networks have a significant impact on the types of places to which he or she goes in the community.* Charlie's extended social network (of family members and relatives, primarily) gives him greater access to private social settings including people without disabilities than either Ellen or Judy. Judy's friendship with a peer who has disabilities gives her access to private social settings with people with disabilities. Outside of family and relatives, however, none of the informants has access to social environments composed of people without disabilities.

In summary, while access to financial resources and independent mobility increase the number of places to which people with disabilities go, they do not in and of themselves increase the likelihood that such individuals will go to places characterized by social interaction with people without disabilities. Likewise, support from family or human services agencies assists people in gaining access to certain places to which they would not otherwise go, but does not result in significant use of social settings with others without disabilities. Finally, people's social networks have increased their participation in private social gatherings; at the same time, these networks are composed almost entirely of family members or others with disabilities and thus do not provide entry into social settings that include peers without disabilities. The following section explores the social connections in people's lives in relation to various dimensions of community membership and participation.

SOCIAL NETWORKS AND DISABILITY

Social networks influence and are influenced by the time we spend in various types of places. Thus, a person's social network could be based primarily on neighborhood or on interests or other activities. Sociological literature (e.g., Bell & Newby, 1974; Macionis, 1978) points to the general decline of neighborhood-based social networks in our society concomitant with the expansion of networks based more on interest and other associations. Some segments of the social network are less voluntary than others. For example, people generally have less choice about social connections to family members, coworkers, and neighbors than they do about social connections to friends or associates in community organizations and interest groups (Fischer, 1982). People's choices with regard to social network are based on varying alternatives, resources, opportunities, and constraints (Fischer, 1982; Maguire, 1983). This section examines the informants' social networks in relation to the types of connections and the types of places in which they spend time. These include disability connections, community and neighborhood connections, family connections, and connections based on common interest.

Disability Connections

According to Fischer, "commitment to, or restriction to, a social context promotes social relationships in it, perhaps to the exclusion of relationships outside it" (1982, p. 106). For all three people in this study, outside of family members, their social networks are composed largely of people whom they met at environments for people with disabilities (i.e., other people with disabilities and staff, or professionals in the disabilities field). All of the friends mentioned by Judy, Charlie, and Ellen are people with disabilities whom they met in special education classes or through human services agencies.

Besides family members, virtually all of the people without disabilities with whom they have relationships are human services professionals—job coaches, social workers, agency staff members, and the like. The few exceptions are either volunteers (e.g., the person who drives Ellen to church) or casual acquaintances (e.g., clerks in stores that they frequent).

Ellen, living in the group home with seven others, is surrounded by service workers and others with disabilities. When asked to name her friends or those to whom she is closest, both Ellen and staff members identified predominantly other staff people and people with disabilities at the group home or at the human services office where she spends time on weekdays. The only people without disabilities with whom she has a social connection are her sister as well as her piano teacher and the woman who drives her to church on Sundays.

For Charlie, the one unpaid, nonfamily member who is identified as Charlie's friend at this time is a young man who was in special education with Charlie and who lives nearby. Charlie also talks about a past significant relationship with a young woman, whom he also met through special education classes. At work, his primary interaction is with his job coach.

The people Judy identifies as friends are all others with disabilities whom she knows either through special education, through an introduction by a social worker at a disabilities services agency, or through recreational activities for groups of people with disabilities sponsored by a disabilities services agency. Judy used to be involved in recreational activities at a neighborhood center. There her strongest connection was with one of the staff members; she did not develop any connections with other teens.

Community and Neighborhood Connections

Outside of their families and the disabilities community, the informants have very few significant connections to people in their neighborhood or the broader community. Most of these connections are based on business, not social, interactions because they take place primarily in places characterized by social anonymity.

Support, or lack thereof, for positive social interactions has contributed to people's lack of relationships in their neighborhood and community. For instance, at work, Charlie had limited, superficial social contact with his coworkers. This was influenced by his job coach's decision that he not take breaks with coworkers. "It didn't work out. It was too hard for him to get back to work." With regard to this, Charlie's sister commented, "I don't know why they just didn't help teach him to get back to work after the break." Judy is very resentful of the lack of interaction and the negative experiences she had with other high school students outside of her special education classroom. When asked if she was able to form any friendships with people other than classmates, Judy responds, "No . . . 'cause they think we're dumb and don't know anything. They make fun of us; that's why I'm so shy."

Regular use of certain spaces has contributed to some social connections for people. These are not close, intimate connections, but rather are characterized by familiarity or acquaintanceship. For instance, because of the time that they do spend in their neighborhood and their use of neighborhood places, Judy and Charlie are known by some members of their community, if not by name then by sight. For instance, Charlie's sister Karen talks about his participation in the neighborhood alongside his older siblings: "He always went everywhere we went. He was just seen as part of the family." She and other family members tell stories of him getting lost in the neighborhood and how other people's recognition of him assisted in his return home. Also, it is through his regular patronage of an ice cream shop near home that Charlie became acquainted with a young woman who works there.

Both Judy and Charlie each are in contact with a person with a disability in their neighborhood. In Charlie's case, the relationship, with a former school classmate, is still maintained because of the residential proximity (living only a few houses apart), which enables them to exchange visits independently. Judy was introduced to her friend through their mutual social worker, who knew that they lived in the same area. Thus, this relationship is also reinforced by residential proximity. Neither Judy, Ellen, nor Charlie has anyone without a disability who is just a friend (e.g., not also a staff person or volunteer) in the community.

Family Connections

Family connections play a different role for people at different stages in their life cycle. Typically, for a child, connections to family are nonvoluntary, whereas for an adult these connections, or the degree thereof, are more voluntary, depending on proximity to family as well as the presence of other connections. With respect to family connections for people with disabilities, two scenarios are prevalent. First, because of lack of support for alternative connections, many people with disabilities have relied all their lives on their family as their primary social connection. Second, others have had their ties with family members severed or significantly diminished due to placement in the human services system.

Family is the primary and almost exclusive social network for both Judy and Charlie, whereas for Ellen family members play a significant emotional but less practical role as a social connection. Charlie's family and extended family members are the most important part of his social network. It is with them that he spends the most time, goes to the most community places, and is involved in the most social settings (private and public). Judy's immediate family members constitute the most significant part of her social network. However, this does not result in many other social connections for her, since the family as a whole is relatively isolated from extended family members, neighbors, and other community members. Finally, while Ellen's family, particularly her sister, are important to her, they live in another city and consequently she only sees them at holiday times.

Interest Connections

Interests play an important role in how we define ourselves and in providing opportunities for connections with others who share those interests. O'Brien and Lyle (1987, Section 1, p. 35) highlight the importance of interests:

> Interests link the personal and the social. They express individual gifts, concerns, and fascinations and call for activities, information, and tools. Shared interest founds associations. People point to interests when they describe what gives their lives meaning.

Traditionally, people with disabilities have been placed into special, segregated programs, such as bowling or square dancing, with very limited opportunity to explore a range of other interests comparable to those of people without disabilities. As a result, they have had minimal if any opportunity to form social connections or relationships with people without disabilities on the basis of interest.

Judy, Charlie, and Ellen engage in various activities and go to various places based on interest. However, due in part to the types of places they go (e.g., large public and private places; places characterized by social anonymity), they don't develop social relationships based on interest. This lack of opportunity to meet people based on interest is also related to such factors as family attitudes and human services system structures. For instance, Charlie is interested in movies and television, sports, and cars. However, when asked about his possibility of developing relationships with coworkers, his mother commented: "They wouldn't be interested in the kinds of things he talks about." Both Judy and Charlie take part in human services agency–sponsored groups of a recreational and academic nature. The agency offers these as separate programs for people with disabilities, rather than encouraging people with disabilities to participate in groups, based on their interests, alongside people without disabilities who share those interests. Ellen has developed a relationship that is important to her (her piano teacher) in the pursuit of her interest in music. Beyond this, however, her group home staff have assisted her in further developing this musical interest by performing for residents of nursing homes, which places Ellen in a segregated devalued setting of another sort.

Summary

Whereas Judy and Charlie have their strongest social connections through family, Ellen's are through the human services system. Although friendship with peers is a significant aspect of social life (Bulmer, 1987; Lutfiyya, 1991), the people in this study have very limited relationships with peers. Those they do have are almost exclusively through their disability connections (i.e., with people they have met through special education or through connections within the human services system). Outside of family members, most of their relationships with people without disabilities in the community are of a staff–client or helper–helpee nature rather than a mutual, peer interaction. They have minimal connections to others based on interest, and those to whom they are connected are invariably people with disabilities.

Some of the factors that seem to affect people's social networks include the following:

1. *The degree to which a person's family is connected to or disconnected from extended family members, neighbors, friends, and others can have an effect on the individual's personal connections.* Many people acquire some of their social connections to others through their family members. The degree to which this occurs, however, will vary depending on the family's connections. For example, Charlie's family is very connected to extended family members and other community members, and they provide a vehicle for him to be connected to these people also. Judy's family, on the other hand, is isolated from extended family members and other neighborhood and community residents, which contributes to Judy's personal isolation as well. Ellen, who lives a few hundred miles from her family, does not have access to their social connections.
2. *The types of places people go can contribute to their social networks.* Certain places more than others provide opportunities to get to know people and form relationships. However, by and large, the types of places that Judy, Ellen, and Charlie go provide little if any opportunity for sustained social interchange.
3. *The way support is provided by family members or service system staff can have a significant impact on a person's social networks.* Support can

either be restrictive or facilitative of social connections and relationships. The support that people in this study receive tends to promote relationships with family members, staff, and others with disabilities, but not with coworkers, neighbors, and other community members without disabilities.

CONCLUSION: REFLECTIONS ON THE SOCIAL MEANING OF COMMUNITY FOR PEOPLE WITH DISABILITIES

There is widespread agreement that the idea of "community" is not just about place, but about social and emotional attachments and connections to and within a place (Gusfield, 1975; Wellman & Leighton, 1979). While living in the community, the people with disabilities highlighted in this chapter have had very limited opportunity to develop a sense of community membership. This is the result of a separation from the social worlds of peers without disabilities that is based on two interrelated dynamics: 1) the social context of the places they spend time with others outside of family members and others with disabilities (i.e., places characterized by social anonymity rather than social interaction, friendship, and intimacy); and 2) the limited dimensions of their social networks, consisting primarily of family members and connections through the disabilities services system.

Family members and service system workers play a significant role in the types of connections people have and places to which they go. This role can either facilitate or inhibit the formation of meaningful social connections. In order to facilitate such connections, effort is needed in two areas:

1. *We must increase awareness of the role of place in either promoting anonymity or providing opportunities for social connection.* When one looks at the types of places where people with disabilities spend time, they are largely places that provide little if any opportunity for social relationship. It is not enough to simply assist people with disabilities to go out into "community places." Rather, it is important for people to spend time in places that foster a sense of community among the people there.
2. *We must increase our awareness of the limited dimensions of social networks (family and disability) for many people with disabilities and place emphasis on the expansion of these dimensions (e.g., friends, neighbors, coworkers).* Although many more people with disabilities live, work, and recreate in community-based settings, this has not in and of itself significantly diversified their social networks. It is through their chosen social networks that most members of society

experience a sense of community and belonging. Typically, the social networks of people with disabilities have been prescribed for them by family members and the human services system. Thus, for many people with disabilities, increased and ongoing intentional efforts by professionals, family members, friends, and others may be important in helping them to find opportunities to develop social connections and relationships with people who are nonfamily members and nondisabled people, but who may share common interests, occupations, identities, or geographic communities.

All of us choose our relationships and locales based on a variety of choices and constraints. Our experience and sense of community derives from these connections to people and places. Because of a variety of factors (low income, service system structures, family protectiveness), these choices are much more limited for people with disabilities than those without. In part, through increased opportunities to participate in community activities that foster social connection and relationships with a greater diversity of community members, people with disabilities will be able to more fully experience community membership and belonging.

REFERENCES

Agnew, J., & Duncan, J. (Eds.). (1989). *The power of place.* Boston: Unwin Hyman.

Bell, C., & Newby, H. (1974). *Community studies.* New York: Praeger.

Bell, W., & Boat, M.D. (1970). The city man's neighbors and friends. In H.M. Hughes (Ed.), *Cities and city life* (pp. 101–119). Boston: Allyn & Bacon.

Bercovici, S.M. (1983). *Barriers to normalization: The restrictive management of retarded persons.* Baltimore: University Park Press.

Blumer, H. (1969). *Symbolic interactionism.* Englewood Cliffs, NJ: Prentice Hall.

Bogdan, R., & Taylor, S.J. (1987). The next wave. In S.J. Taylor, D. Biklen, & J.A. Knoll (Eds.), *Community integration for people with severe disabilities* (pp. 209–213). New York: Teachers College Press.

Bulmer, M. (1987). *The social basis of community care.* Winchester, MA: Allen & Unwin.

Edgerton, R.B. (1967). *The cloak of competence.* Berkeley: University of California Press.

Fischer, C.S. (1982). *To dwell among friends: Personal networks in town and city.* Chicago: University of Chicago Press.

Gans, H.J. (1962). *The urban villagers.* New York: Free Press.

Gorman, B. (1979). Seven days, five countries: The making of a group. *Urban Life, 7*(4), 469–491.

Gusfield, J.R. (1975). *Community: A critical response.* New York: Harper & Row.

Katovich, M.A., & Reese, W.A. (1987). The regular: Full-time identities and memberships in an urban bar. *Journal of Contemporary Ethnography, 16*(3), 308–343.

Keller, S. (1968). *The urban neighborhood: A sociological perspective.* New York: Random House.

Liebow, E. (1967). *Tally's corner.* Boston: Little, Brown.

Lutfiyya, Z.M. (1991). "A feeling of being connected": Friendships between people with and without learning difficulties. *Disability, Handicap & Society, 6*(3), 233–244.

Macionis, J. (1978). The search for community in modern society. *Qualitative Sociology, 1*(2), 130–143.

Maguire, J. (1983). *Understanding social networks.* Beverly Hills: Sage.

McGill, J. (1987). Our leisure identity. *Entourage, 2*(3), 23–25.

Minar, D.W., & Greer, S. (1968). *The concept of community.* Chicago: Aldine.

Nathe, P.A. (1976). Prickly Pear coffee house: The hangout. *Urban Life, 5*(1), 75–104.

O'Brien, J., & Lyle, C. (1987). *Framework for accomplishment.* Decatur, GA: Responsive Systems Assoc.

Wellman, B., & Leighton, B. (1979). Networks, neighborhoods, and communities: Approaches to the study of the community question. *Urban Affairs Quarterly, 14*(3), 363–390.

Whyte, W.F. (1955). *Street corner society.* Chicago: University of Chicago Press.

12

More Than They Bargained For

The Meaning of Support to Families

Susan O'Connor

Over the past 15 years in the United States, child care and parental leave have emerged as important issues for all families (Knoll et al., 1990). In the field of disabilities, the past 25 years have presented a movement away from services dispensed at institutions toward more community-based services. Parallel to this trend has been increased acknowledgment of the importance of the family as a provider of care and support for its children with disabilities (Fujiura, Garza, & Braddock, 1990).

This recognition of the importance of the family has given rise to the concept of family supports. Over the past decade, a unifying set of principles has emerged that acknowledges the uniqueness of every family and designates the family as the most important determiner of its own needs. These principles call for support to be community- and family-centered, flexible, directed toward the whole family, and collaborative (Bradley, Knoll, & Agosta, 1992). Individual need is the defining determinant of what a family might gain from the system. Family support efforts have taken on many forms, offering families respite, case management, equipment, and/or cash subsidies as needed.

Current professional language describes the goals of family supports as being "family-centered" and "family-determined" and doing "whatever it takes" (Bersani, 1987; The Center on Human Policy, 1987; DeLuca & Salerno, 1984; Walker, 1988). Family support programs and community service organizations using this language reflect much diversity in the kinds of support and services that are actually given and received. In many family support efforts, the professional's role is that of a facilitator or broker of services, someone who gets to know the families' needs and then connects them with what they (the professionals) determine to be the appropriate services.

A recent study reports that 42 states are taking initiatives to provide family support services (Braddock, Hemp, Fujiura, Bachelder, & Mitchell, 1990). However, the percentage of funds allocated for such services remains only 3% of the total budgets of mental retardation/developmental disability agencies (Fujiura et al., 1990).

Although family support services continue to expand (Knoll et al., 1990), it is only through a more in-depth examination of the meaning of support to families that we can hope to understand how services affect individual families' lives. This study attempts to understand what happens when families seek support services for their children with disabilities. It looks at four families from different racial, cultural, and socioeconomic backgrounds, all of whom live in or around a central New York community. Two of these families are headed by single mothers and two by both parents. Although the families differ greatly in terms of makeup and life experience, this study contrasts what they saw themselves as needing from the human services system with what they actually received. This contrast indicates some of the distinctions between the private world of the family and the public world of the support services system.

THE FAMILIES

The following is a description of the four families included in this study.

The Foster Family

Kevin and Peter Foster are 7-year-old twins. They live with their mother, Karen, and two of their three sisters, Peg and Linda, in a middle-class suburb. The third sister, Katy, recently moved in with their father, who has not lived with the family for 6 years. The Fosters are of European American descent. At the time of this study, Karen owned and ran a small business. Both Kevin and Peter have severe multiple disabilities resulting from a viral infection that they both contracted within the first year of life. The children's extensive care needs and the parents' disagreement about whether to keep the children at home precipitated a divorce. She explained, "[Their father] wasn't involved from the day the boys got sick. He called them things and couldn't accept them . . . I kicked him out. I made a choice to keep them [the boys]!" For the past 6 years Karen has cared for her family alone.

Over the past year, Karen's life has changed. She became engaged to Jeff, who, to her great delight, has grown close to her sons and Peg.

She stated, "I have thought of finding a place for Kevin and Peter, but Jeff insists they stay with us."

The Henry Family

Verna and Nate Henry are heads of a family that can best be described as proud. They moved north from Georgia 25 years ago and began to raise their family of three boys: 20-year-old Martin, who works on and off at different jobs; 12-year-old Mitchell, who is in the sixth grade; and 9-year-old Charles (Chas), a fourth grader. Chas has autism.

The Henrys are African American and, despite their having gone through a variety of financial ups and downs over the years, would presently be considered to have a lower economic status.

Verna and Nate begin their day about 5:00 A.M. Both work full time but nevertheless can "barely make ends meet." In the quiet of their living room, talk concerned the current health problems of Verna and her need to be off work to recover. Verna expressed anxiety about the bills getting paid: "We just keep gettin' in the hole it seems, [but] we keep gettin' by."

The Salah Family

Thomas, a young adult, is the only son in this Arab American family. His three sisters—Mary, Nora, and Madeline—are also young adults. All three sisters live in the family home in a middle-class suburb with their mother, Clare, and grandmother (who because of her age came from the Middle East to live with her daughter and family). With the grandmother came a young woman from the Philippines who had lived and cared for the older woman previously. The Salahs came to this country approximately 25 years ago. Mr. Salah died 3 years ago. Clare continues to work as a seamstress in a local department store. Thomas was born with Down syndrome. Up to a year ago, he lived at home with his family, which is common in the Arab culture. His mother described what his life was like when he lived at home:

> He knew everyone in the neighborhood—people we didn't even know. He spent time with people when they were fixing their cars. He knew more people than we did. The group home, there is a difference between that and home.

The Valdez Family

Jaime and Gloria are Latinos who have lived in the United States for 20 years. They have two elementary school age children, Barbara and Miguel. The Valdez family moved to their community about 2 years ago.

The Valdezes live in an area of the city known to have a strong Latino community. Many people living here are of low socioeconomic status, as are the Valdezes. Although Jaime does not work in the traditional sense, he has repeatedly stated that he does not want to be on welfare. His daily activities involve managing the family's interaction with the outside system of teachers, doctors, and workers. He also manages property owned by his nephew who lives in another city. Gloria, his common-law wife, has the more traditional role of taking care of the children and the home.

Three people in this family have been labeled with either mild or moderate mental retardation. Gloria and Barbara, the youngest child, have been labeled as having mild mental retardation, and Miguel moderate mental retardation. As a result, the children are in special education classes, and all three receive Supplemental Security Income (SSI).

It is important to mention that Jaime Valdez speaks some English, enough to communicate with social workers, school personnel, and other English speakers with whom he must interact. On nearly half of the occasions I was at the Valdez home, there were other workers present who could clarify for me when I didn't understand what was said. On other occasions the conversation simply took on a longer, more descriptive means of expression. Gloria Valdez, the mother, speaks no English except for a few words and phrases, and both children prefer to use English at home and in school. Beyond my initial explanation of my intentions to each of the four families, there were seldom questions or discussion about why I continued to visit.

My level of involvement with each family took different forms ranging from seven interviews and observations with one family to an ongoing and continued relationship with two families. The families were chosen as part of an attempt to gain an understanding of people of a variety of cultural backgrounds.

Finally, it is important to identify myself within the context of these families' lives. My understanding and insight into the experiences of their lives and cultures is influenced by my background as a European American who has not had a person with a disability in the family. Although I have worked in the field of special education for the past 15 years, 5 of which were in Arab countries, the interpretations of their experiences were likewise influenced by my values and perspectives.

THE AGENCIES

The agencies involved with the families in this study ranged from a private, nonprofit agency serving families within a particular county to a state-run agency under the auspices of the Department of Mental Retardation and Developmental Disabilities. The nonprofit agency has a reputation as being parent-focused, and a majority of the staff are parents or relatives of people with disabilities. Other services provided by the agencies range from standard case management services to a small community-based neighborhood center that provided, among other services, programming and social work support to families in their immediate area.

FAMILIES' DEFINITION OF THEIR NEEDS

Whether or not there is a child with a disability, the needs of individual families vary greatly. These variations certainly existed for all of the families in this study. Each family entered or was referred to the social service system to receive a specific form of assistance or support, at least initially. This section discusses the ways in which these families defined their needs, focusing on two main areas: 1) needs of the family versus the needs of the individual with disabilities, and 2) the need of families for practical and concrete assistance.

Family Versus Individual Needs

One of the precepts that has emerged in providing supports to families is a focus on the family as a whole rather than just the child with a disability (Turnbull & Turnbull, 1990). When the families in this study described themselves, they talked about who they were as a family and how what they wanted from the system would help them as a family unit. In the Henry family, for example, Nate Henry did not focus on Chas but rather talked about his and Verna's way of life and current priorities:

> We used to do a lot of things; we would go out from time to time. We used to bowl on a team . . . but we haven't done that in years. Now all of our time is spent for the children.

Even when discussing the child with the disability, families often express concern about how the child's disability affects the family as a whole. Karen Foster talked about how her time is divided between work and her family:

> It has taken its toll on the girls [having the boys at home]. They are both so good and I don't spend enough time with them.

Jaime Valdez looked toward concerns for the future and how his children would fare:

> I think of the kids out on the streets and what trouble they can get into, and now I think in my head about Miguel when he gets older and I already got ideas of that in my head.

Concrete and Practical Needs of Families

The families identified their needs clearly and simply. In each case, these needs were very concrete and practical, such as 1) respite care, 2) financial assistance, and 3) help in obtaining postschool services.

The Need for Respite Services   For two of the families in this study, as for a large percentage of families of children with disabilities, the need for a break is consistently expressed (Cohen & Warren, 1985; Levy & Levy, 1986). In many cases, it is the only request that a family makes. This was the case for the Valdez family.

In the Latino culture (Sanchez-Ayendez, 1988), as in other cultures (Hanson, Lynch, & Wayman, 1990), the extended family plays a major role in the lives of family members. It provides for much care of the children as well as other family needs. It also encompasses a sense of reciprocity. For the Valdez family, moving to this city meant moving away from family. Because of this, they have moved from the informal support of the family to the formal support of the social service system in order to care for their children. They are extensively involved in this system with six different workers (case managers, social workers) from at least three agencies. To Jaime, their needs remain simple: "We need someone to take the kids sometimes." Finding that support was the major topic when he and Gloria discussed their needs. Jaime stated this repeatedly:

> I don't need any money; we just need to have a break! They gonna get me someone, but we only got it once one weekend for Miguel; I don't know what's happenin'.

Karen Foster talked about both the family's needs and her sons' needs. Much of her frustration was due to the strain of unremitting time together:

> Getting caretakers is always a struggle; I really have to work at that; I had to put out $4,000 this year for caretakers and got nothing from the state.

Jeff talked about why this was so important:

> I get tired after being the primary care provider all day long, my back hurts at the end of the day, and I don't know how Karen does it amidst all of this.

Getting and keeping people to help her and her daughters care for Kevin and Peter at home became a major concern to Karen. She tried in different ways to obtain money with which to pay people to come into her home and work with the boys. She had become very politically involved and aware of the system and how she might obtain respite and support in the home. She explained:

There is nothing in place and there has been nothing in place since I have come into the handicapped world. The only way we survived is for this family to have participated in pilots and for myself to have fought for program after program. This system isn't set up to support. I'm tired of fighting.

Financial Needs For some families, it is difficult to identify their needs on a predetermined list of specific services such as respite care or equipment. They may need financial assistance, help in locating services, or any number of other factors that are not on the checklist offered by a particular program. They see little potential in getting what they really need within the confines of the available programs. Nate talked about his family situation in relation to the support program. "What would really help us they can't do; see, money is our problem. If we could just get ahead or put together all of the things we owe and refinance, that would really help."

The Need for Help in Obtaining Postschool Services Thomas Salah lived with his family for most of his life. After Thomas graduated from school, his mother looked for assistance in finding her son a job with the assumption that he would continue to live at home as her daughters did. Clare Salah described her son's likes and dislikes:

He doesn't like being around other handicapped people; he tries to go away from that and has always wanted to be around regular people. You know, he sees the difference and he was always around us and why not? Before he got his job at McDonalds he worked at Progressive Industries [a sheltered workshop]. As soon as it was time for a break he would rush into the offices and spend his time with staff. He just loves his job at McDonalds, I think mainly because he is around normal people.

She was clear as to what integration meant for her son: "All that therapy didn't do nearly as well as just living with people." She also discussed his transition from school and his desire to get a job at a fast-food place. It was in the context of finding a job that they sought out services for Thomas once he left school.

CHANGING IDENTITIES: FROM THE PRIVATE ROLE OF THE FAMILY TO THE PUBLIC ROLE OF CLIENT

All families confront troubles daily. Matters arise that threaten the family unit. In many families these issues remain private, to be dealt with according to the family's norms and values. However, these families' problems were taken out of the private realm of the home and subjected to scrutiny by the human services system.

The families entered this system because a member of the family needed support and practical assistance in connection with a disability. This support ranged from help caring for their children in the home to help finding a job, to acquiring Medicaid and other benefits. But rather than simply receiving the assistance they sought, the families found themselves involved in a process of changing the family identity, with professionals sometimes viewing them as clients, judging them as good or bad parents, counseling and advising them, and attempting to modify their attitudes. The service system often labels the family deficient; even models of intervention designed to empower families (Deal, Dunst, & Trivette, 1989) adopt this focus. This section will discuss six factors by which agencies challenged families' views of themselves, defined them as deficient, or encouraged them to change their behavior: 1) clienthood, 2) changing from good to bad parent, 3) learning the rules, 4) changing the family attitudes, 5) dispensing information and advice, and 6) exploring the meaning of labels to families.

Clienthood

One of the roles taken on by families seeking human services support is that of client (Gliedman & Roth, 1980; Sonnenschein, 1984). In order for a family to receive the support they need, there are certain rules by which they must abide and roles they must fulfill. This is a departure from the private world of relative autonomy and anonymity to the public world of exposure, scrutiny, and judgment. Assumption of the client role takes place subtly and gradually as a result of worker–family interactions.

The experience of clienthood and the type of identity that develops in such a role is common (Bush, 1988; Scott, 1969). People who become clients are thrust into a dependent and passive role in relationship to their caregivers or those who support them. According to Bush, the term *client* frames a person such that the most significant salient aspect becomes the person's need (Bush, 1988). Systems often oversimplify people's lives and homogenize situations by categorizing them according to needs, interventions, and outcomes. Service administrators frequently concentrate on means at the cost of ends (Bush, 1988), with emphasis placed on a deficits model and what needs to be corrected. Often families' needs must fit into predetermined categories, with little attention paid to outcome. For example, a family may need financial assistance, but find that only respite care is available. If this "assistance" is provided, it will not meet the family's need but will show on paper that the family received support.

Families entering a system for support often anticipate receiving help, but they become increasingly aware that they are losing some privacy. Karen Foster explained, "You know, I'm a private person and don't appreciate having to divulge all of the personal information."

This comment came after Karen had shared her life story over and over to different service workers, administrators, and school personnel. Often this awareness of loss of privacy accompanies the realization of how information they have shared has been used. When talking about the social worker who 7 months earlier had empathized with him and expressed approval regarding the way he took care of his family, Jaime Valdez said: "She can't come in my house anymore—she try to take my kids away."

In a sense, families' attempts to receive services place them in the same status as their son or daughter. They now need therapy, or to be "fixed" (Gliedman & Roth, 1980; Sonnenschein, 1984; Turnbull & Turnbull, 1990). This was exemplified clearly in the Valdez family when Elena, a social worker, told them what would have to happen before they could be dismissed from her case load:

> I will be working with you for only a few more months. I would like to work on organizing the people who work with your family as well as all of your relationships, between you and the kids, you and Gloria, and Gloria and the kids. I want to see what you take on as your responsibilities and how you provide for your family and the communication with Gloria. I want to work on and look at how you take care of the children together. After this I will step back and see if it is necessary that I be here and I will maybe close your case.

For this family, support meant having to change a fundamental part of their identity. Whether or not this change was brought about in an acceptable manner would be determined by someone outside of their world, a social worker or case manager, someone who did not really know them but spent time with them because they were deemed to have problems.

Part of accepting the role of the client involves a change in identity with respect to who has the power to make decisions. For example, decisions concerning families are sometimes made during meetings from which the families are excluded. This was the case for Jaime Valdez during an agency meeting with six professionals on the subject of respite. After an hour Jaime was dismissed by the moderator, who said, "Well it looks as though the biggest thing that needs to happen here is respite. I guess we're done then." Jaime was told that the meeting was over and that the others needed to stay to discuss another family. He left reluctantly and the real agenda was addressed. I later talked to one of the workers who said,

> Whew! There is a lot more going on in that family than what came out, some problems with Jaime. Gloria has been complaining and might leave, and they are really concerned about what that might mean for the kids. Someone will be talking with Jaime.

The Continuum: From Good to Bad Parent

The concept of life as a continuum, that is, a process of preparing for experiences and choices to come, is paramount for people with disabilities. It profoundly affects their experience at work, at home, and with education (Taylor, 1988). Upon entering the human services system, families are moved along a continuum whereby they must acquire certain parenting skills and make major changes, as determined by social workers, in order to be considered competent to manage their lives. A family's place on this continuum is not static. It can change based on the discretion of those working with them and how members of the family follow the rules of the system. Jaime went from being defined as a "good father" to a "problem" within 5 months, as he began to disagree with the social workers and not follow through on what they had asked him to do. Likewise, his wife, who was seen as "needing a lot of work," instantly became the "better" parent when Jaime was placed on the low end of the continuum. "I don't know how she can live with him; it would be better for her to move out with the kids," said one worker.

Yet this idea of competency is based on the values and standards of individual professionals who bring their own experiences and problems to their work (DeLuca & Salerno, 1984; Schon, 1983). As one social worker assigned to the Valdez family stated about her own life,

> My husband used to abuse me physically. We weren't married, but I have been through it all and drugs too. He drank and did drugs, and I would kick him out. We have been together 20 years.

Workers, too, have a multitude of problems in their personal lives. The difference is that their lives remain personal and are not judged by outsiders who come in to change them.

By exposing their lives, families become vulnerable and their actions are left open to judgments about whether they are good or bad. This was demonstrated in the Foster family when they were reported by a teacher for child abuse and neglect after Kevin came to school with what was described as a "red bottom." Karen explained:

> One of the boys got spanked for tipping over the TV; you know, he could have been killed doing it. And they mark very easily; if you put em in lukewarm water they come out all red. So I spanked him to scare him, and he went to school Monday morning and the teacher saw the red and called the police. She turned me in for child abuse! We had to go and get my son out, interrogated, the whole nine yards.

The focus is taken away from basic needs that the family thought would be met when they entered the system and placed on the need for the family itself to change. In many cases, that change means they must perfect themselves before they are actually able to determine what they want for their families.

Learning the Rules: "Gloria Usually Has the House in Order"

Families in the human services system must learn how and when to demonstrate acceptable behaviors, as determined by those in power, in order to be considered as following the rules. Such compliance may potentially increase their opportunity to determine what they receive from the system. Families are aware of this when workers enter their home as well as when children go outside the home. Nate Henry was concerned about Chas's swearing at school, using words he had picked up from watching a video of the "Black Godfather." As Nate put it,

> Seems Chas is goin' to school sayin' those swear words. Now you know what you would think first, that he is hearin' them around the house. The first thought is that he heard it from his parents.

Likewise, Gloria Valdez, in the eyes of the professionals, kept a very clean house. As one worker, Elena, commented on our first visit: "Gloria usually has the house in order and very clean." When I visited alone on subsequent occasions, the house was in less-than-perfect order. However, it was always clean for the workers. Despite her not speaking English, Gloria had early on picked up the cues of what it meant to be acceptable when visited by workers.

The need to follow rules became apparent in connection with caring for the children and the house. The youngest child, Barbara, loved to play with the dog. On one occasion when a worker named Maria was present, Barbara lay on the floor kissing the dog's snout. Maria said, "No, no, chica [girl], don't touch the dog like that! Animals sometimes carry sickness and insects that could make you sick." After repeating this several times to no avail, Maria turned to Jaime and indicated that he should intercede. At first he ignored her request but then finally acquiesced, making Barbara stop. When I visited by myself on numerous other occasions, the children were allowed to play similarly with the dog undisturbed.

Parents learn quickly how to adapt their lives when workers visit. They know how to create the appearance of abiding by the new rules set for their family. Any infraction of the rules is noticed by the service providers. Karen Foster experienced this with the boys' teacher, who expressed her feeling to me regarding the care they receive at school versus that at home: "I think we make them do a lot more for themselves here. I send all of the programs to Karen but she hasn't been involved at all." Invariably the parent becomes the focus of the interventions and shoulders the responsibility for what is not right. This often results in a back-and-forth flow from being labeled as a good parent to being labeled as a bad parent, depending on how well that parent has abided by the subscriptions of the particular programs.

Often a family's own ideas, once expressed, are viewed by workers as problematic. Responding to a comment that the Henrys are a great family, one worker said hesitantly, shaking his head: "Yeah, but they definitely have their own ideas."

The Henrys notwithstanding, families tend to take on a different persona in the presence of workers, manifesting a need to do as they are told. They have been taught to accept all advice from workers as being correct for their family. There is a tendency on the part of workers to encourage such acquiescence. Families that do reject advice learn, as a child does, at least to comply when workers or teachers are present.

Changing Family Attitudes: "She Cried and Cried; She Just Wasn't Ready"

Changing parents' attitudes is another major component of support service. This was the case for the Salah family when Clare Salah was encouraged to place her son in a group home. Mrs. Salah said, "They told me that it would be better to place him now because this nice place was opening up, and it might be a long time before there would be another opening." A friend of the family commented: "She had such a hard time with that decision; she cried and cried and just wasn't ready."

The encouragement came with good intentions in relation to the norms of this society in which becoming part of the community as an adult has meant moving away from the family in an attempt to achieve independence (Turnbull & Turnbull, 1990). Yet cultural distinctions are not always accounted for within the structure of a large system. It is the norm within many cultures for children to stay at home, as all of Thomas's sisters did. Often professionals are unaware of the cultural differences and recommend services that may be the norm for people of the dominant (middle-class European American) culture but not for those of different backgrounds or traditions (Kalyanpur, 1988). Families with backgrounds other than that of the dominant culture are placed on the same continuum, with little attention paid to their individual needs. The differences are treated more as negative attitudes to be changed or overcome than traditions to be respected and supported.

Teaching and Advice: More Than What They Bargain For

The work of support becomes a matter of 1) educating the family through professionalized teaching techniques and 2) producing results that can be measured and proven to administrators. This determines how successful the worker has been in delivering service to the family. This became clear as one worker discussed how it seemed as if all her work with the Valdez family had not paid off, indicating that both she and the family had failed:

> It doesn't look like we have done anything in all this time. He's just awful. We thought of having a meeting with our supervisors, but they wouldn't understand. There has been no change to show them.

Again, successful service delivery seems to be measured according to preconceived norms. This raises some very important questions for all families, but most especially for families of differing races and cultural backgrounds who might be placed at a disadvantage. Should these families be asked to submit to a set of norms outside of their culture? Must they assimilate into the mainstream? Within the area of disability, this is important on two levels. First, by simple virtue of having a child with a disability, a family is an outsider, considered not typical within the dominant culture. Second, families from outside of the dominant culture must deal successfully with stereotypes based on their racial and cultural identities, as well as on societal attitudes about people with disabilities, in order to be considered acceptable by the dominant culture. Often the number of outsiders coming into the home can in and of itself be perplexing. The job of each worker was confusing to Gloria. On numerous occasions when asked what this or that one did, she shrugged and in her few words of English said, "I dunno, just talk!"

The Meaning of Labels to Families:
"What Is This Mild and Moderate Mental Retarded Anyway?"

In some families, disability may not be a major problem. The disability is incorporated into their identity as a family. This is true in a number of cultures. Frequently in dominant U.S. culture, a disability is considered something to be fixed or treated. In the private world of some families and in some cultures, disability does not create such problems. In these families' worlds, the child may not be viewed as having a disability or as a problem at all.

Jaime Valdez felt confused during a meeting with a committee on special education at which his children's school placement for the next year had been discussed in terms of disability labels. Jaime's question after leaving the meeting was, "What is this mild and moderate mental retarded anyway?" According to Jaime, his children played with peers in the streets of the neighborhood, and his wife took care of the home and the children—a highly valued role in their culture; yet all were labeled by the system. The public attitude toward and current treatments for persons with disabilities are based on contemporary medical models that presume there to be a specific cause, whereas private explanations may allow for many causes (Joe & Miller, 1987).

THE COST OF HELP TO FAMILIES

In looking at what each of the four families received as a result of their involvement in the human services system, one is struck by the fact that in two of the families the children with disabilities were placed outside of the home. This could be viewed as the parents' choice. Indeed, parents may even describe it as such, as in the case of the Foster and Salah families, where it appeared as though the parents chose their outcomes freely. There can never be adequate documentation of how tired these parents grew of the battles and struggles with the system and why they eventually gave up caring for their own children. Karen said:

> Once a child crosses over your threshold and into a community care facility, all the things that I personally had wanted and that they denied me my child now gets: Social Security, Medicare, every single thing paid for that I have struggled for.

The Salah Family

The Salah family placed Thomas in a group home with seven other people with mental retardation about five miles from his family, friends, and the community where he grew up. For the Salah family, placing Thomas in a group home meant accepting a change in the extent of their involvement with him. Clare Salah explained:

> We brought him home every week at first. They told us no, we would have to stop, that the state pays for a certain number of days and he is gone too much. It isn't that the group house cared; they were glad to get rid of him. It was the state that cared.

The state determined when and for how long she could interact with her son, imposing rules and regulations on her family that led her to believe, "It's not a home."

Thomas eventually got a job at a local fast food restaurant when he moved from his family home to a group home. Although this can be viewed as a natural process in mainstream U.S. culture, within the

Arab culture the idea of caring for family members is fundamental. Thomas' sisters remained at home and his grandmother was brought over from another country to be cared for by family. Yet based on recommendations by a social worker, Thomas was separated from all of these primary connections. The anguish that Mrs. Salah experienced in deciding to place Thomas in a group home was solely the result of her being encouraged to do so in the name of support.

The Foster Family

For all 7 years of their lives, Kevin and Peter lived at home. However, during the time I was involved with the family, it was decided that the boys would be placed in an intermediate care facility located approximately an hour away from the family. Because of her impending marriage, Karen decided to sell the family home and move to a community about an hour away, which would mean a 2-hour journey to see her sons.

The decision to place Kevin and Peter out of the home was a big step for the entire family. Karen explained, "The boys have always been part of the family and you learn what they give you, what they add to your lives. It has been a long struggle, though, and I'm tired of fighting."

Karen was indeed exhausted by her struggles of the past 6 years. Most of those efforts had been made alone, but, after having arrived at the decision to place her sons, she was offered considerable emotional support not only by the workers involved with her but also by the teacher who had reported her for child abuse. The teacher said, "She has worked hard; it's the best decision."

The Valdez Family

For the Valdez family, the threat of having their children removed from the home depended on how workers viewed their performance as parents. At one point, Jaime was reported to child welfare for not providing adequate food and clothing for the children. His response was that he no longer wanted one particular worker in his home: "They can't take my kids away from me." An investigation by child welfare showed no abuse.

The Henry Family

For the Henrys, daily life went on as usual. The financial struggle was primary, but the family remained intact. However, their interactions with the system increased after Chas was referred for counseling so he would refrain from touching and hugging people.

CONCLUSION

All parents have expectations of what they will receive from any service system they enter with their child. Although the benefits and services sought by parents of children with disabilities may be different from those sought by most parents, such parents also have expectations in terms of what they might gain through support services (Featherstone, 1980; Greenfeld, 1986). Every family has its own life circumstances that shape its members' identities as individuals and as part of a family and are the basis for the rules and conventions by which they live. A family's way of life is related to the particular values and beliefs of its members as well as their ethnic, class, and racial backgrounds. Families seeking support from the human services system possess as much diversity of lifestyle as the professionals who enter their homes to give support. However, the families in this study were given little to reflect or uphold that individuality. The discrepancy between what families think they will get when entering the service system and what they actually receive becomes greater as their time spent within that system increases. By requesting services, families bring their private lives to a public arena to be scrutinized, judged, and influenced by professionals who may have little knowledge of their concerns or needs. Workers must be sensitive to the feelings of exposure and mistrust on the part of some families in connection with the professionals who are involved in their lives.

Professionals should feel challenged to cultivate a posture of learning from and respecting the differences among families rather than pressuring all families to adhere to the same rules. We must get to know families in ways that help us to appreciate who they are in terms of their values, fears, and concerns. Often, getting to know a family results from simply listening to members talk about themselves and each other: Standing back and observing family interaction can provide more insight than the numerous evaluations and assessments to which a family is typically subjected. We give frequent lip service to respecting families but seldom examine on a personal level how to demonstrate that respect. At the same time, we can never know everything about a given family; nor should we. Sometimes knowledge of their personal world is eventually used against them in ways that neither they nor the worker intended. Professionals must learn to appreciate the expertise of the family and the significance of their fundamental bond. They must relinquish the role of expert and decision maker who judges what is best for each family in favor of forging a partnership with them and allowing families to accept and reject advice that is offered. This presents a challenge to professionals, who at times find themselves having to address questions of safety or having to determine when children are at risk; however, creating such a partnership is the only way to make social services truly family centered.

As the diversity of families who are served grows, so too must the perspective of service providers. The lives of families are filled with many problems, challenges, joys, and day-to-day experiences that do not directly relate to their child with a disability. For example, medical or financial factors may need to be addressed, and service providers must be aware of this.

In summary, it is critical that professionals entering homes to offer support be cognizant of the values and beliefs of the family whom they wish to help. It is equally important that professionals examine their own attitudes and beliefs so as not to impose these on their clients. In most cases, support must be offered on the families' terms, which may often conflict with present models and the limited array of supports that are offered. Without a change in how services are provided, the cost of support to families may in many instances be greater than the benefits they receive by opening their lives to public judgment and advice.

REFERENCES

Bersani, H. (1987). *Calvert County ARC, Family Support Services*. Syracuse, NY: The Center on Human Policy.

Braddock, D., Hemp, R., Fujiura, G., Bachelder, L., & Mitchell, D. (1990). *The state of the states in developmental disabilities*. Baltimore: Paul H. Brookes Publishing Co.

Bradley, V.J., Knoll, J., & Agosta, J.M. (Eds.). (1992). *Emerging issues in family supports*. Washington, DC: American Association on Mental Retardation.

Bush, M. (1988). *Families in distress: Public, private, and civic responses*. Berkeley: University of California Press.

The Center on Human Policy. (1987, September). *Families for all children*. Syracuse, NY: Author.

Cohen, S., & Warren, R.D. (1985). *Respite care: Principles, programs, and policies*. Austin, TX: Pro-ED.

Deal, A.G., Dunst, C.J., & Trivette, C.M. (1989). A flexible and functional approach to developing individualized family support plans. *Infants and Young Children, 1*(4), 32–43.

DeLuca, K.D., & Salerno, S.C. (1984). *Helping professionals connect with families with handicapped children*. Springfield, IL: Charles C Thomas.

Featherstone, H. (1980). *A difference in the family: Living with a disabled child*. New York: Basic Books.

Fujiura, G., Garza, J., & Braddock, D. (1990). *National survey of family support services in developmental disabilities*. Chicago: University of Illinois, University Affiliated Programs.

Gliedman, J., & Roth, W. (1980). *The unexpected minority: Handicapped children in America*. New York: Harcourt Brace Jovanovich.

Greenfeld, J. (1986). *A client called Noah*. New York: Henry Holt.

Hanson, M.J., Lynch, E.W., & Wayman, K.I. (1990). Honoring the cultural diversity of families when gathering data. *Topics in Early Childhood Special Education, 10*(1), 112–131.

Joe, J.E., & Miller, D. (1987). *American Indian cultural perspectives on disability* (Monograph Series No. 3). Tucson, AZ: Native American Research and Training Center.

Kalyanpur, M. (1988). *We look after our own: The impact of cultural differences on service delivery*. Unpublished research report. Division of Special Education and Rehabilitation, Syracuse University, Syracuse, New York.

Knoll, J., Covert, S., Osuch, R., O'Connor, S., Agosta, J., & Blaney, B. (1990). *Family support services in the United States: An end of decade status report*. Cambridge, MA: Human Services Research Institute.

Levy, J.M., & Levy, P.H. (1986). Issues and models in the delivery of respite services. In C.L. Salisbury & J. Intagliata (Eds.), *Respite care support for persons with developmental disabilities and their families* (pp. 99–116). Baltimore: Paul H. Brookes Publishing Co.

Sanchez-Ayendez, M. (1988). The Puerto Rican American family. In C.H. Mindel, R.W. Habenstein, and R. Wright, Jr. (Eds.), *Ethnic families in America* (3rd ed.) (pp. 173–195). New York: Elsevier/North Holland.

Schon, D.A. (1983). *The reflective practitioner: How professionals think in action*. New York: Basic Books Inc.

Scott, R.A. (1969). *The making of blind men: A study of adult socialization*. New York: Russell Sage Foundation.

Sonnenschein, P. (1984). Parents and professionals: An uneasy relationship. In M.L. Henniger & E.M. Nasselroad (Eds.), *Working with parents of handicapped children: A book of readings for school personnel* (pp. 129–139). Lanham, MD: University Press of America.

Taylor, S.J. (1988). Caught in the continuum: A critical analysis of the principle of the least restrictive environment. *Journal of The Association for Persons with Severe Handicaps, 13*(1), 41–53.

Turnbull, A.P., & Turnbull, H.R. (1990). *Families, professionals and exceptionality: A special partnership* (2nd ed.). Columbus, OH: Charles E. Merrill.

Walker, P. (1988). *Family supports for children with severe disabilities and chronic illness in Maryland*. Syracuse, NY: The Center on Human Policy.

Epilogue

Steven J. Taylor, Robert Bogdan,
and Zana Marie Lutfiyya

The Introduction to this book started with the question, "What is life in the community like for people with developmental disabilities and their families?" The book's title, *The Variety of Community Experience*, suggests the answer. As the chapters in this book demonstrate, the experience of living in the community varies dramatically from one person or family to another. Although the community experience cannot be understood in terms of simplistic generalizations, several lessons can be drawn from the studies contained herein.

First, the concept of community should neither be romanticized as utopian nor ridiculed as anachronistic. For many people with developmental disabilities, living in the community means little more than physical integration. They are in the community but not really a part of it. People with developmental disabilities can function in the same places as other people yet be isolated from community life.

For some people with disabilities, however, life in the community has resulted in social acceptance and inclusion. There are towns, associations, and organizations in which people with developmental disabilities are included as full-fledged members. In many instances, people with developmental disabilities are included not as a result of professional engineering but as a consequence of ordinary social processes. Their participation in these settings is taken for granted and viewed as natural by all members.

Many of our current notions about the community stem from the early stages of deinstitutionalization, when opposition to group homes dominated attention in the field. Too often we have expected rejection and exclusion of people with developmental disabilities. When such people are not accepted in neighborhoods or included in community groups, it is viewed as a normal and natural outcome of backward attitudes and prejudice. We need to pay more attention to how our own practices, such as grouping of people with developmental disabilities, tend to discourage inclusion; we also need to devote greater care in identifying the kinds of communities or associations in which people with developmental disabilities will be accepted.

Second, human services professionals should be viewed neither as saviors nor as villains. To be sure, state institutions and bureaucratic service organizations have not been responsive to the needs of people with developmental disabilities and their families. Today the rhetoric of human services can obscure the reality. It is difficult for impersonal bureaucracies to provide person-centered or family-centered services. Even the most responsive human services agencies cannot fulfill the human need for a caring network of family and friends.

Yet it would be misleading to suggest that all of the problems of people with developmental disabilities and their families would disappear if human services and the associated professionals simply went away. Some agencies have found unobtrusive ways of supporting people in their attempts to live and participate in the community, and some professionals have developed skillful ways of facilitating inclusion and building relationships. Within large bureaucracies, some—perhaps many, perhaps few—service providers have been willing to bend the system's rules to do what is right for the individuals they support.

Third, despite the fact that people with developmental disabilities and their families have been subjected to prejudice, discrimination, and even abuse, they should not be regarded as passive objects who happily conform to what is expected of them. Although the phenomena known as the "self-fulfilling prophecy" and the "client role" are real and undoubtedly exercise a strong influence on how individuals and families feel and act, defining people solely as victims is just as dehumanizing as defining them solely as clients of human services. As human beings rather than robots, people with developmental disabilities and their families sometimes conform to the dictates of the human services system and societal expectations—and sometimes do not. Families may reject negative stereotypes of their children and construct positive definitions of them. People with developmental disabilities may not view themselves in terms of their deficits and may take an active role in trying to control their lives. One of the most striking aspects of institutionalization is that some people emerged from the experience as survivors, with their dignity and self-respect intact.

Thus, this book concludes on an optimistic note. We have observed, documented, and attempted to understand instances in which communities and associations accepted and included people with developmental disabilities, human services agencies and individual professionals actively supported community inclusion, and people with developmental disabilities and their families were not passive victims.

As qualitative researchers, we cannot say exactly how common such instances are. But their occurrence gives cause for hope and provides examples to emulate.

Index

Page numbers followed by "*n*" or "*f*" indicate footnotes or figures, respectively.